Tobias Jones studied a   College, Oxford. He was on the staff
of the *London Revie*   and the *Independent on Sunday*
before moving to Par   *The Dark
Heart of Italy* he has   s for Rai 3:
Ricchi d'Italia and C

TOBIAS JONES

Utopian Dreams:
In Search of a Good Life

faber and faber

First published in 2007
by Faber and Faber Limited
3 Queen Square London WC1N 3AU

This paperback edition first published in 2008

Photoset by RefineCatch Limited, Bungay, Suffolk
Printed in England by Mackays of Chatham plc

A CIP record for this book
is available from the British Library

ISBN 978-0-571-22381-7

2 4 6 8 10 9 7 5 3 1

For my parents, Bob and Jane, and
their Combe Mead community

Contents

Acknowledgements

I am, above all, grateful to everyone out there who let us come and stay: to the members of the communities mentioned here who were unfailingly hospitable. I feel very fortunate to be published by Faber: the trust, intuition and guidance of Walter Donohue and Stephen Page have been invaluable. Georgina Capel, Philippa Brewster and everyone else at Capelland continue to make writing unexpectedly enjoyable. Maia Bristol and Justin Wildridge have been stalwarts. Frankie Elston, Christopher Lewis and Edward Bailey gave excellent advice. Thanks to all the other people who lent me money or books, bought us meals or beers or just suggested leads: Daniela Calebich, Keith Jones, Rickie B, lo Zivo, il Gallo, il Davo, l'Albe, Elisabetta Salvini, Harry Seekings, Euan Wallace, Lisa Kerr, Enrico Basaglia, Stefano Mercurio, Mario Casartelli, John Foot, Richard Pendlebury, Diego Saglia, Richard Hepwood, Alfred Giannantonio, Glen Alessi, Erica Scroppo and Richard Newbury. I'm very grateful to various commissioning editors in London, Milan and Rome – in particular to Jacopo Zanchini and Giovanni De Mauro – who have made me feel a little less out of the loop over the last two years. My siblings, Dave and Vandana and Paul, have been sterling. I'm indebted to The Society of Authors for a generous grant from the K Blundell Trust which enabled us to linger in places rather than racing through. Finally, I'm full of admiration and respect for my two travelling companions, Francesca and Benedetta. Any errors are, obviously, all mine.

Introduction: Going Astray

I originally intended this book to be only about those alternative communities that live on the fringes of our society. And that is still, in some ways, what the book is about: it's a series of journeys to modern, self-contained communities, a pilgrimage to centres of – depending on your taste – idealism or escapism. I've travelled to the far-out and far-away to listen to people describing the strange, surreal beauty of their dreams.

But I haven't written about the counter-culture or about hippie communes and dysfunctional ashrams. There are already hundreds of books like that. Using a stand-offish voyeurism, they have always had a similar narrative trajectory: whether the writer uses the term 'utopia' (somewhere that's nowhere) or 'commune' (slightly sixties) or 'Intentional Community' (the dull, modern denotation), the aim of the writer is invariably the same: to pry into alternative types and conclude that they're doolally, if not actually dangerous. The books may be more subtle in the way they say so, but the bottom line is normally gentle derision: they tend to echo Samuel Johnson's weary warning about those who 'listen with credulity to the whispers of fancy, and pursue with eagerness the phantoms of hope . . .'[1] And understandably so: it's much easier to sell a book which shores up our complacency by denying the alternatives than one which challenges it by quietly listening to them.

I wanted, though, to cross-examine the values by which we, in the so-called 'real world', live. That, at least according to Matthew Arnold, is what culture means; it implies 'turning a stream of fresh and free thought upon our stock notions and habits'.[2] So I decided, somewhat gingerly, to try and live inside, rather than just visit, these communities. I wanted to immerse myself in optimism and idealism, spend time with people who still believe in potential and possibility, those who still 'expect that age will perform the promises of youth, and that the deficiencies of the present day will be supplied by the morrow'.[3]

Only in retrospect can I understand the hazy reasons for that decision. In the old days, those promises about progress were to be found everywhere, be they in religion or politics, in Christianity or Communism. There was a Whiggish, millenarian belief that tomorrow really would bring something better. But the generation which came to maturity in the aftermath of 1989 has had minimal idealism. There might be micro-beliefs and single-issue sacred cows, but there's no macroscopic, universal, cosmic creed; only incessant cynicism and a dippy kind of relativism. Having grown up in that cultural humus I was too cynical to expect to find that elusive cosmic creed; but I was fascinated simply to find out what it feels like to believe in something, actually to believe that the world could get better rather than worse. And, having read Nathaniel Hawthorne's fictional book about his utopian experiences, I recognised that whilst idealism might often be erroneous, it's also rather noble: 'I rejoice that I could once think better of the world's improvability than it deserved,' he wrote. 'It is a mistake into which men seldom fall twice, in a lifetime; or, if so, the rare and higher is the nature that can thus magnanimously persist in error.'[4] I wanted, for once, to be idealistic; I hoped to find imagination rather than resignation.

It was more than just idealism per se that aroused my curiosity. Another thing that the majority of Thatcher's children have never experienced is, possibly, even more elusive: a sense of community. Our society is, by now, so atomised, privatised and individualised that most people under, say, thirty, have no idea of what a community, a real community, is truly like. I, along with most of my peers, had only heard of this quaint idea from the wistful descriptions of elders who had grown up in one. There was, moreover, an interesting connection between idealism and community. Émile Durkheim suggested that idealism only ever emerged through the communal because it was only 'at the school of collective life that the individual has learned to idealise. It is in assimilating the ideal elaborated by society that he has become capable of conceiving the ideal.'[5] Over recent decades many have taken issue with Durkheim, but he provided interesting parameters for a debate about the interplay between idealism and community; if idealism is dead, I began asking myself, was it individualism which bumped it off? To what extent does our contemporary obsession with individual rights preclude communal aspirations? And is the true cost of community an acceptance of a limitation on freedom? As I spent weeks and months living in these communities, I began to be fascinated by the debates about the permeability of the communities, about different forms of leadership, about alternative ways of structuring families and finances.

Slowly, the vision of the book became bifocal. The more time I spent in these unusual villages, the more I found myself outside what Coleridge called the 'lethargy of custom'. I was at one remove from reality, beyond the habitual and mechanical movements of normality. So the focus of the book became not only the communities themselves, but also, from their vantage point, our own, now-defamiliarised, world; that world against which they were defining themselves. I wanted, in short, to discover if the 'credulity' and the foolish 'pursuit of phantoms' were actually our side of the fence, not theirs.

In shifting the focus between these – for want of a better word – utopias and the 'real world', one theme kept coming back again and again. I realised (one shouldn't probably think about such things, but I did) that to write about this theme was to forfeit the sympathies and offend the tastes of the vast majority of readers. And yet it was, I reluctantly admitted, the key which unlocked the whole book. It provided the clearest, black-and-white contrast between the communes and the real world, it was at the epicentre of what community, at least in the past, has always meant. It was, according to taste, the greatest or else the daftest idealism of them all: religion.

It was only through acknowledging that religion, rather than politics, was the choreographer of these communities that their difference and distinction emerged. It was that which really set them apart and gave me, as I moved between the real and the removed worlds, the stark contrast between the sacred and the profane. My intention wasn't to test their doctrinal logic or veracity. It was something much simpler: I merely wanted, as with the yearning to rub shoulders with idealists, to experience what religion feels like. Again, religion is something with which only a minority of my generation has had any contact; even as far back as the 1940s, society had been so thoroughly cleansed of belief that Dietrich Bonhoeffer wrote: 'we don't worship anything now, not even idols. In that respect we're truly nihilists.'[6] By now, religion, when it's dealt with at all in the mainstream media, is dismissed out of hand as the redoubt of cranks and authoritarians; tiny articles on religion are only commissioned if there's the suitable peg of sexual orientation or gender. In certain circles, if someone confesses to being a believer, they're met with the same fear and loathing that was once reserved for atheists. There's a sort of theophobia at large which quickly becomes evangelical and it's rarely long before certain words come out, 'intolerant' and 'fundamentalist' top of the list. At a time in which understanding religion is, for obvious reasons, more important than ever, there seems to be a knee-jerk derision from the 'sophisticated' corners of the country. The 'melancholy, long, withdrawing roar' of the 'sea of faith' (described in Arnold's 'Dover Beach') happened so long ago, and the retreat of the tide has been so relentless, that some of us have never even seen the sea. We have no idea what it was like to live in an age in which religion seeped into all corners of the community. That was the opportunity which these communes afforded. I could spend time with people who looked to Jacob's, rather than the property, ladder; with people who displayed animation rather than anomie.

There's nothing new, of course, about disdain for religion. What is extraordinary and unprecedented, though, is our ignorance about it. Even Nietzsche (always first to be name-checked by anti-religionists) wrote that loving men for the sake of God 'has been the noblest and most remote feeling attained to among men'. He did, of course, dismiss it as 'an abundance of superstition and nonsense', but he also said that if we love man without the sanctity of an ulterior objective we're guilty of mere 'stupidity and animality'. 'Let him be holy and venerated to us for all time', he wrote of *homo religiosus*, 'as the man who has soared the highest and gone the most beautifully astray.'7 Going 'beautifully astray', I thought, is rather a good intention for a travel book. I would rather, I thought, get lost in sunshine and enchantment than remain in the dark at home. At least that way I could pick up the gauntlet eloquently thrown down two centuries ago by Friedrich Schleiermacher: 'I wish only,' he wrote to those who are contemptuous of religion, 'to call upon you to be properly informed and thorough-going in that contempt.'8

Moreover, it became obvious that any debate about the meaning of community required meditation upon religion and vice versa.

The etymological origin of 'religion' implies community; it means to 'tie in', to bind, to *ri-ligare*. Community and religion have always been intimately linked and the debate about which came first has been a fairly chicken-and-egg one. For believers, religion is clearly the architect of community; its values provide the foundation stone for society. For others, religion is the means by which society endorses and legitimises itself, it is the deification of the established order. The connection between the two was clear and I was keen to trace the ways in which the two played upon, were even dependent upon, each other. Because something very unusual has happened to religion recently. It, like everything else, has become privatised. Years ago, Cardinal Basil Hume observed that shopping was the new religion; whereas, in truth, it's also the reverse. Religion is the new shopping. As anyone who has ventured into the boom industry of 'retreat centres' offering spiritual detox knows, religion has been privatised in both senses of the word: in the commercial sense, in that it increasingly involves a financial transaction, thereby mistaking the believer for a buyer; but also in the sense that the communal, shared experience of religion has been eroded. Gone are the nationalised religions with their monopolies. Everything has been deregulated, opened up to competition. Religion has gone into retail and what we now have is one huge spiritual supermarket. One can walk up and down the aisles picking and mixing according to taste. Or, to use Peter Berger's metaphor, the sacred canopy no longer covers us all; at best we might have sacred umbrellas. Someone might stand under your umbrella with you for a while, but more normally that sacred umbrella – the personalised, privatised and individualised religion – only adds to our sense of isolation. Even if it only covered a small community, I hoped to crawl back under that sacred canopy to see how much religion really is communal, and how much it is always, necessarily, private.

All of which, I appreciate, makes for a bemusingly ambitious book and the result may fall far short of the intention. But that, in some ways, is the book's central question: whether it's better to have aspirations, idealism and beliefs even though you know you'll fall short and fail. The book is, I know, fairly inchoate. On the journey I've often felt like a blind person standing next to someone describing the view: you admire their eloquence, but occasionally doubt that the scenery is really there. Or maybe they, too, are blind and are only consoling you.

The selection of the communities probably requires explanation, but I'm not sure I'm able to provide one. When I told friends about this book, they all assumed I was off to Japan or India, or exotic destinations in far corners of the globe. In reality, I chose three communities in Italy and two in Britain because I think the failing of books on community is that they're normally too exotic, not only ideologically but also physically removed from the writers' native habitat. In order to do justice to profound and complicated beliefs, I only wanted to write about places where I'm linguistically or theologically fairly fluent. That meant I stayed on home ground, meaning Italy and Britain. In three out of the five chapters, I stayed within Christian communities; one stridently so, the other two very subtly so. There are numerous and admirable 'retreat centres' and communes of non-Christian faiths, and I have visited many of them; but – out of respect for their depth, rather than disdain for their difference – I haven't felt competent to write about them. Beyond that, however, the actual selection of the communities was very random, almost unprofessional. I followed hunches. Someone would say something in a pub or during a weekend with mates, and we would be off. My method of selection – as much as there was one – was simply to stay in places I found thought-provoking (with the result that I often write not so much about the communities but the directions in which they pointed me). I was also intent on finding places I admired. Only in one of these communities (Damanhur) am I less than lukewarm, but I included it because it seemed an appropriate point of departure for reasons which will become obvious.

To all but the first location, I was accompanied by my wife, Francesca ('Fra'), and our baby daughter, Benedetta ('Benny'). I dislike writers who yank their partners and kids into books through pride or a need for light banter. But they were with me on the road, they made the trek fascinating and fun, and I wanted to write the book exactly as it happened. Taking my family wasn't intended as a cynical entrance voucher, but I slowly realised that if you show up with a woman and a tiny girl under a year old, the reaction to your visit is extraordinarily different. All sorts of gender and generational issues are thrown up and the interaction is

6

subtly altered. Nor did I ever go, as it were, undercover. If anyone ever enquired why I had rolled up in their midst, I normally said more or less what I have written here. I didn't go anywhere which charged admission. Not for miserliness, but because it would have skewed the relationship and negated integration, however temporarily, into the community. I paid with time rather than money, offering to do any job going: teaching, washing up, gardening, farming. Hopefully that investment will benefit the book more than it did various gardens.

Choice

Before I leave home on this strange pilgrimage, it's only fair that you know why I'm leaving in the first place. Most pilgrimages have an object in sight: a shrine, a chapel, a Madonna or a mountain. I have no end in mind. And, in a way, I don't mind where I end up; I only know that we have to leave home. I can't stay here, like this. I find everything false and fanatical.

If you want to know why I'm stepping off the exhausting, hedonistic treadmill, it's enough to look at the way I live now. I drive thousands of miles every year to see friends and relatives who live the other side of the country or the continent. None of us live in the same neighbourhood any more and mobility is the neurotic result. We're never at home for the weekend. I seem to be suffering from an inability to stop and belong. Where I stand used to be the centre of my world, but it's no longer like that. The world has shrunk exponentially and now, instead of feeling at home where I actually am, I imagine home is wherever I'm not. I've become like the permanent passenger described by Ivan Illich:

> His inherited perceptions of space and time and of personal space have been industrially deformed. He has lost the power to conceive of himself outside of the passenger role. Addicted to being carried along, he has lost control over the physical, social and psychic powers that reside in man's feet. The passenger has come to identify territory with the untouchable landscape through which he is rushed. He has become impotent to establish his domain, mark it with his imprint and assert his sovereignty over it. He has lost confidence in his power to admit others into his presence and to share space consciously with them. He can no longer face the remote by himself. Left on his own, he feels immobile.[1]

Community is obviously difficult in this strange world. By 2003, the annual distance covered by passengers in the United Kingdom was 794 billion kilometres. That is only domestic travel and doesn't even include all our manic flights abroad. 678 billion of those kilometres are travelled by car (an increase of 68 per cent from 1980), whereas on average we each travel only 191 kilometres per annum on foot (a decrease of 19 per cent since 1989).[2] We've all become consumers of distance, breaking down boundaries as we career from one destination to the next. We're perpetually ahead of ourselves, trying to get to somewhere before everyone else. It's a truism of our way of life that we're constantly in-touch but out-of-place. We're always wanting to be somewhere else, and when we arrive there we find ourselves talking to someone who's not there and immediately start thinking about the next journey, the next stop. By now, even the word 'stop' is misplaced: 'fleeting pause' would be more appropriate.

Speed becomes paramount. Computer connection or five-gear estate, I've got to get there quickly. If I ever get caught in traffic, or in a shop queue, I'm insufferable, impatient, moody: 'Get out of my way,' I whisper through gritted teeth. I'm addicted to a way of life. Like all addictions, it gets worse the longer it goes on. The joys are more intermittent, the sorrow always increasing. I'm spending far too much money and working harder to earn more so that I can travel further and faster and screw the neighbours. We pride ourselves on being democratic, but have a caste system according to speed and time. We're speed capitalists obsessed with the exchange value of time – time spent, invested, employed, wasted. We all realise the bane of being always busy, and that's compounded because we rarely know why we're bothering to be busy in the first place. Even sources of knowledge suddenly boast not that they're accurate, but that they are based on speed (the internet's *Wikipedia* derives from the Hawaiian 'wiki' meaning 'fast' or 'quick'). We're all search engineers, racing around for important information delivered in a thousandth of a second. Truth is a secondary consideration and is relegated to whatever you can get away with saying.

I thought I might find the solution to such things in high culture but it seems to have become infected not by satire but by cynicism. Satire is both pessimistic and idealistic: it points up hypocrisy by recognition of something superior. Cynicism is different because it makes hypocrisy disappear; it has no means to measure aspiration and the falling-short. The whole point, I always thought, about art or fiction or drama is that they allow us the magnificent luxury of stepping into a world other than our own. That is precisely why they could be idealistic or offensive or satirical, because they take us out of our context and show us alternatives. But the vengeance of cynicism precludes all that. Art must be realistic to the point of brutality because realism is identified with honesty. No stretch between reality and possibility is allowed. For all our vaunted mobility, we're actually mired in the mud. In modern art, shit literally wins prizes.

Our culture is by now based on the exclusion of any idealism. We've convinced ourselves that the greatest ideal is not having one; the absolute truth is that there is no absolute truth. Tolerance as it's conceived today is really about serving two or more masters, or none at all. It's vague, predicated on being noncommittal. It borders on chaos because we're building communities, if they can be called that, which have nothing in common. Our universalism is based on difference, on my identity being different from yours. We delight in diversity to such an extent that it becomes the only definition for what unites us. What appears to its proponents rather mystical appears to most of us insanely vacuous.

I work very hard, but never have any money. Every choice I make seems stupid as soon as I've made it. I have a chronic case of consumer melancholia: objects which, when they're on the shelf, promise to remedy problems of self-worth turn out to be, well, just objects. I spend hundreds of pounds a year on books I never read, on clothes I never wear. I've spent years believing that retail is the way out of existential angst. I make wrong choices, stupid purchases, but at least there's always another purchase around the corner to remedy everything (for a price). That's what I love about retail: it's so forgiving. It always lets me back. I haven't yet worked out why, if there's so much choice, we're all wearing the same logos, all bringing home the same Ikea lampshades. The pushchair (now called an 'integrated travel system') my nephew in Parma uses is exactly the same as the one I bought in Bristol. We delight in diversity, whilst actually becoming production-line consumers.

Our nearest high street has a shop called a 'Lifestyle Centre', where the word 'lifestyle' has become so stylish it's become a registered trade mark, canonised by having an encircled 'R' above it. There's even a church a few hundred metres away called the 'Lifestyle Church'. Everything is about adopting a pose. It all seems the relegation of style, its reduction to something much more material: your life is communicated to others by the style you have and that is dependent upon the lines of your new stereo and so on. The surprising thing is that we don't actually realise that our feeling of dehumanisation is created by that wholesale identification of ourselves with what we own. It seems as if we no longer have any vocabulary or argument to confront what we instinctively know is damaging, even devastating, to our human ecology: rampant consumerism. Such is the climate of shrugging accommodation to advertising and greed that even to take them on makes one sound like a prig. Talk to advertisers about their trade, and you'll never again misunderstand cynicism. Some pretend to think advertising is dedicated to idealism because it's the purest form of democracy, in which you give people exactly what they want. But it's manipulative and invasive. It's the advertisers who puppeteer the cold-callers, those cheap-as-chips workers in Asia who repeatedly call you out of the blue at home, trying to be intimate by manically repeating your name. They're the customer-profilers, paid to ask you questions about your lifestyle and possessions so that they can report back to the marketing or advertising campaign team who will create the perfect commercial to persuade you there's something missing in your life. There are focus groups whose job is the same: they study us by analysing our desires and allow advertisers to pronounce themselves the high priests of democracy because they give us what we want. It's supply-and-demand, that perfect equation between them and us: we need, they deliver.

But actually all those promises have turned out to be false. The promise of happiness has created an epidemic of depression. It's us who are being consumed, not the objects. The idealistic promise of post-modernism (that we tolerate all opinions, allow absolute autonomy to individuals, grant rights and choices in abundance) has turned out to be scintillatingly cynical. Post-modernism is the hidden fuel of the consumer culture. It allows everything to be erased, replicated, replaced. Nothing even aims for permanency or perfection and thus the throw-away-buy-again society finds its cultural justification: we're constantly buying because we're cool chameleons. We're ceaselessly changing, dressing up to assume new roles. We never have to remain the same because we can always move on. We mustn't ever belong, ever hint at commitment, because that would be the death-knell of rights and choices. That way no door is ever closed to us, no purchase or partner ever precluded. Sounds good, huh? But it's not. The promise never comes to fruition. We can't even remember what the promise was, because any promise relies upon patience and a degree of permanence and they, in this weird world, are outlawed.

I simply can't continue living like this. I'm feeling increasingly apocalyptic. We're rushing towards the economic and energetic bankruptcy of the planet. Very shortly we'll be unable to pay back the loans. We're taking everything for ourselves. Our children and grandchildren will remember us as the unnatural ancestors who left the world infinitely worse than we found it. I used to think 'egomaniac' was hyperbole, but now I don't think it's strong enough to describe myself and the vast majority of Westerners. For the first time in human history, certain societies have an extraordinary surplus of goods. They have no memory of what it was like to struggle to meet essential needs and have now replaced need with desire. The same survival drive is present, the same ruthlessness in pursuit of the new need. New objects are never lacking.

Already the first or second question people ask on looking for a house is about storage space, because we've all got too many possessions. We just haven't got enough space to put them, so we have to work harder and earn more aggressively to have a couple of extra square metres of floor, which will then get filled up with more rubbish. The city of Bristol alone produces 190,000 tonnes of rubbish a year. That, I'm reliably informed, requires a land-fill site twenty-seven times the size of Bristol's massive cathedral. That's every year. As a society we've got exactly that collective addiction to consumerism which is evoked in Italo Calvino's 'Leonia'. This is a place, described in *Invisible Cities*, which delights in pristine, new products, a place which, on the surface, is spotless and happy. And yet that glorified comfort can be measured not in what is bought, but what is expelled:

It is not so much by the things that each day are manufactured, sold, bought that you can measure Leonia's opulence, but rather by the things that each day are thrown out to make room for the new. So you begin to wonder if Leonia's true passion is really, as they say, the enjoyment of new and different things, and not, instead, the joy of expelling, discarding, cleansing itself of a recurrent impurity. The fact is that street cleaners are welcomed like angels, and their task of removing the residue of yesterday's existence is surrounded by a respectful silence, like a ritual that inspires devotion . . .3

Leonia is a place, like our own world, which prizes cleanliness and novelty, where it would be bad form to mention the existence of waste and want.

I hear myself grumbling and begin to suspect that I'm becoming a fogey. Perhaps this is what ageing feels like. The world suddenly seems tawdry, ineluctably more tacky and vulgar than you remember it. And yet, if you look closely, the fogeys are getting younger . . . which is amusing but also intriguing. Why are people barely in their thirties, having gulped down every elixir in the cupboard, suddenly saying 'this is wrong'? 'This is vulgar and silly and unsatisfying,' they think, but rarely admit it because they think to do so would appear, well, fogeyish. Some do say so, and with humour: the 'Chap Revolution' is an amusing movement for more politeness, etiquette and class. It's a sideshow which barely registers on the media radar, but it's delightful precisely because it tries to recuperate what we chucked away in the rush for that cupboard. It takes a leaf out of the cool, non-conformist's manifesto and turns it, tongue-in-cheek, against the vulgarity of modern life.

But everywhere else I look there's something to depress me. When I walk home in the evening the pavement is covered with the greasy shreds of kebab cabbage. Red-eyed smokers with centre-partings are screaming abuse at each other. Train carriages smell of warm polystyrene and fries. Rugby pitches are covered in blue paint because of banking sponsorship.

Whenever I go out I'm surrounded by people looking lonely merely by the effort they're putting into not looking lonely: talking loudly, guffawing louder. A few weeks ago I went to a club in Parma. It was frenetic: two dance-floors, an illuminated swimming pool, private tables. This is Italy, but it could be anywhere: the music's the same everywhere, so are the people. I've seen the symptoms and, having suffered from them myself, recognise them: the manic desperation to live some colour-supplement lifestyle. There are video screens showing the latest risqué snaps from some modelling agency;

there's advertising around the dance-floors for a local furniture chain called (in English to get in the musical meaning) 'I love my house'. When we go home there's so much traffic, at 3 a.m., it seems like rush hour. It's all so depressing. It's institutionalised rebellion, absolute conformity under the disguise of radicalism. It must be Fate (or whatever's) way of laughing at us that the bright lights that we think will make us ecstatic are actually isolating.

If we're not addicted to shopping or alcohol, it's something else. More than half of my friends or relatives have been on anti-depressants. Me too. Many still have blips and have on-off relationships with their therapists years after the initial darkness descended. The cost comes second to the mortgage in the 'out-goings' accounting column. Many of my friends now talk about their 'life coach' as casually as, presumably, people used to mention their parson fifty years ago. Everyone seems caught up in a vortex of debonair desperation. We're all yearning for perfect relationships at the same time as insisting that rootedness and belonging are alien to our vaunted autonomy.

I don't know why, but I have a problem with the globalised universalists. They seem to be starting at the wrong end of the cosmos: leaping for planetary glory before they know what a microcosm might be. Our modern universalists seem to be the cause of, not the cure for, our malaise. They suggest we can be at home anywhere, which means we're at home nowhere. They persuade us that charity begins abroad. Charity itself is now measured not in humans but in figures. It's something done at arm's length, with a mouse or a telephone. We can all by-pass our neighbours now. No one needs to have anything to do with the person eating and sleeping a few metres the other side of the wall. As with television, the universalists stretch our horizons so far that we forget where we're from and where we belong.

So we're all paranoid that we're not where it's at. We keep travelling. I've lost touch with many great friends: not just because we have divergent taste in tipples (they prefer a couple of lines of coke to a simple beer), but because they go to New York or Barcelona for a weekend rather than to Somerset. They're busy. They work until ten or eleven every night and as a reward feel authorised to blow the money on the international stage. I miss them and wonder if they're happier than the rest of us. Maybe they really are where it's at.

In case you haven't noticed, I'm constantly complaining. I've turned ranting into my default pastime. I go red in the face when a booking is forgotten or the courier doesn't come. I'm constantly miffed about something. And, after years like this, I realise that I've been living without gratitude. I'm not obliged to anyone and, as a result, I've lost any sense of *oblige*. Our society now bears all the scars of decades of failure to teach those gentle virtues of gratitude and obligation. In an ideal community, the onus for you to take responsibility for other people is borne out of a thankfulness that someone, here, has taken responsibility for you. It's symbiotic, joyous almost, because your relationship is based on love. In contemporary Western society, however, the instinctive mood is vindictiveness born out of years of being told one is a victim. Complaint becomes knee-jerk, litigation second nature. We can be spiteful to people because we'll probably never see them again.

The result is that we furiously defend our territories. What for years was symptomatic of American suburbia is now present all over Europe: the wealthy are creating ghettos, they're 'forting up' in response to fear of the outside world. Not only gathering in gated communities where they can live behind bars and buzzers in exclusive, segregated spaces (11 per cent of all American housing developments as long ago as the mid–1990s were for forms of gated communities)4; there's also been a spatial revolt of the elites whereby the elitism is expressed by never being in one place long enough to call it home. Either way, people now shelter behind either a gate or the passport-and-wallet combo. There's no need to mix. For all the rhetoric of integration, it's ever easier to live amongst a clique: our society is more atomised than ever before. Programmes are narrowcast or podcast as much as broadcast: they're made to order, 'pulled' not 'pushed'; we can shop from our bedroom. It's the walkman syndrome, in which everyone struts to their own soundtrack. By now, 31 per cent of all households in Britain are occupied by just one person living alone (a figure which has almost doubled from 17 per cent in 1971)5. The old methods of throwing open the doors to fate – hitchhiking or train-carriage conversations – are almost extinct.

Many people have said to me in the last few days that it's crazy for a young family to go to live in communes for a year. 'They're bound to be narrow-minded,' friends said, 'they're just escapists from the real world.' One mentioned the famous cartoon of a grassy meadow with the wooden sign for the commune: 'Blissful acres: an ignorant community'. But we're leaving home because we feel imprisoned in this so-called open society where we've banished chance and replaced it with choice. We screech about rights, but are unable to understand why we remain unloved and unhappy. We're miserable despite enjoying a freedom which is unprecedented in human history.

It's very difficult when noble ideas have been deified to suggest that they may have ignoble consequences. And it's deeply unfashionable to offend those twin objects of modern desire, choice and rights. But they have become millstones around our neck, hindering our ability to raise our voices to other virtues. I want to get back on the road not to contradict rights and choice, but to find the complementary virtues they require to remain themselves virtuous. And I want to observe whether, in the ether of human relationships, a sense of the sacred is a hindrance or a help. Is it possible that we only become fully human by accepting that certain things are hallowed? Or is the sacred just a sophisticated way to worship ourselves even more than we already do?

So that's why I'm leaving home. I admit that a pilgrimage without a destination doesn't sound particularly promising. I don't know if this is going to go anywhere. And I realise that there's something paradoxical about travelling to cure myself of pathological wanderlust. But it's done: the bags are packed. We're on the road again. Or rather, I am: Fra is heavily pregnant with Benny and sits this one out.

I'm on the dual-carriageway north of Turin taking you to the fringes of Piedmont, 'the foot of the mountains'. Come here during the skiing season and the traffic is terrible, full of cars bombing towards resorts like Cervinia. Now, though, it's a peaceful drive. It's late September and the sky is a deep blue. I can just see Monte Viso as I climb into the hills outside Ivrea. I'm headed towards Val Chiusella, near the French border. Somewhere close by is the 'Great Paradise' national park, the former hunting reserve of Vittorio Emanuele II.

As I get closer, there are advertising boards along the side of the road. Most are announcing the 'great opening' of some new commercial centre or car outlet. Every now and again, though, there's one advertising Damanhur. The road meanders over mountain rivers, barely a trickle now. There are vineyards stretched across steep hills. It's an impressive valley: a deep chasm straddled by the hydroelectric dam built in 1922.

I first read a reference to the Damanhur community in a book and during the following years I occasionally came across mention of it: once, outside Vicenza, I met a music-loving dentist who played me a CD of his duo-tonic Tibetan singing recorded at Damanhur. Then, a year later at the summer fair in Fornovo, outside Parma, I saw a middle-aged man selling rainbow-coloured jelly plant-feed on a stall covered with fliers for the 'utopia'. But otherwise Damanhur is unheard of. Unless they remember a curious news incident from a decade ago, no one in Italy knows of its existence.

I've come here because this community says very intriguing things. As you walk around with me, you'll think they're all wackoes, that this is a classic hippie commune. But this is a very shrewd place, a commune which privatised itself and discovered big, international fame on the spiritualist circuit. It's been the subject of various academic monographs. Damanhur is the first stop on the road out of the 'real world' because, for all its strangeness, it is the community most faithful to it. It isn't at odds with the world I know, but one which, in some ways, faithfully reflects it.

Damanhur is announced by a line of flags by the roadside: the UN, the US, the EU and the rest. Pride of place is the Damanhurian flag: two superimposed squares which form an eight-pointed star against a yellow background. A display shows the time and temperature in red neon. I stop at the barrier of the car park and get my visitor's pass.

'You know the rule? No smoking on any Damanhur territory.'

It's Year 29 *anno horusiano*. People are rushing across the large car-park carrying filofaxes and chrome lap-tops. The women are wearing long linen dresses and many men are wearing flowing hemp clothes, but they're mostly talking into mobile phones. As I walk up to the main reception centre, there's a cashpoint. A few metres away, there's an automatic machine for changing my euros into crediti, the Damanhurian currency. I feed in my 50 Euros and three perfectly minted coins drop out the bottom: two twenties and a ten. The credito is what's called a 'complementary currency': one credito equals one euro.

I walk past the various boutiques towards the Soma Chandra bar. The strange thing is how normal everything seems. People are drinking prosecco in the evening sun. Men are reading about the football results in *La Gazzetta dello Sport* or else joking in hushed tones with beautiful women. More than any other commune I've ever been to, the people are decidedly bon viveurs. There are wafer-thin slices of prosciutto and melon laid out on large plates. A dapper middle-aged man sits down beside me.

'I'm Sparrow Hawk,' he says.

'Sorry?'

'Sparrow Hawk. That's my name.'

'Oh. OK.'

I introduce myself and we get talking. It doesn't take long for him to pick up my daft accent and he's immediately curious as to why an Englishman should come all the way to Damanhur. I give him my spiel.

'There's no religion here,' he says quickly once I've finished. 'Damanhur is a school of thought, a philosophy. It's a continual spiritual research to discover a unitary and coherent vision of life. A religion, by its very nature, would limit that research by pronouncing its dogmas and beliefs.' Sparrow Hawk has been part of the community since the beginning in the mid–1970s. He brings out a map of the world covered with lines drawn with a felt-tip pen. These, he explains, are 'synchronic lines' which criss-cross the globe. 'These lines are capable of catalysing the great cosmic forces. They're the communication channels of the universe, the nervous system of the planet.' He explains that the intersection of these synchronic lines create centres of great spiritual importance. A couple cross at Glastonbury or Jerusalem, but only at two points of the globe do four lines intersect: Tibet and Damanhur.

Sparrow Hawk heads a cashmere consortium. He passes me his business card and then puts his hands together in praying position and bows slightly before moving off: *Con te*, he says. 'With you.'

I go to the bar to get a coffee and meet Talpa, 'Mole'. We get talking and she starts telling me about how much she loves Tibet, it's one of the most beautiful countries in the world, she says.

'When were you there?' I ask.

'Oh, this was in a previous life. I was a monk in Tibet before I was reincarnated as Mole.'

'Oh. OK.'

'It's very similar to Tibet here,' she says.

Damahurians believe in utopia. Their various brochures tell me that 'yesterday's utopia' has become 'today's reality'. They believe that improvement, even perfection, is possible, that humans are good. 'Damanhur was born to realise the dream of a society based on optimism . . .' says one of the glossy brochures at the welcome centre (called 'Olami').

I leave the Soma Chandra bar and begin wandering around. To the left is the Via della Speranza, 'Hope Street'. It leads to an open-air temple with huge, terracotta columns rising towards the sky. This is the piazza which is used to take the periodic photographs of the *popolo*: about once a year, between the columns, the entire community (currently about 600 residents; there's a wider diaspora of a thousand 'citizens' and sympathisers) gather, all dressed in white, for a photograph. It's an amazing sea of smiling faces which extends way beyond the temple and into the hills and woods beyond. The open-air temple is now deserted and you can see hundreds of coloured lines, like in those gymnasia used for a dozen different sports: these are meditation routes and as you meander around the community you often see people walking, head down, along the lines.

Damanhur is actually called a 'federation of communities'. It has no boundaries but instead spreads over the valley in what they call *macchia di leopardo*: 'leopard-skin' formation. There are outposts of Damanhur all across the Valchiusella: forty-four nuclei, with about fifteen people living together in each. Some are as much as ten or twenty miles away from the central reception area, called Damjl. You can be walking idly across the valley when you suddenly come across a mountain hut which looks slightly unusual: probably with one of Damanhur's yellow flags flying or else giant flowers, painted over two or three floors of the external walls. It's one of the distinctive features of Damanhur that its boundaries are very porous and yet very marked. There's continual contact with the outside world; indeed many Damanhurians have jobs in Turin, Ivrea or Milan. They are nurses or engineers or sculptors or farmers and so on: all the normal careers. Ivrea is the silicon-city of Italy, and in Damanhur there is one computer to every six citizens. So the interaction with the 'real world' is frequent. And yet, the boundaries of the community are precisely maintained by its idiosyncrasies: no smoking on Damanhur territory, the use of animal species for Christian names and vegetables as surnames, the use of *con te* instead of *ciao* and so on. 'With you, Prawn,' you might hear someone saying by way of 'goodbye'.

That porous but distinct boundary means that life at Damanhur (named after the town on the Nile delta meaning 'the city of the hawk' or, symbolically, 'of the sky-god' or 'of light') is an unusual combination of the extraordinary and the everyday. Often it can seem entirely normal: you can be sitting around a table with good-humoured conversation and a bottle of Barolo and it feels like a standard evening in the Italian Alps. Then, suddenly, in walks Shark Hemp, who purifies the food by reciting a prayer with his hand over the *bagna cauda*, and everyone gets to talking about 'the mountain of the initiate'. There are a lot of middle-aged divorcees wearing purple and reinventing themselves as Wiccan priestesses. Cars have 'Protected by Angels' stickers on the back bumpers.

The community is the brainchild of Oberto Airaudi (who is now known as Falcon). Born in Balangero, just north of Turin, in 1950, Airaudi was a precocious child. He published a melancholy novel at the age of seventeen, *Cronaca del Mio Suicidio* ('Chronicle of My Suicide'), and quickly became interested in the alternative spirituality for which Turin is famous. Indeed, urban legends from the nineteenth century (prompted, almost certainly, by Catholic dismay at the role of Piedmont in annexing the Papal States) talked of a 'Turin triangle' in which sinister, satanic goings-on occurred. Turin was, for decades, nicknamed 'the city of the devil'. It is, certainly, an area more tolerant of difference than many other parts of the peninsula: it has a rich Jewish and Protestant heritage and – influentially for Airaudi, who aimed to reverse Exodus and lead his people back into Egypt – the largest Egyptian museum in Italy. Airaudi's day job was selling insurance, a role in which he enjoyed extraordinary success. In 1975, however, he and friends established the Horus Centre, a small unit conducting research into spiritualism, esoteric physics and various forms of healing, particularly pranotherapy. Within a year, Airaudi and his followers pinpointed a plot of land between the small villages of Baldissero Canavese and Vidracco as a point of 'synchronic' importance. They rented, and subsequently bought, the land. Damanhur and its philosophy – the *Via Horusiana* – was born. Airaudi is, by now, in his mid-fifties, and has been the 'spiritual guide' of the community for almost thirty years. He has slightly bulging eyes and a greying pencil beard. He dresses a notch or two below the Italian impeccable look: he's normally seen walking swiftly in jumpers, slacks, baseball caps and such. As so often with Damanhur, it's the apparent normality, as much as its opposite, which strikes you.

I'm walking through the woods with a young girl. It's early autumn and the undergrowth is dappled by the sunlight. We're talking idly as we wander along looking for firewood. We were hoping to cook up polenta for lunch, but the stove has no wood and we're supposed to bring back a couple of armfuls.

'Do you think we should look out for mushrooms?' she says.

'I don't know,' I say. 'What were we going to put with it otherwise?'

'I don't know either. Hang on.' She runs back to the cottage and I can hear her shouting through to the kitchen. A long, loud debate ensues that disturbs the pigs and geese and they join in. I'm leaning up against a tree trunk realising how much of a hippie I'm becoming. I catch myself stroking the bark. The scene is idyllic. At my feet I can see a long, praying mantis walking sprightly over my toes. There are birds everywhere and, since the wood is on a hilltop, I can see through a clearing to the valley below.

She comes running back with instructions: she'll collect the mushrooms and I'll do the heavy-duty labour of finding and cutting the wood. It takes a couple of hours, covering barely more than a couple of hundred square metres of woodland. She's singing as she looks for the mushrooms. I've got a blunt, rusty axe which slowly hacks enough wood for lunch and dinner. It's a blissful way to spend the morning: meeting the most simple, immediate needs. I realise, for the first time, the extraordinary solace of manual labour.

We're starving by the time we get back to the house. A large woman in an apron is in the kitchen, already frying the onions. Others come into the kitchen bit by bit and all help out: opening wine, laying the table for eighteen, slicing the thick rye bread they bake themselves. Within minutes the entire room smells rich but simple: onions, wine, earth, flour and sweat. Everyone is assigned a role and integrates harmoniously into the whole. As we start eating, one of the men tells me about his theory of community. He, like many at Damanhur, appears both eloquent and erudite: 'Aristotle said that if you live outside a *polis* you're either an angel or a beast. I reckon that almost everyone in isolation is a beast; there are very few angels. Better to live in a community where it's the reverse: the beasts are in a minority, they have to be. You know that the word "idiocy" is descended from the Greek *idiotes*? It meant, originally, a private person. Interesting that equation of privacy with stupidity, with the implication that wisdom resides in community. I certainly believe that the only way to lead a profound, simple life is to share it completely with other people.'

One day I'm walking through the fields and come across a crowd. On a nearby noticeboard is a list of competitors divided into their respective teams: Dingo Onion, Penguin Fresia, Giraffe Ribes, Orang-utan Rice, Lamb Radish, Armadillo Chilli, Ant Coriander.

I recognise someone and ask what's going on.

'These are the Horusian games, our equivalent of the Olympics,' he says.

'Oh. OK.' I stand on tiptoe to look over the crowd and see two or three men crouching down with their faces close to the earth. Their hands are put palm to palm as if praying but the fingers are rubbing furiously one against the other and thus twisting a vertical stick in between.

'What's the sport?' I ask.

'This is the final of the fire-lighting competition.'

'Oh. OK,' I say smiling. In a way it seemed to capture the atmosphere at Damanhur. Whilst billions of people around the world watch the real Olympics, glued to the television to glimpse the planet's supermen, here they compete to produce the first hand-made fire. The Damanhur version was infinitely more enjoyable. Everyone was laughing. The spectators, instead of sullenly watching the heroes on TV, were involved, shouting raucous support.

'Over there,' he points to another part of the field where two women are standing twenty metres apart with their eyes closed in concentration, their finger-tips to their temples, 'are the heats for the telepathy competition.'

By now I was openly giggling. The man alongside me was laughing too and I think for the same reason. One may have reservations about the reality of telepathy, but that, in a way, was a side issue. Here a large section of the community had come together in a field to enjoy themselves.

'*Con te*,' the guy said as he drifted over to the semis of the oratory competition.

'*Con te*,' I say, putting my hands together and bowing slightly.

The community has recently bought a large factory on the outskirts of the town of Vidracco and transformed it into a series of artists' studios and boutiques: the new retail space is called 'Damanhur Crea'.

Interestingly, the building was part of a previous 'utopian' project promoted by Adriano Olivetti. Olivetti, president of the famous typewriter company, had founded a political movement called 'Comunità' and was mayor of Ivrea before becoming a parliamentarian. He also co-founded, in 1955, the weekly magazine, *L'Espresso*. A few years later he conceived a project called 'I-RUR', *insediamenti rurali* or 'countryside settlements'. The idea was to give work to people in their own communities rather than disrupt those rural communities by offering work only in the cities. The Vidracco building opened in 1961 and at the height of the mid-sixties employed over 200 people making cases for portable typewriters. By the late 1980s, however, the company was in difficulty and the building stood empty for fifteen years until Falcon and his disciples bought it in 2003. In exactly a year, they had completely restored it: beyond the artists' studios and the school, the building now has a conference centre, a shop for selling the community's organic produce, an engineering office specialising in solar panels, a company selling laser shows, a laboratory researching GM food and so on. People in white overcoats, looking like scientists, walk briskly along the corridors. This is the cutting edge of the community's commercial operations and it looks, like everything at Damanhur, exceptionally efficient.

One particular boutique takes my eye. Behind the counter there are three or four women working quietly under spotlights, twisting and bending metal. It's a light, airy workshop with large windows overlooking the valley. It sells 'Selfs' (they use the English word) and 'Spheroselfs'. I see Stork, an old acquaintance: she's a very beautiful woman with emerald eyes. She shows me her 'Selfs': they are coils and spirals of copper and other 'high-conducting' metals. The more expensive models have little wooden stands and stones; the top of the range have light-bulb-shaped balls of glass filled with pink 'alchemic liquids'. Stork explains their purpose. It is one of those points at which my resolution to be accepting and open-minded is stretched to breaking point.

'The particular energies that the selfic structures call upon,' she says, 'are in fact living forms, border intelligences that can pass from one reality to another acting as a go-between from one plane of existence to another. Selfic energies belong to a sector of our universe characterised by ultra-light speed and when they are called inside an object it is as if they undergo a kind of deceleration. Selfica was widely used in Atlantis . . .' She talks about the phases of the moon and changing valences. There's the memory Self (worn inside a yellow pouch for men, a blue pouch for women), a menstrual-pain Self, neck-pain Self, the environmental-energy balancer (which 'changes the polarity of psychic and discordant emanations'), a Self for pot plants, the dream Spheroself (which 'selects the most useful dreams and facilitates their understanding'). I glance over the price tags: between tens and hundreds of crediti.

By now it's early evening and hundreds of people are arriving from all over the valley to hear Falcon's weekly sermon. Since I'm not an official member of the community, I have to pay 10 crediti to enter the conference hall. Coyote is on stage, doing the warm-up, going over last week's lecture, but as soon as Falcon arrives he drifts off-stage in mid-sentence. Falcon is informal, sitting in an office chair with a radio-mike wrapped around his jaw. Dozens of foreigners are being offered simultaneous translations as he speaks. As in church-going in Italy, there's not exactly silence during the sermon: there's a constant background hiss of the congregation's whispering. Questions come and go: Falcon is asked about everything from the environment to American militarisation, from politicians to astral libraries. He frowns and smiles at naïve questions; at other times, he jokes and archly raises his eyebrows and everyone laughs loudly. All the while a woman writes the gist of his sermon on the blackboard: 'Damanhur – esempio (+ magia = amplificatore)'.

I try to scribble down his words as he speaks:

The rule of what doesn't exist is that it doesn't exist; thus, to fill what doesn't exist – the vacuum – with something has meaning only for what is doing the filling and not that which is filled, precisely because it doesn't exist. The principle is another, it's to transform that which exists into inexistence. The principle of the adversary of the complexity of man is to make inexistence win, which means to eliminate that which exists and thereby action is on the form and not on inexistence.

Falcon has the same hindrance that theologians have always suffered: he's trying to enunciate and elucidate something unknown, unknowable, unspeakable. He's a great talker, though; one might say, almost, that he had the gift of the gab. I'm not sure I understand much of what he says, but he speaks with infectious conviction about the divinities and knows exactly where the parallel windows and doors are to be found.

When you meet him, Falcon doesn't seem like a charismatic leader. He's more like a managing director of a large company: not self-important, but simply very busy keeping the balls in the air. The kind of man you should only way-lay if you have something important to say. He speaks of Damanhur as the 'holy city' of the future and hopes that a 'new species' of human will emerge from his mass experiment. When you speak to him, you know that he knows exactly what he's doing. He has thought everything through and, invariably, seen everything through. He exudes contagious self-confidence.

'Community,' he tells me, 'means the point at which the individual and the community find each other, in which the individual isn't lost but manages to maintain his own singularity. Of the people who come here, there are those who need reassurance, who come to take rather than to give. By contrast, there are those who come with the idea of getting things done. There's a net distinction between those who are looking for Disneyland and those who come for a spiritual pilgrimage. With the first, you do the little tour, you're polite and you try to lead them to the exit.'

What makes Falcon's vision original, and his community exceptional, is that it has become, as he says, a community of individualists.

In concrete terms that means Damanhur has done something extraordinary for a commune: it has privatised itself. 'The community in 1970s style doesn't exist any more,' says Falcon dismissively. 'They were idiocies in which people didn't want responsibilities, in which they were only looking for a way out. Here, we have tried to generate responsibility. We tried to privatise four times. In 1984, people weren't adequately mature, it didn't work. We managed it only ten years ago.'

In the 1990s businesses began to spring up at Damanhur: sculptors, potters, bakers, and – the mainstay of the economy – Self-sellers. Falcon issued licences for what he calls 'measured competition' on the communal land. Originally there were five different bakers on the commune; it was decided that the supply exceeded demand and three of the licences were revoked. For every business – from the mosaic-makers to the *caseifici*, the cheese producers – there are always two licences to guarantee internal competition. But the businesses run privately, autonomously. They stand or fall on their own. It has caused friction but Falcon has tried to stress the difference between interests and ideals: 'As you create responsibility, it's necessary to reassure the citizens, persuade them that there is a collective solidarity, that we have shared ideals. That way you manage to obtain the balance between competition and belonging.'

The use of the currency system of crediti bears witness to the inventiveness and financial nous of Falcon. Originally intended as a means to 'clean up' the concept of money, to return it to a means of exchange rather than an end in itself, it now doubles as a useful way to attract custom. Some petrol stations in the valley, for example, accept crediti. To redeem them the pump attendants come and shop at 'Damanhur Crea'. It creates a financial, and philosophical, affinity. When you visit comparable communes like Findhorn in Scotland you often find something rather threadbare where they charge you £14 to wash up for the day; Damanhur, by contrast, is financially buoyant. Not least because everything has a price. It costs 55 crediti to visit the temple; 10 to hear Falcon speak. Even his previous sermons are on sale, along with his books, at the back of the conference hall. 'The idea of becoming rich never scared us' was one explanation I heard when talking about the well-oiled operation. Damanhur has international duty-free shops in Abu Dhabi and Saudi Arabia. Its members export produce (organic food, art, furniture and clothing) to all corners of the globe. Damanhur has become a mini-multinational and there's a sharpness about money which would make even an indulgence-peddler of the Middle Ages blush.

'Our philosophy is capable of modulating itself,' says Falcon, 'it is rethought, always looking for comparisons. By contrast, religions are made up of dogmas, they're scared of comparisons. We haven't got a good relationship with Catholics; in fact, before, we had a dreadful relationship with them. They automatically assume that theirs is the only truth. External enemies are important in building a community and undoubtedly they helped us. With an enemy one gets stronger.'

I wonder how difficult it would be for Damanhur to survive without their iconic leader. 'I've always thought about the succession,' Falcon says. 'They can do without me, I'm not worried about their strategic ability. It's necessary to recognise authority, if you elect deputies not to criticise them immediately afterwards. Damanhur is a body which moves and I am the inspirational part, it's as if I were already dead.'

This is a strange corner of Italy. I go to Foglizzo one day and there are two constants on the roadsides: the shrines of the Madonna with electric candles in front of the saintly woman and then, at equally regular intervals, there are black prostitutes in colourful bikinis sitting under parasols. I wander from one Damanhur nucleus to another: I meet Crab carrying huge watermelons and then meet Vulture, the former Sanyassin (a follower of the Indian guru Osho) from Germany who's been living here for years. Then, I find myself sitting opposite Lepre Viola (Hare Violet). An attractive, rotund blonde, she's been here since year 7 (1982). 'Then,' she says, 'it was another world, there was the community and nothing else. There were about thirty people, most of whom have remained. Instead of the car park that you see now there was a campsite where we cultivated earthworms. There was mud everywhere. My first winter it was bitterly cold.

'The first people who came here were very courageous. They wanted to form a non-hippie commune, something very unusual at the time. They were very determined people and for me, at eighteen years old, it wasn't easy to be accepted. There was a distance, a diffidence. The summer of 1983 made the difference. In a van a group of youngsters, including me, travelled all over Italy with Falcon. The people came to listen to us on the beach. It was magical, everything seemed possible. We spoke about our philosophy and somebody always came away with us. We returned to Damanhur with another thirty people.' As often happens at Damanhur, the imagery is almost biblical: fishing for men and women on the beaches; I'm later told that work on the community's sacred, underground temple was begun after seeing a star in the east.

'There was a lot of friction between the two groups,' Hare Violet continues, 'between the older and younger people. Falcon decided to mix them up. Half the older people were sent to live with us and vice versa. There were two mentalities which clashed,' she says laughing. 'They were proud, but there was the danger they might become obsessive. We were from the artistic and alternative scene. For example, in the middle of the night we would decide to paint a wall and we would do it. The real integration between the two groups only happened ten years later. That gave us a constancy but now I miss the adaptability, the belief that everything is possible.'

The taking on of animal names dates from that summer. It was, says Hare Violet (in a phrase you constantly hear at Damanhur) a way to *mettersi in gioco*, 'to get into the game'. One of the three 'bodies' at Damanhur is called 'the game of life' (again, conceived in 1983). It's described as a 'path to illumination' and consists mainly of constant role-playing, personal experimentation and reinvention. 'It's a personal challenge,' says Hare Violet, 'a real challenge.' The more 'out there' you are, the more you're standing alone and learning about yourself and your surroundings. What that amounts to in reality is an unusual mixture of honesty, responsibility and inconstancy. There are, at Damanhur, *leggi individuali* in which you register with the 'Collegio di Giustizia' – personal traits of which you should be aware: selfishness or timidity or whatever. You register your self-regulation publicly and others become involved in analysing your behaviour. It's a rather byzantine way to invite self-criticism. But at the same time it creates inconstancy because everything is a game, it's all an enjoyable adventure and whenever I return to Damanhur after a period away everyone seems to have changed completely. There's a kind of frenetic inventiveness in which nothing is allowed to stay still. 'Evil is being static,' a Damanhuriano once told me. Which makes describing the political structure of the commune very difficult. No sooner is the ink dry on one description than the entire thing alters.

Coboldo is one of the elders of the community. A man with a round, kindly face, he tries to explain to me the philosophy here: 'Religion doesn't give valid replies any more. It's as if it described your country, but now we've discovered the borders of that country and gone beyond them. Here there's no dogma,' he says proudly. 'We don't give you any certainty, only doubt. One thing is clear: there is no certainty. It's best to accept changes, never remain set on one single point. One should be evermore flexible. Whereas in religion you stop thinking, everything is already fixed and immobile.'

I begin to hint that I have a problem with the huge amounts of money charged for twists of metal. Do they really have magical properties?

'A crystal or a Self is a piece of furniture. It's an object. The object in itself isn't important; it's the use you put it to which renders it relevant or challenging.'

'It's like Pirandello,' says Hare Violet. '"Tutto è se vi pare": "so it is, if that's how it seems to you". Any interpretation is valid.'

It mirrored many conversations I had over ensuing weeks. There was an almost pathological aversion to positivism, as if it somehow implied the colonial imposition of fact on error. Every utterance at Damanhur was valid and valued because the object of conversation was only the departure point for your own evaluation or interpretation. Nothing you could say could ever be contradicted or wrong because hermeneutics was, unconsciously, king: the meaning of anything – the crystal, the symbol, life itself – wasn't there to be learnt or discovered, but was actually conferred by you.

I spend a day at the school. It's like any other Alpine house in the mountains, except that this one has been painted bright yellow. One of the teachers tells me proudly that here they reduced the hours of the school day because some of the students complained. They have classes which are 'mixed', not by gender but by age. I sit in on a few classes and am introduced to various children: Alicos,

Ariel, Iside. The teacher's mobile starts ringing during a lesson. Everywhere there are photographs of Falcon and on a notice board are the children's letters to 'the god of the black moon'.

The walls of the community's gymnasium are covered with strange signs: curvy rectangles with wiggly lines coming out the top as if they were sprouting hair, a circle in one bottom corner. Once you've been at Damanhur long enough, you begin to recognise these symbols. They are, everyone tells you, 'our hierogrammatic language'. It's a hieroglyphic form of communication which contains 300 different signs. 'Various levels of meanings have been taught to us by Falcon,' says one girl emerging from the gym, still drying her hair as she walks to her car. She introduces herself as Goat.

She translates a few symbols for me: 'to be' or 'divinity' (a sort of curvy W). Once again, you're struck by the social cement in this community, at the brilliance with which the normal is spliced with the unusual: here is an exceptionally modern, well-equipped gym but on the walls is what everyone refers to as the 'sacred language'. Like everything at Damanhur, it's both accessible to an outsider and yet impenetrable; it's intriguing and yet bemusing in equal measure. It's explained in *La Via Horusiana* (the book subtitled 'The principles, concepts and traditions of Damanhur's school of thought') as

> an ancient language which belongs to the esoteric tradition, an ancestral language which existed even before languages started to specialise. It was born before the subdivision of logic: it permits one to travel from one logic to another and is therefore a magic language. It's a language of power which has eight levels of interpretation that correspond to different levels of perception. Who knowingly uses it operates on the physical and non-physical world. If the archetypes could be written, they would be written only in this language. It's called 'sacred' because it's a bridge-language which serves to translate human things into divine concepts.[6]

Goat tells me that Falcon teaches the various levels of meanings; Damanhur's Olami university then runs courses to pass on his teachings. She runs her fingers over the garish wall and picks out a couple of common nouns.

The longer you stay at Damanhur the more you recognise these symbols: they are present in the stained-glass mandalas, on the covers of books, on throws and rugs. Concepts are repeated, and the more repetitious they are the more their meaning, to retain meaning, has to have another meaning, if that makes sense. It is actually in continuous, rapid evolution. What one hieroglyph means today might be different tomorrow. And what you think a symbol means depends on your level of esoteric knowledge. The symbols become part of the community's hermeneutic defence mechanism whereby only the experts understand what it's all about; and the initiates' knowledge is always dependent upon Falcon. Egypt, he once said in an interview with an Italian academic, has 'been used as a convenient external symbolism, in order to hide more esoteric truths that Damanhur is not prepared to share with the outside world.'[7] Paradoxically for a community whose whole existence is based upon vehement rejection of Catholicism, it is in some ways very similar. Unlike Protestant's 'priesthood of all believers', the Horusian Way is acutely hierarchical: the locus of the sacred is distant from the average believer and only the suitably studious intermediary can interpret and explain it for him. There are even coloured scarves which Damanhurians wear to denote their placing within the pyramid of ecclesiastical power.

I run into Goat a few weeks later. I ask her why a young, attractive girl from Berlin, someone who still works as a management-consultant, should want to come and live on such an unorthodox community in the Italian Alps. 'There's such a strong sense of sense here,' she says. 'In Berlin I had such a lack of direction, of destiny. Consumerism was everywhere. But here we're pioneers, always conquering new terrain, creating ideas that never existed before. And we only do it, as it were, by doing it. By getting on with it, using goodwill and intuition.'

Goat explains that the success of the community – and, whatever one's opinions, there's no doubt that measured by human happiness and financial well-being, the community is exceptionally successful – is due to satisfying people's need for both autonomy and inter-dependency. Here, she says, the two seem reconciled. 'Esoteric physics is about power over events. Damanhur represents a promise that you can pursue the life you want. A lot of people don't understand it because it's very Faustian.'

'But to make that society of free individuals work, you need a myth big enough to make you dream, close enough to feel its effect. Its *mysterium* is in the temple, something that you intuitively get but your mind doesn't. You remember what Nietzsche wrote? "Without myth every civilisation loses its healthy and creative natural force: only a horizon drawn by myths can hold together a process of civilisation in a single unit." I think that's very true.'

'Like Bettelheim's "uses of enchantment"? We have to look outside realism to be wise about reality?'

'Right. And in the temple you feel the presence of another being; other entities are present as if the temple is its own intelligence, it harbours sacred forces. I have contacted divine forces, a non-material reality which isn't real but which is very real. The difference is we don't worship the divine, we recognise it.'

I ask her to describe that experience of divinity.

'The experience was a sensation of humility and had to do with love when all thought melts together in one instance; there was a concentration on touching truth, a warm wave in you. I felt enormous acceptance, I was seeing everything there is and honouring it. I encountered a force and realised it was there and sensed that it is supreme . . . sensed it while I'm incarnated and consciously perceiving it. It was a moment of incredible intensity: a respect from the divine towards me as a human being, an acknowledgement that he would honour in me something similar to divinity. We're here to become gods and be recognised as such.'

I'm sitting, lotus-position, on a cushion in the Hall of Mirrors in the Temple of Mankind. The four mirror-lined walls are inclined slightly inward so that the surface area of the ceiling is smaller than the red granite floor. 'Under the floor and inside the walls,' I was told before I came in, 'there is a complex selfic system of copper, precious stones and other metals. One of its many functions is to amplify the various activities of the underground citadel, so that it can be used as a planetary transmitter.' Above me is a huge cupola in Tiffany glass ('the largest in the world'). The sun is enclosed in the wings of a falcon. A serpent ('considered an ancient symbol of knowledge' says one of the accompanying high priests without irony) is depicted nearby. In one corner a two-metre-diameter gong is suspended. Hare Violet is hitting it and the noise and vibrations rebound off all that glass and rattle your ribs. I'm there cross-legged, the soles of my feet facing the ceiling. The gong sounds extraordinary. Booming and frightening but almost quiet.

The temple is an incredible, bizarre creation: a series of rooms and corridors created underground. It was dug by hand, in secret, over more than a decade. It's like a cross between a Salvador Dali painting, James Bond gadgetry and Indiana Jones adventure. The entrance is obscure: it's next to what looks like a garden shed at the back of a house. There's a cement-mixer nearby. Before entering we had to put blue plastic bags over our shoes to protect the mosaics and sign a legal form absolving Falcon from any legal responsibility in the event of injury. The lift which takes you down into the temple is broken so we go down via the old entrance: there's a narrow corridor painted with Egyptian figures. It looks like a dead-end until Hare Violet clicks on her remote control and one of the walls opens outwards into a room. Everywhere is damp and humid and smells of wet sand.

The location of the temple was chosen with care. It is placed, they tell me, where the Eurasian continental plate meets the African one; moreover, it has been dug where an ancient, important mineral, mylonite, is found. Mylonite, they tell me, is 'characterised by the faculty of transporting the physical energies of the earth'. The other aim of this sacred space is that it resembles the interior of mankind, intestines and all: hence labyrinthine passageways, halls, side-rooms and so on.

In room after room you hear the verb *simboleggiare*, to symbolise: nothing is casual here, everything is a symbol for something else. 'Water symbolises memory' or else 'five warriors defend a fire that symbolises the evolving spiritual life of Humankind' and again 'this hall is in the shape of a chalice, symbol of receptivity, offering and a capacity to welcome'. One room, The Hall of Water, 'is a genuine, authentic library, containing written texts in twelve extremely ancient alphabets. Serpent-dragons executed in gold leaf indicate the flow of the Synchronic lines in the Hall.' On one floor there's a dandelion, symbol of Damanhur: yellow, sunny, ever-changing. It takes over an hour to walk through the entire temple and very quickly you begin to suffer from sensory and semantic overload. Every wall is painted from floor to ceiling (which are themselves often mosaics). Once again, although determinedly against native Catholicism, Damanhur is almost instinctively influenced by it: the preaching, albeit very different, is pictorial. Here, though, the iconography is a little more naïf. There are big-bosomed women and naked men with penises halfway down their thighs; smiling crowds running through glens and moors and waterfalls; there are, on most walls, recognisable faces from the community, fighting their battle against the grey forms of darkness. I can't remember who it was that said 'religion is the way a society worships itself', but that's certainly the sense that one gets here. There are images of the beginning of the world: a man blowing the primordial goo from the palm of his hand, with the result that foetuses fly through the starry night. There are spheres and chalices and terracotta caryatids. Then there is the alchemic laboratory for the preparation of magical liquids. It looks like something from a children's Disney film: test-tubes lined up next to bulbous containers, white smoke, like dry-ice, cascading around. As you emerge above ground again, there's a reception room where you can sign the faux-antique visitors' book. Inside there are tens of thousands of signatures from around the world; pages of admiration. Then they ask if you would like to help the magical community in a concrete way: maybe buy a mouse-pad depicting the Tiffany cupola, or a T-shirt, or a CD of their sacred music.

The discovery of the temple catapulted Damanhur, for a year or so in the 1990s, to international notoriety. Because the temple was being dug out from the rock in secret and at night, almost all the work was done without the use of mechanical instruments. For years members of the community would dig through the night with pick-axes; the work was even kept secret from some other members of the community. 'The secret was a very strong glue for us,' Hare Violet once told me, 'something to protect inside and outside of ourselves.' It went on for years, a kind of prolonged bonding session conducted by Falcon in dead of night. Whether or not they believed the place was a 'planetary transmitter' (and many are serious about it), the members of the community shared a secret, and an illegal activity, for almost a decade.

The outside world knew nothing of its existence until, in the early 1990s, a disgruntled former member, Filippo Maria Cerutti, began demanding payment for the investment of his time and money in the Damanhur project. As there was no likely settlement in the offing, Cerutti informed various local authorities of the existence of the temple. Damanhur was subjected to a nocturnal raid complete with armed *carabinieri* and helicopters; during the following days and weeks camera crews descended on the 'cult'. Damanhur was being discussed or derided across the country.

Unfortunately, of course, the temple had been built without planning permission. They had created a huge hole (some 5000 cubic metres underground, according to the Guinness Book of Records certificate proudly displayed at the temple's reception area) in the middle of the mountain. It was *abusivismo*, illegal 'building', at its most blatant. In 1993 the nearby town Vidracco, under whose jurisdiction the temple came, ordered its destruction. Eventually, however – as usually happens with these cases – the national government passed a *condono*, a general amnesty for illegal building, and the temple survived.

For years, the prospect of the town of Vidracco confiscating the temple has hung over the community. It's quite possible that the town could do this and lease the temple back to the community, or even (as Damanhur is profitably doing itself) open it up to thousands of tourists a year. All of which has encouraged a new stage in the development of Damanhur: a political party called 'Con Te per il Paese' ('With You for the Country') has been formed. Bison Oak recently became mayor of Vidracco with 77 per cent of the town's votes, not all of them from Damanhurians. The temple, for the time being, is safe.

The ambitions of Falcon, however, are boundless. He says that only one tenth of the temple has actually been built. He is planning a mile-long tunnel which will link the temple to an auditorium large enough to house a thousand people. Indeed, if you leave the temple and walk up the mountain road towards the peak, you can see the huge bowl where it will be built. He also intends to build a library to house the 'largest collection of esoteric books in the world'. Damanhur is only at the very beginning of its long, spiritual journey, he says.

Over a century ago, Émile Durkheim was explicit about the retreat of religion:

Originally it extended to everything; everything social was religious – the two words were synonymous. Then gradually political, economic and scientific functions broke free from the religious function, becoming separate entities and taking on more and more a markedly temporal character. God, if we may express it in such a way, from being at first present in every human relationship, has progressively withdrawn. He leaves the world to men and their quarrels. At least, if he continues to rule it, it is from on high and afar off.[8]

That paragraph set the template for almost a century of 'secularisation theory', in which historians and sociologists mused upon the decline and imminent extinction of religion. Humans were waking up from a dream. In the process, even the word secular was secularised. It no longer implied *saeculum* ('this century' or 'this age', which could contain, for example, secular priests outside monasteries) but instead came to imply merely the opposite of religious. Many were gleeful about reason's conquest of superstition, but others, whilst acknowledging the moment of 'God's funeral', were still full of admiration for the beauty of the deity created by humans. Thomas Hardy coupled mourning with the affection for what had passed, imagining the bleak bereavement and epic solitude of humanity: 'uncompromising rude reality/Mangled the Monarch of our fashioning,/Who quavered, sank; and now has ceased to be.' He wrote of 'our myth's oblivion' and pondered 'who or what shall fill his place?'[9]

Despite the funeral notices, however, it's clear that the spirit of the age is now . . . well, spiritual. The New Age is everywhere. It has seeped, almost unnoticed, into every corner of modern life – and you don't realise quite how much until you step back from it. If you go into any bookshop the religion section will, very likely, be no more than a few feet long. The Mind-Body-Spirit section, by contrast, extends along entire walls and contains monographs on everything: Bach flower remedies, Reiki, Alexander Technique, Channelling, Astral Guidance, Craniosacral massage, near-death experiences, chakras, the consciousness of crystals, anything Celtic, holotropic breathing, angel-tracking, Wicca, shamanism, yoga, tantric sex, druidry and so on. Few self-respecting publishers are without their own Mind-Body-Spirit imprint, not least because successful titles sell millions of copies. Every bed-and-breakfast in Britain, and most corner shops, have notice boards offering a whole range of services which are loosely described as New Age. Religion, by contrast, is a dirty word. The song which, for many, epitomises utopian aspiration – John Lennon's 'Imagine' – lists 'no religion' as one of the prerequisites for the perfect society.

The key words of this mushrooming spiritual industry are 'growth', 'awareness', 'ancient' or 'native wisdom', 'enlightenment', 'awakening', 'energy' and, always, 'paradigm shift'. It's a world of seers, healers, prophets, astrologers, cosmologists and holistic apothecaries. It's indicative of a spiritual hunger which has outlived the eclipse of traditional religion and which thus seeks sustenance wherever it can get it. That there remains a spiritual hunger at all is an eloquent rebuttal of the secularisation theorists, who expected all such illusions and supernaturalisms to melt away. But the trouble is that many people – myself included – now find it difficult to distinguish what is religious from what is merely moody or 'deep'. Even *Private Eye* – more renowned for comic than serious content – has underlined how sinewy belief has been turned into an easygoing aesthetic experience: '[TV] regulators should either allow completely secular schedules or insist that the religious programmes shown are seriously about belief. The current view that any programme which is solemn or arty or has music or suffering in it is somehow religious is failing to serve either the religious audience or the secular one.'[10]

The New Age is a movement that defines itself against all Graeco-Roman and Judaeo-Christian influences, against all the so-called 'patriarchal' archetypes. Since the emphasis is on the exotic and esoteric, there's a centrifugal movement towards the edges of obscurity. Although on the surface it appears determinedly alternative, Damanhur is actually very much a child of its era; ironically, an almost obedient child visibly following the mores of the cultural milieu in which it was nurtured. Most noticeably, its rejection of anything that forms part of the heritage of the Western world chimes perfectly with the prevailing fashion, widespread far beyond the confines of Damanhur, of denigrating anything our ancestors did. Prompted by a powerful combination of postcolonial guilt, curiosity about the esotericism of Eastern religion and by a vague idea that Christianity only implied conquest and crusades, the New Agers relish anything which will distance them from their own heritage.

In all this, Damanhur is merely an exaggerated example of a very widespread tendency in both Italy and Britain. There's a desperation for anything which comes under the label of 'ethnic'. But despite that, it's easy to trace the multi-coloured threads of the New Age back to more mundane and recognisable origins in the West. The British monk Pelagius (c.355–c.425) is an ancestor of the new spirituality. His denial of original sin, his notion of the ability of humanity to take steps towards its own salvation independent of divine grace, still finds echoes today. Gnosticism is another, obvious precursor. It is the belief in *gnosis*, a secret knowledge which permits individuals to transcend their corporeal existence. Sects like the Cathars, Bogomiles and Albigensians, and groups like the Beghards and Beguines, identified divinity as something internal to every individual. The sixteenth-century Dominican monk from Naples, Giordano Bruno, is also influential: his monistic notion of the universe's fundamental unity has been, probably unconsciously, relevant in the creation of the ecological concerns of the New Age and Gaia theory. Rousseau, too, provides an undercurrent: the unspoken notions sacred to the New Age – that society corrupts rather than civilises, that nobility is to be found in the primitive, that structure and etiquette and obedience are psychologically damaging ploys of authoritarian figures – are all descendants of Rousseau's writing. Other Enlightenment figures, particularly Voltaire, are influential not because they extolled rationalism, but because of the attack on the priestly caste of conformist Christianity.

That liberationist side of the Enlightenment is coupled with the individualism and interior exploration of Romanticism. As one observer wrote during the boom years of the New Age, 'Nineteenth-century Romanticism was strikingly like the contemporary counter culture in its explicit attack on technology, work, pollution, boundaries, authority, the inauthentic, rationality and the family. It had the same interest in altered states of mind, in drugs, in sensuousness and sensuality.'[11] Romanticism involved not only a dreamy contemplation of nature but also, as Friedrich Von Schlegel noted in 1803, an 'Oriental Renaissance',[12] a rediscovery of the Middle and Far East. The New Age continues the tradition: it is, in the words of the Preface to the *Lyrical Ballads*, a 'spontaneous overflow of powerful feelings', a coupling of 'passion' with 'pleasure'. It all creates a kind of spiritual promiscuity which flees from the stern monotheisms of the Western world.

Despite that, the American transcendentalists, particularly Ralph Waldo Emerson, are important influences. 'Nothing is sacred but the integrity of your own mind,' he said; 'the centuries are conspirators against the sanity and authority of the soul.'[13] His message of the sacralised self, living free of fetters amidst holy nature, is paramount to his New Age descendants. They long to be epistemological individualists, meaning that all knowledge would come from within themselves and they would no longer be subject to outside rule. It's all about the 'internalisation of authority'[14] in which the repository of truth is the individual, not an institution. Everyone is enfranchised. Hence the popularity of spirituality (by which most people, as far as I can work out, mean interiority). That's why the name of a particular and popular tour operator is 'Inward Bound Adventures'. Nothing is imposed from without; instead, everything emerges from within.

It's a reflection of the old marketing adage that 'people hate to be sold to but they love to buy'. As long as the impetus and initiative is thought to lie with us, we accept what we might otherwise reject. We don't want to be given something; we want to take it because that implies it's our decision, our call. Interiority thus becomes the redoubt of authenticity, the place of protection against the coercive, authoritarian outside world. Only inside ourselves, goes the New Age logic, is there purity. It's a short step from there to the old notion that sincerity is a synonym of truth. It's impossible to be wrong if we feel so sincerely about something. Teaching becomes equated with indoctrination, an imposition from without. The only legitimate source of knowledge and understanding is the sacred, sovereign self. The name of Stork's expensive sculptures, mainstays of the economy, is no coincidence.

This suspicion of authoritarianism is one of the consequences of secularism. Secularism began not only as a strategy, in the late seventeenth century, to maintain the unity of the body politic after the unity of the Church had been shattered. It was also, paradoxically, a noble ally of the spiritual quest. In theory, no organisation or church was granted a monopoly on the sacred because cosmic truth was considered so essential that every individual was asked to bring their own, personal opinion.[15] Secularism wasn't, in itself, a creed, but rather a broad church where all creeds could be peacefully accommodated. Damanhur is eccentric precisely because it exemplifies that 'breadth': it excludes no one and every opinion, however whacky, is as valid as the next. That's the reason the place is admirable as well as frustrating. I admire the fact that it constantly challenges authoritarianism and is permanently on the look-out for exclusion and intolerance (something institutional religion hasn't always been particularly good at). But it frustrates me because I suspect that the instinctive, unquestioning rejection of authority is as dangerous as the instinctive, unquestioning embrace of it. I'm beginning to feel that one extreme is as pernicious as the other, and that what's required is balance between the two: an ability to distinguish good authority from bad authority.

The trouble is that the philosophy here doesn't sound, to me, like a promising foundation for a community. Relationships would be like the clinking of billiard balls: never really symbiotic, but bouncing off one another at the first clunk. Captivated by his own 'authenticity' and 'sincerity', the New Ager becomes a kind of psychic flasher. As always, Dietrich Bonhoeffer was ahead of his time when he saw the danger decades ago. His criticism arose from a Christian position, but any rationalist would take his point:

> Exposure is cynical, and although the cynic prides himself on his exceptional honesty, or claims to want truth at all costs, he misses the crucial fact that since the Fall there must be reticence and secrecy . . . I'm trying to draw a sharp contrast between trust, loyalty and secrecy on the one hand, and the 'cynical' conception of truth, for which all these obligations do not exist, on the other . . . Anything clothed, veiled, pure and chaste is presumed to be deceitful, disguised and impure; people here simply show their own impurity. A basic anti-social attitude of mistrust and suspicion is the revolt of inferiority.[16]

In the New Age existentialism is, paradoxically, blended with something almost its opposite: the numinous. Psychology is spliced with mysticism; the Human Potential Movement is stretched to the point at which our potential is nothing short of divinity. One of the most eloquent commentators on this bizarre blending speaks of the 'sacralisation of psychology' in which Jung, particularly, 'not only psychologised esotericism but he also sacralised psychology, by filling it with the contents of esoteric speculation. The result was a body of theories which enabled people to talk about God while really meaning their own psyche, and about their own psyche while really meaning the divine. If the psyche is "mind", and God is "mind" as well, then to discuss one must mean to discuss the other.'[17] The irony is that psychology, born in some ways to deal with the trauma of no longer believing in God, has become a back door for a return to the realm of the numinous.

In many ways, New Agers are lapsed atheists. They're psychic survivalists who, prompted by the modern epidemic of depression, have stepped back from the brink of materialist rationalism and are desperately searching for serenity in things other-worldly. The New Age is full of promises that you can radically alter your life, that you can suddenly empower yourself and discover true content-ment. The trouble is that the wilful, conscious pursuit of such things often, somehow, precludes their appearance. We never get what we most fervently desire and the more people desperately seek either happiness or their perfect partner, the less likely they are to appear. In the late eighteenth century the philosopher Jeremy Bentham invented Utilitarianism (the greatest good for the greatest number) and spoke of a felicific calculus (a sort of abacus on which to calculate happiness). It was a theory which made utility the criterion of virtue: if it made you, and others happy, it was good. And yet, it causes disquiet because there's no patience, no notion that such gifts can't possibly be subject to rational calculation but are always inadvertent. Happiness which is centred on the self is tinny and hollow and that's the problem: most depressed moderns display Keats's 'egotistical sublime' without the sublime. Victor Frankl expressed the problem succinctly:

For success, like happiness, cannot be pursued; it must ensue, and it only does so as the unintended side-effect of one's personal dedication to a cause greater than oneself or as the by-product of one's surrender to a person other than oneself.[18]

The longer I stayed at Damanhur, the more I began to feel that they were so desperate for happiness that they would never countenance 'surrender to a person other than oneself'. Strangely, the desperation to be individual, to throw off all vestiges of external authority, actually creates a loneliness and lack of direction and the individual becomes almost pathologically reliant upon gurus and guidance. The ideal might be Emerson's self-reliance, but the reality is desperate dependence.

Another result of the retreat of religion, and cause of New Age's central contradiction, is the sense of cast-iron fatalism. In a world ruled by the scientific analysis of cause-and-effect, our free will comes to seem illusory; our actions are merely the predictable consequences of some cause. The knock-on effect is endless exculpation: nothing is ever your fault if you had no responsibility for your action in the first place. Concepts like good and evil are abolished when free will is replaced by biological and psychological contextualisation, even inevitability. They offer excuses and explanations for the way in which the past comes to bear upon the present and the most liberating, exhilarating claim of religion – that the human can break with his past and enter an entirely different future – is discarded by the wayside. For all its talk of personal transformation, the New Age, with its tarot experts and the rest, is searching for causal outcomes rather than trying to transcend them. It is looking for secret or forgotten knowledge which will unlock the universe and allow certain practitioners of that knowledge to become magicians. It's not escaping the mechanistic, scientific world which derides it, but actually aspires to be the best operator of the system.

Many Christians hope the New Age is a sort of 'Trojan unicorn' for a return to the gospel. They say its existence bears witness to the spiritual hunger of the age. Others are more dismissive. The problem, say austere monotheists, is that, ironically, gullibility actually increases in times of scepticism. Their basic objection is the line, anecdotally attributed to Chesterton, suggesting that when people no longer believe in God, they won't believe in nothing; they'll believe in anything. And the problem with the New Age, as I discovered at Damanhur, is that there seems to be a permanent injunction against ever saying 'cobblers'.

Either way, it's hard to know now quite how healthy the secularisation theory is. Evangelical atheists ridicule religion's claims on the grounds that they by-pass the gold-standard of empirical proof;

religionists counter that for a rationalist to write on religion is akin to a deaf critic reviewing an orchestra merely by watching the movements of the musicians. The academic debate between the two tends to be confusing and circular: rationalists only see new outposts of religion like Damanhur as an example of how daft all religion is, to which monotheists complain that religion is a far more serious enterprise than this and that Damanhur is daft, to which Damanhurians would reply that it doesn't claim to be a religion but rather an 'esoteric quest', to which sociologists ask if it's not a religion why does its existence disprove the secularisation theory, and others (myself included) reply that by now we're totally confused.

Something that is noticeable and understandable in every commune is the attachment to a charismatic founder and leader of the community. Many people had described parts of the overall ideology and theology of Damanhur, but it was only reading Falcon's book, *La Via Horusiana*, that the project became clear: something called the *Operazione Triade* was an attempt to awaken divinities which had 'fallen asleep' because 'the civilisations which created and devotionally nourished them have by now disappeared. At the end of this magic work we will have one divine essence representative of the globality which we have hinted at above, and which will take the name-frequency HORUS.'[19] The interesting thing isn't the unusual theology, but the insistence on Horus as the unifying deity. Horus is a generic name for various Egyptian deities and is often symbolised by a falcon. For a community so acutely aware of the symbolism of ancient deities, it's an extraordinary coincidence. The deity they are all lauding shares the same symbol as their leader. Horus was the creator, the falcon which flew into the sky at the beginning of time. The falcon was also the attribute of the god Ra, symbol of the rising sun. Indeed, falcon is the principle of light, which is why Renaissance printers used a falcon with the motto *post tenebras spero lucem*: 'after darkness I hope for light'. When you know what to look for, the iconography of Damanhur becomes curious. Throughout the temple are pictures and sculptures of falcons, often holding the rising sun in their wings; or else the sun is encircled by a cobra, symbolising fire. There are stained-glass portraits of Falcon himself in recesses. After a while, one begins to wonder whether a personality cult is teetering on the brink of worship.

One evening I go to Castellamonte for a pizza. It's a small town a few miles from the centre of Damanhur, famous for its ceramics and for the fact that it was the birth-place of Antonio Lebolo, the Egyptologist whose papyri were 'translated' by the Mormon prophet Joseph Smith for the Book of Abraham.

I'm sitting in a pizzeria. Next to me is a man sitting alone, drinking a beer.

'Have you heard of Damanhur?' I ask him.

'Damanhur?' he says, almost choking on his drink. 'Don't go there. They're a bunch of loons. They give you everything – swimming pool, sauna, gymnasium, house, job. Everything they provide. But you work for one man, the leader.' He has a strong Sardinian accent and keeps making me promise never to go there. He repeats allegations which have always been levelled at any experimental community, especially Damanhur, regarding sexual behaviour.

But funnily enough, the sense one gets from New Age communes is not – as critics of à-la-carte morality always suggest – that dangerous vices are let loose. It's that the virtues are. It's very difficult to explain, but live long enough at Damanhur or any other rainbow community and you get an inkling that there is, as it were, no geometry to their morality. (Deliberately so, since this is an aquatic age and ethical architecture is a thing of the dark, Piscean past.) But virtues which are incessantly extolled and eulogised without mention of their moral opposite end up having little meaning. It's like someone who's trying to paint a portrait but is so enamoured of white that the entire canvas becomes a cloud. There's no contrast, there's no context, no reality. Perhaps, of course, that's what utopia means: the exclusion of reality, the wilful ignoring of evil. For Damanhurians, evil doesn't exist. There's only imperfect knowledge because actions are determined by enlightenment or ignorance. All of which, for me, only brings to mind Edmund Burke's description of the paper-thin line between benevolence and imbecility. Those who (and they're invariably revolutionaries and utopians) rush headlong towards a conception of good without due heed of its opposite are often as dangerous as those who espouse evil from the outset. One needs what Burke called 'provisions, preparations and precautions'.[20] Without them, the intentions might be right, but the consequences can be disastrous.

Damanhurians, meanwhile, are adamant that their project isn't a religion. As Falcon writes in *La Via Horusiana*:

> A religion – we have said it so many times – is limitative, closed, it doesn't grow because it's dogmatic and most of the time it doesn't allow an expression of an idea of liberty; often a religion tends simply to give commandments and by commandments I mean indications for life which become elaborated according to various ethics and fashions. A type of philosophical process like the one we are witnessing at Damanhur is much broader because it doesn't commence from one or two principles, on which the truth has to pivot, but commences from a series of ideas which, thanks to knowledge and techniques, can slowly become broader and augmented by the same, singular individuals, which allow us, considering the multitude of shapes of reality, to make choices about which one is truly conscious. Where a religion demands faith, a philosophy demands a continual choice.[21]

The last two sentences identify *consapevolezza*, 'knowledge/consciousness' with *scelta*, choice. It's perhaps that, more than anything else, that makes Damanhur what it is. It's all about choice. In some ways, monastic or communal existence has always been 'intentional' rather than 'inherited': given names are laid aside, new ones are chosen. But at Damanhur the emphasis on choice is almost identical to the extreme, post-modern position in which any restriction of choice is seen as a denial of freedom. Choice is idealised whilst acceptance is scorned. You can say and think anything as long as it doesn't preclude any other utterance or thought . . . it's a kind of neurotic democracy, an enfranchisement of every possible opinion. When you seriously sit down and talk to New Agers, nothing ever seems conclusive. You never, as it were, end up with an omelette because no one ever wants to break any eggs. There doesn't seem to be an awareness that choice, like freedom, is only a means to an end, not the end itself. When it is upheld as the ideal it naturally creates disquiet and profound dissatisfaction. Because to have, always and for ever, a choice means, really, never to make one. If any choice we make can always be trumped by another, no decision is ever final and rather than relaxing and enjoying our decision, we're hostage to the dismay that we've made the wrong one. Either that, or else there's a paralysis of choice in which we are reluctant even to make one lest we thereby rule out another. All of which, of course, is music to the ears of the producers and salesmen of the world, because choice is related to greed. It means you want everything and settle for nothing. You make one purchase and, like a toddler discarding his toys, immediately look for another. And the crux is that we become less able to make choices. We are neurotic about making a wrong one . . . so we deify choice *per se* while our willingness and ability to make a choice, which actually takes us beyond choice, are inexorably diminished.

'When the possibilities of choice', wrote Simone Weil in her manifesto for the perfect community, *The Need for Roots*

> are so wide as to injure the commonweal, men cease to enjoy liberty. For they must either seek refuge in irresponsibility, puerility, and indifference – a refuge where the most they can find is boredom – or feel themselves weighed down by responsibility at all times for fear of causing harm to others. Under such circumstances, men, believing, wrongly, that they are in possession of liberty, and feeling that they get no enjoyment out of it, end up by thinking that liberty is not a good thing.[22]

Choice, once a promised land of individual liberation from fate, has turned out to be a disappointment; choice means we have less and less in common. It means we mourn what we haven't chosen rather than enjoy what we have. It means we can never feel at home because we have no notion of what the right choice might look like. Metaphysical belonging is impossible because doors have to be kept open to alternatives.

Because we have no yardstick by which to make the right choice, the labels which used to imply judicious competence like 'discrimination' have become dirty words. They imply the existence of that yardstick that New Agers and their post-modern allies are keen to deny. 'Discrimination' has been sent to the linguistic dog-house because it's associated in the modern mind with racism, sexism and so on. What used to be a compliment ('she's very discriminating') is now exclusively a slur, a suggestion that the person in question is intolerant.

So everything becomes reversible, subject to erasure. There's no solidity and, in a strange way, never any consequence. Heresy (another word which finds itself, in English if not in Italian, in the linguistic dog-house) is an etymological cousin of choice (from the Greek *haíresis*, meaning choice). The point is that without a notion that some choices are wrong, no choice that we eventually make will ever seem either consequential or correct. The actual criteria by which we make choices have become themselves subject to choice: anything goes which means that nothing stays. There's no permanence. The tyranny of relativism has replaced the tyranny of orthodoxy. The trouble is that we're caught in a conundrum. In the stark words of Peter Berger, we're presented with 'an unattractive choice between thugs [fundamentalists] and wimps [relativists].'[23] Obviously, anyone who doesn't want to make a choice is automatically in the second camp. We seem to have come to a dead end in which most of us want to be neither thug nor wimp but can't see the alternative. We don't want fundamentalism because it implies a reduction of our freedom, but relativism renders that precious freedom meaningless because it has no aim and no ideal.

I don't know how I got here. It's gone midnight and I'm sitting in a sauna with two girls in bikinis. We had a barbecue and then a party, and then had a swim in the outdoor pool. Then it got cold and now the others have gone home and I'm sitting here. They're throwing vodka on the coals. I'm breathing alcohol and beginning to feel light-headed. The girls are in their early twenties with, I can't help noticing, slim, muscular, tanned bodies. The thermometer says it's over 75 degrees here and we're all sweating. One of the girls throws more vodka on the coals. I need more oxygen but seem to get more drunk with each breath I take.

'So, do you have a girl in your life?' she asks.

'I'm married.'

'Until when?'

'Sorry?'

'How long are you married for?'

It was only then that I was told that marriages, at Damanhur, are *a termine*. They last as many years as you stipulate in the

48

ceremony. Some people get married for three years, some with more commitment cut a deal for five. (It's an interesting point as to whether a time-limit on your marriage improves or weakens it. Some, naturally, say you would try harder and treat your partner better because you would hanker after 'contract renewal'. Others would maintain that the effort involved would be reduced precisely because in, say, five years the contract would expire.) It sounded rational, but bizarre. I tried to explain, without slurring too much, that I imagined marriage as the renunciation of other choices. I mentioned Chesterton's idea that the most romantic things in life – posting a letter or getting married – are those things that are irrevocable. They're given flavour by being final; that's why wed-free would be much less romantic than wed-lock. The two girls looked shocked. I flattered myself that this was due to my chivalrous reply to what I had imagined to be their advances . . . but then I realised it was actually because I had precluded from my life what they held most dear: choice itself.

It's a beautiful evening. Children are running around in the fields, and fifty or so pilgrims, mostly from abroad, are gathering to listen to Falcon. This time the talk is at Damjl, in the open air; it's an introductory chat to explain more about the community to various German, French, American and Norwegian visitors. They are all offered headphones and simultaneous translations.

I vaguely listen to Falcon's words: '. . . astral travel is a splendid technique for another type of work. Time travel, by contrast, requires a very refined technology . . .' Time travel is the centrepiece of the Damanhurian narrative. In terms of mythological or theological importance, it is their equivalent of the crucifixion. Inside the temple I had seen what looked like the glass tubes of strip lights hanging vertically, surrounded by miles of metallic coils and high-power magnets. When I heard descriptions of their experiments in time travel, I sometimes wondered whether it was really an experiment to test the gullibility of the outside world, whether it was all an elaborate fiction to tease those who thought they were teasing Damanhur. As usual, the descriptions were eloquent, full of unusual words ('pirogue', 'bight' and 'filiform') which make everything sound almost scientific (and, amusingly enough, if it sounds improbable in English, in Italian – being such a soaring, rhetorical language – it sounds almost plausible):

'There are two possible experiences: travelling with your own body and taking over a body already extant in another time. The risk is to move consciousness, strength and material enough to be able to operate. The navigability of time isn't new for magic. The novelty is that with technology one is able to render these experiences possible even to the unenlightened. The first experiment dates from 1994. I went back 6000 years. I reached a village and cut some conventional signs on a pirogue and made sure it was lost. A year later, in 1995, a group of archaeology students, as all the newspapers bear witness, found it stuck in a bight of a river. With our experiments we have arrived up to the Renaissance. The closer in time one wants to arrive, the more difficult it becomes, one needs much more energy. And then, past time is longer than ours: 20 minutes of experimentation here can last three or four hours there . . . you digit codes, you get over an initial, light nausea and you have the sensation of floating inside yourself. Your eyes are closed and you see a sort of shadowed opening in the shape of a serpent, or a door the shape of a comma, and you dive. You actually do the physical gesture and from that moment you're no longer here. You disappear here and reappear in the destined time. But one needs a long training and a long preparation to reach certain time packets, as we call them. Sometimes you're expected by them on the other side, sometimes not. I once found myself inside a kind of bubble, observed and studied by filiform beings of various shapes, coloured violet, and with wide, flat heads. In certain cases the bodies in which you land, if they are sleeping, live you as a dream or a nightmare. During training you learn to feel the arrival of the temporal doors which pass every two or three hours. If you miss the expected one for the return, you have to look for the next one . . .'[24]

It's not the amazing claims which perturb me. After all, every religion makes extraordinary claims and expects you to believe the unbelievable. But I have a gut instinct that the essence of being a temponaut is the inverse of what religion might, normally, mean. It's an extension of the self, spatially and temporally. Ironically, for a community founded, consciously or not, on the neuroses of post-colonialism, it seems a peculiarly imperial aim: one is transported to places not your own, the very aim is to stretch yourself, extend your boundaries, expand. There's something hungry, maybe rapacious, to it all. Not for the first time, I began to feel that, for all its esoteric claims, Damanhur was rather mundane: tourism (albeit temporal) was a kind of consumption, discovery was blended with desire. It's impossible to enunciate properly because it's only a hunch, but I just had the feeling that things were the reverse of what they should be. Freidrich Schleiermacher wrote that 'the basic intuition of religion can be nothing other than some intuition of the infinite in the finite . . .';[25] it's comparable to Bonhoeffer's description of 'the beyond in the midst'.[26] The religious inkling derives from a sensation of a presence from another inexplicable realm which illuminates our own world, throws it into sharp relief. Some external, unknown element enlightens our reality. The temponauts from Damanhur, by contrast, were extending their own presence, placing their midst in the beyond, stretching the finite over the infinite. It was a projection of the first person as far as possible.

The difference between Damanhur and religion was not unlike the distinction Coleridge drew between fantasy and the imagination. Fantasy obscures reality whilst the imagination enlightens it. Fantasy is the puppet of desire, obedient to the whims and strings of the puppeteer. Fantasy is an escape from truth, whereas the imagination is an invention which illuminates it. Where fantasy flees from reality, the imagination distances us from reality in order to deepen it. Since fantasy originates with us, and creates something unreal for our own satisfaction, it has no perfection to point to. Whereas, Coleridge wrote

> both poetry and religion throw the object of deepest interest to a distance from us, and thereby not only aid our imagination, but in a most important manner subserve the interest of our virtues; for that man is indeed a slave, who is a slave to his own senses, and whose mind and imagination cannot carry him beyond the distance which his hand can touch, or even his eye can reach. The grandest point of resemblance between them is that both have for their object (I hardly know whether the English language supplies an appropriate word) the perfecting, and the pointing out to us the indefinite improvement of our nature, and fixing our intention upon that.[27]

There's a difference between the unthinkable and the inexplicable. Time travel, for many, might be unbelievable but it's not unconceivable. It's not subject to empirical proof, but that doesn't mean humans haven't thought of it; actually, it's one of the staples of science fiction. Whereas, as Kierkegaard wrote in his mystical vein: 'the supreme paradox of all thought is the attempt to discover something that thought cannot think.'[28] It's the very fact that religion remains not only unbelievable but also unthinkable that distinguishes it.

I was determined at the outset to be positive about the communes, and I remain impressed by Damanhur. It was, I'm sure, well-intentioned: the idea that anything dangerous could ever come out of Damanhur is hilarious, which is in itself a serious compliment. And I was fond of the people I met. But if I had started off imagining, with Sparrow Hawk, that religion was dogmatic and restrictive, I was beginning to realise that Damanhur was, for all its exoticism, rather predictable. There is no transcension. Gaia is god, the natural is supernatural: idealism is folded in on itself and the 'beautiful frontispiece of eternity',[29] as Thomas Traherne described our world, is mistaken for eternity itself. It's a reduction, rather than an extension, of the horizon. I had been looking for a religious community, but had found one based instead upon magic: 'that form of transcendentalism which does abnormal things, but does not lead anywhere: and we are likely to fall victims to some kind of magic the moment that the declaration "I want to know" ousts the declaration "I want to be" from the chief place in our consciousness . . . Magic is merely a system whereby the self tries to assuage its transcendental curiosity by extending the activities of the will beyond their usual limits . . .'[30] It was a place which spoke repeatedly about the sacred, but could countenance no sacrifice. No demands were made and that, in a curious way, made it surprisingly unsatisfactory.

Danièle Hervieu-Léger has written about religion as a 'chain of memory'. The fact that change is 'a function of modernity itself' means that modern societies are 'less and less able to nurture the innate capacity of individuals and groups to assimilate or imaginatively to project a lineage of belief.'

It requires the slackening of the tradition (of authorised memory) to have reached a sufficient degree for it to be possible to invent an alternative memory. Hence logically it is the periods of significant change . . . which have seen a major flourishing of utopias.[31]

It reminds me of that mournful paragraph written by T. S. Eliot about the erasure of our cultural patrimony: 'If Christianity goes, the whole of our culture goes. Then you must start painfully again, and you cannot put on a new culture ready made. You must wait for the grass to grow to feed to sheep to give wool out of which your new coat will be made. You must pass through many centuries of barbarism. We should not live to see the new culture, nor would our great-great-great-grandchildren: and if we did, not one of us would be happy in it.'[32] Knowing this, each generation urges the next to accept with gratitude and good grace what it has received, only to see its descendants scorn the collective heirloom. The newness appears shallow and we realise, wistfully and too late, what we have discarded. That is precisely what has happened in the Valchiusella. The official chain of memory hasn't only broken at the weakest links; it doesn't even seem to have any strong links left. Falcon has flown down into that spiritual breach and his people have begun putting the pieces back together in a radically new order. I admired the experiment but I'm leaving, I suppose, because Damanhur appears strangely similar to the world I've just left behind. It idealises the subjective and that, necessarily, hinders the possibility of the creation of a true community. Their window on the outside world is a mirror which reflects themselves. There's a kindness, a softness and gentleness which is affecting. But one comes to suspect, rather guiltily, that it's also rather affected.

The strange thing about writing, at least in the haphazard way I go about it, is that you only realise what book you're writing as you go along. It takes you to unexpected places and points in unexpected directions. Having stayed at Damanhur, I'm beginning to think that the reason I wanted to visit communities in the first place is that I'm intrigued by stability and tradition rather than change and choice. Utopia has usually been associated with innovation rather than antiquity because it's about creating a new environment; and living in a community is always an act of dissent, an expression of a counter-culture. But in an age in which ceaseless change and dissent are the norms, the communities which really interested me weren't escaping the real world for the promotion of novelty, but for the preservation of antiquity. True dissent, I thought, might entail stability and permanence. I wanted to glimpse not the dawning of a New Age but the eclipse, if it was an eclipse, of an old one.

Brotherhood

A few months later. I'm on a train rattling south. We're running parallel to the sea and as I squint out of the window to the right I try to
catch a glimpse of the islands of Elba and Corsica. I get off at
Grosseto, halfway between Florence and Rome and walk out of the
station wondering if I will recognise – amongst all the smartly-
dressed Italians – the man from the Catholic commune. It isn't hard.
After about ten minutes a car drives up with wonky hub-caps. It's
not exactly caked in mud, but it's so covered in dust I can barely tell
what colour it is. A short man steps out. He's dressed in heavy,
woollen clothes and a cloth cap. He has a gingerish-grey five-o'clock
shadow. This is Domenico. The car has that unforgettable smell of
old vehicles: an aroma that combines wood and old clothes.

We drive the few miles to Nomadelfia. It's a community which,
to any Italian over fifty, is very well-known: it's one of the most
famous social experiments in Italy. But its post-war renown has
declined and almost no Italian of my generation knows of its existence, let alone any foreigners. I first read about it when reading a
book by Danilo Dolci, an architect from Trieste whose altruism in
the impoverished south meant he was given the nickname of the
'Sicilian Gandhi'. He spent a year or two here in the early 1950s
and it profoundly influenced him. I found the website, read a
couple of books about the place, and decided to visit.

As we arrive, a tablet of ochre stone announces in Latin, Greek,
Cyrillic, Hebrew and Arabic scripts that this is Nomadelfia. 'Legge
di Fraternità,' it says underneath: 'law of brotherhood'. Domenico
and I go for a walk. It's a beautifully clear day. Sandwiched
between the sea and the Apennines, it's a stunning spot: the hills
form a sort of horseshoe which faces the sea. In the plateau below
you can see the thin arms of vines stretched into long parallel lines.
As you get closer you glimpse, through the green, hundreds of
knuckles of rich, purple grapes. In other fields there are horses or
cows. Nearer the houses are pigs and hens. There are poplars and
cypresses and pines. Hundreds of trees have the first two metres of

trunk cut away and Domenico explains that they are cork oaks, the bark being used to make cork for wine bottles. You can hear swallows and wood pigeons. Everywhere there are rich, orange-coloured rocks. I feel as though I'm in a blissful, Tuscan hybrid of the Waltons and the Amish – a serene cross between a farm and a monastery. But one of the first things Domenico says to me is 'Non è un paradiso.' In many communities, especially Damanhur or Findhorn, the first thing they say to you is what a special place it is, how magical this realisation of utopia, how it has become a paradise. I was relieved to hear Domenico, realistically, warning me from the outset that all the normal rivalries and disagreements happen here just as everywhere else.

We get out of the car and start walking: past the dairy and the farm buildings, towards the dam at the far corner of the community. We double back through more fields and come to a circular, walled cemetery just as the land rises slightly towards the woods. This is where Don Zeno, the founder, is buried along with other Nomadelfi. Inside the shrine to the founder is the long text of his dying words: '. . . all that I can say is that I have come to know a new world on Earth: the sons of God, the true sons of God, I have met them on Earth . . . and I will meet them in Heaven . . . Nomadelfia – the world and the Lord need Nomadelfia . . . It is right to say "Your will be done" because I would not know what my will consists in . . .'

Nearby is the full-size football pitch: perfectly painted lines, immaculate nets and fencing. Next to the football pitch are the prefab school buildings: lots of Portakabins with a library at the centre. We go inside and I poke around whilst Domenico is chatting to the librarian. It's well-stocked: not at all restricted to either Italian or Catholic works.

'Complimenti,' I say to the librarian.

'Grazie,' he says. There's a long pause whilst he just looks at me. 'Ti posso chiedere un favore?' he goes on: 'Can I ask you a favour?' I nod, and he starts searching for a book which he says someone from Cambridge once lent him. 'A copy of Cardinal Newman,' he says. He finds the volume and then searches for the address of the Cambridge academic. I flick through the book: it's scary enough reading Newman in English, but in Italian it's bizarre. It seems so remote from the Christianity I was brought up with:

> It's perfectly true that the Church cannot permit its children to cultivate the smallest doubt about any of its teaching. This for the simple reason that one is Catholic by virtue of a faith incompatible with doubt. Nobody can be Catholic without believing simply that what the Church declares in the name of God is the word of God and, because of this, is true.[1]

Newman was, to put it lightly, confident. There was, for him, no difference between faith and certainty. I take down the address in Cambridge, having read, at complete random, that paragraph. I never did track down the man in Cambridge, but the book was a baited hook. I would spend the next few nights in my guest room (a chilly but comfortable out-building miles from anyone) reading the arch-Englishman in arch-Italian.

Nomadelfia was started by an extraordinary man called Zeno Saltini. He was born in August 1900, the ninth of twelve children. He had that benevolent stubbornness common to many Emilians. Having left school at fourteeen, he fought in the First World War where, in a debate with an anarchist, an event changed his life: the anarchist argued that religion enslaved people and that revolution was the only possible future for the destitute and neglected. Lacking the intellectual equipment to counter the arguments, Zeno vowed to educate himself and prove the anarchist wrong: 'Gli risponderò con la mia vita,' he vowed: 'I'll reply to him with my life.' He returned to school and eventually studied law at the Università Cattolica del Sacro Cuore in Milan. Meanwhile, however, he was living in experimental, Christian communities: living with abandoned children or amongst ex-convicts. He graduated in 1929 and in 1931 became a priest. At his first mass he adopted as his son Danilo 'Barile', a seventeen-year-old who had just emerged from prison. From then on his central idea of *piccoli apostoli*, the 'little apostles', took root in his parish of San Giacomo Roncole. A strange family of priests and young children grew up, aided, later, by what were called 'vocational mothers' – women who would take on and bring up the children as their own. The project was called Opera Piccoli Apostolini.

Short, with thick hair swept back and a round nose, Zeno was tenacious and outspoken. Always aware of the anarchist's challenge, he wasn't political but was socially revolutionary. He frequently, in the local cinema, decried the injustice of Fascism. 'Giustizia' was one of his favourite words; when you listen to old recordings of his sermons it's hammered out time and again. On 30 July 1943, a few days after the fall of Mussolini, he wrote: 'Finally the . . . tyranny inflated by egoism and violence has fallen for ever. A regime which has ruined Italy and cretinised youth has fallen for ever . . . woe to those who believe that being Christian means also being chickens.'[2] The sentence is vintage Zeno: powerful and agricultural, almost aggressive. The Seminary of Nonantola, nearby, became a centre of resistance as German troops moved into northern Italy after the Italian surrender. It protected Jewish children, organised food for partisans in the mountains and offered escaped English POWs shelter. On one occasion, eight out of Zeno's twenty-eight 'little apostles' were hanged outside the seminary. One priest, Elio Molinari, was shot. Nomadelfia is proud of its history and later Domenico gives me a video made by an English documentary film-maker about returning with his father to find the Italians who protected him as a POW: Zeno, of course, was one of them.

After the war, Zeno and his followers decided to turn the former concentration camp in Fossoli di Carpi, near Modena, into a refuge for all the orphaned children from the war. In its heyday, there were almost twelve hundred people living at Fossoli. Meanwhile, Zeno also became the deputy mayor of Mirandola and set up a satellite community, mirroring Fossoli, in Tuscany: Maria Giovanna Albertoni Pirelli (daughter of the tyre magnate) had been inspired by Zeno and had bought, on his behalf, 360 hectares of land in Caprarecce, in Maremma.

Zeno had always been practical rather than theoretical. He wasn't good at political compromises: 'God keep us from the politics of priests, Catholic, Protestant or Muslim,' he once said.[3] He made a habit of provocative gestures: on one occasion he hounded his congregation about their selfish, bourgeois lives and said he would refuse to take the next service unless they found decent clothes for his hundreds of destitute children. His mission was frowned upon by both the ruling Christian Democrat party and the Roman Catholic Church and in February 1952 the Holy See ordered him to leave Fossoli and go to another parish. 'I am amongst the most unhappy men on earth,' he wrote.[4] The Fossoli community itself was closed down. It had huge debts and Zeno was tried, in Bologna, for *truffa*, fraud. He was found innocent, but creditors remained disgruntled and unpaid. Reluctant to leave his little apostles and his nascent community, Zeno requested that he might leave the priesthood. The Holy See acquiesced and for ten years he worked in the community in Tuscany (where the Fossoli community had reassembled) as a lay member. Only in January 1962, when his project was recognised by Rome, did he return to the priesthood. Nomadelfia was recognised as 'popolo civile di volontari cattolici' and it became a parish with, for the next twenty-nine years, Zeno as its parish priest.

There are various extraordinary things about this parish, though. First, there is no private property and no money circulates within the community. There are no isolated family units: there are eleven groups (called 'La Bruciata', 'Diaccialone', 'Sughera' and so on) each with about thirty people (from newborns to nonagenarians) who all live and eat together. Only the sleeping quarters, with spartan bathrooms, are separate.

For the first few days I was sleeping in the guests' quarters but eating at the Nazaret group. Everyone asked me why I had come here: 'Friend, for what purpose have you come?' I don't know if it was a deliberate echo, but it sounded just like the question Jesus asked Judas when he arrived in the garden of Gethsemane: Friend, why you have come? I told them I was trying to write a book, and that one of the reasons I had come to Nomadelfia was because of its fascinating attitude towards television. Here there's a very original approach to limiting the intrusion of the media. The community has its own broadcasting service, RTN ('Radio Televisione Nomadelfia') which records programmes and then rebroadcasts a suitable selection of them internally without any advertisements and with scenes of unnecessary violence or eroticism removed. 'Don't always stay in front of the television because you'll become cretins,' Zeno had written years ago. 'And when you're eating, speak amongst yourselves and switch it off.'⁵ So I told them I had come here because – trying to make them laugh although I was serious – it's the one place on the peninsula where Berlusconi's Mediaset is truly challenged.

I begin to get my bearings over the next few days, helped in part by the huge crucifix on one of the hilltops. It's illuminated at night. To say life at Nazaret is enchanting would be an understatement. There are bachelors surrounded by babies, widows next to teenagers. Tackling the dangers of egotism and smugness inherent in a nuclear family was one of Zeno's most original ideas. When he proposed the notion of living in large groups rather than in isolated families in 1954, sixteen out of forty-eight families left, reducing the community from 400 to 260. But it's that, along with the television 'censorship' that makes Nomadelfia what it is. Basically, every aspect of domestic life other than sleeping and washing takes place in each group's central building. Each group has its vegetable patch, its animals, its eccentrics, infirm, elderly and so on.

The experiment is particularly interesting because one of the earliest sociological observations on Italy, one re-echoed throughout the following decades by historians and other sociologists, was Edward Banfield's idea of 'amoral familism'. It suggested that Italians have such close-knit kinships that anything like loyalty on an anonymous, civic level is inconceivable; it is, by now, a stereotype, but one which is close to reality. At Nomadelfia, however, the amoral familism is inverted; here, there's moral a-familism. There's no ideal unit here. It's hoped that the rivalries and jealousies of nuclear families are diminished; and that the love shown to your own children or parents or siblings is stretched to include every human as a relative. With that same aim, every three years, the entire arrangement changes and the groups are mixed up by the community's president.

In other ways, too, Nomadelfia is very unlike the rest of Italy. It's the only place on the peninsula where I can, sartorially, compete with the natives: people here wear country clothes and, for once in Italy, I don't feel self-conscious about my ill-fitting, charity-shop outfits. And one of the mottoes of this place is 'neither slave nor master'. There is supposed to be no hierarchy. No one uses the formal 'lei' which, to me, occasionally seems like the veiling of contempt with faux-politeness. It's great to live amongst people who renounce it altogether. There's never an issue of status; no one is at pains to display their power. Names are, obviously, fairly biblical or else saintly: there are many Zenos and a Zena, a Nazzarena, Amos and so on. Understandably in a place where the role of women is so central, men often identify themselves by their wife's name: instead of 'di Giovanni' or 'Delvecchio' (surnames based on the male), someone will say 'sono Mario dell'Angela'. When my own family arrived I became 'Tobia della Francesca'. It's like being called Joan's instead of Jones, a feminisation of the family name.

The central aim of Nomadelfia remains that of brotherhood. Its aim is to give a home to orphans and problematic children. Since its foundation it has taken in almost 5000 children. It's one of the most noticeable aspects of the place. Everywhere you go you can hear children playing and laughing. There are kids all over the place with the entire gamut of mental and physical capabilities. The community is, in fact, the perfect size for them: certainly large enough to get lost in, but small enough to feel safe. And it's the children who start helping you understand how this place, although it looks so normal, is actually extraordinarily different.

One night outside Nazaret the children are bored of counting jumps with the skipping rope. They decide to play football. The ages range from about four to twelve. I referee. They're playing on the wide country road which comes with parallel ditches at the edge, which double as the touchlines. I've refereed quite a few games of football in Italy and it is excruciatingly painful. Normally you're verbally abused for an hour and a half. People scream insults and blasphemies because that, I suppose, is what they've seen on television. Here it was rather different. Towards the end I compliment them on how polite they had all been. 'Ma va a cantare,' screams five-year-old Ivan, his open palm pointing at the sky, and everyone laughs: 'fudge off' would be the English equivalent, a childish hint at a swear-word.

Another evening after supper in Nazaret most of the women were knitting or sewing. One older, slightly troubled guy was struggling with a jigsaw. A girl in her early twenties confided to me with a shy smile that she was trying to write a love letter. It all seemed bucolic and old-fashioned, even if the gender roles were traditional to say the least. Women were sitting with dozens of infants and, yes, the men were watching the football (the only thing, along with the news, which is shown in real time). About five of yesterday's footballers wanted to play cards and pleaded with me to teach them something.

'I know a fantastic card game,' I said, thinking of that stunning invention, shit-head.

'Come si chiama? Come si chiama?' screamed little Ivan. What's it called?

'It's called sh–' I adjusted quickly. 'It's called wallop.' I've no idea where the word came from.

'We want to play wallop, we want to play wallop,' they all screamed.

I paused, looking round the table at all these eager, excited children. I can never help showing off in these situations and so did a magician's shuffle, pulling my hands apart and spraying the cards from one to the other. 'The aim of the game,' I said melodramatically, 'isn't to win; it's not to lose.' They all burst out laughing at the absurdity of the concept. 'And whoever loses is called "Wallop" by everyone else. We all point our finger and laugh at Wallop the loser, OK? So don't worry about winning, just make sure you don't lose.'

'Giochiamo, giochiamo.' Let's play.

We played a few hands and it was hilarious. The sheer tension and excitement of choosing and playing the last three cards blind was too much for some of them and they creased up in apprehensive giggling fits. Others, aspiring actors, would mop their brow and demand silence before defiantly flipping their cards. They were simply delightful, impressive children. But that wasn't the point. What happened next was what alerted me to the uniqueness of this place. After an hour or so, the children had become fairly rowdy and the adults were beginning to suggest it was time to go to bed. Some had drifted off, still chanting 'wallop' at each other. Matteo – a ten-year-old with a girlish voice and one of those permanent, natural quiffs at the front of his hair – came up to me. He wanted me to teach him how to play poker and I stupidly came out with my usual challenge: 'So you want to lose some money then?' At that, the room went rather quiet. I could feel the adults looking at me and I knew I had said something crude. In Nomadelfia they have neither money nor private property. There is no cash, there are no possessions. In the awkward silence that followed, I couldn't work out how you could teach poker without the rapacious element of Mammon, without the necessary deceit and bluff and greed. I probably, I thought, shouldn't teach it to Matteo. We decided to play chess instead.

Then, a few nights later, Naomi and I are teasing each other over the dining table. She must be about seven and is the kind of girl who could melt a glacier. She's very obviously missing a couple of teeth and I ask her whether she got a good bargain, financially, from the tooth fairy. The place goes quiet again and I realise, not for the first time in my life, quite how stupid I am.

Doing away with money is one of the oldest of utopian aspirations. When I arranged to come here, money was never mentioned. I've been eating food (and drinking my fair share of wine) for a week, and nothing has been asked for in return. Naturally, there is an interface with the 'real world' which involves financial transactions: the community is about 80 per cent self-sufficient, but it does require, obviously, electricity, gas, petrol, paper, flour and so on. Those external necessities are obtainable because the community receives money from the state pensions of any retired Nomadelfi and also receives contributions from the judicial system, which entrusts the community with the upbringing of orphans and young offenders. Also, the community relies on the generosity of thousands of Italians who are regular contributors to the community's coffers; many clothes and much food comes from the Banco Alimentare and Caritas or else simply from the local shopkeepers around Grosseto who often visit. The community also produces something like 400 tonnes of wine a year and as an agricultural co-operative it sells the surplus. But within Nomadelfia itself there are no transactions. Nothing belongs to anyone. Dostoyevsky wrote that true happiness means never having to use locks. None of the houses in Nomadelfia, of course, are ever locked. All the doors are open and people come and go without compunction or suspicion.

I often got the impression that I was watching the world through a keyhole. There's no way my body could squeeze through it, but I can glimpse what it's like for those who have. They have given up everything the world holds dear: possessions, money, almost family itself and the result really is idyllic. Children grow up surrounded by cows and bees and chickens and horses. Most people walk everywhere. There's a football pitch and a library. It comes close to my description of the perfect society. After an idyllic week, I call Francesca and suggest that we come and live here for a while.

The whole place feels a bit like I've always imagined an Italian village from fifty or more years ago. At night, you can hear the wild boars burrowing around the undergrowth and youngsters gather under the one lit lamp on the street corner. On Saturday nights, almost the entire youth of the village head up to the central area to watch the week's film. Men work in the fields, do the carpentry and mechanics and dairy, and women do the *faccende*, the housework, the cooking, the cleaning and so on. Many women also teach. I'm slowly introduced to people as I wander around with Domenico. Some have been part of Nomadelfia since the 1940s, and thus many are natives of Emilia, where the whole project started. One of the strange things is that it feels, more than any other community, like an organic village, a real place, but actually of course the accents are from all over Italy. Some have the missing consonants of the south, others the Tuscan 'C' which becomes like an English 'H', a breath in the back of the throat. They talk about a glass of 'hoha hola'. There are quite a few from the Veneto.

The older men have earthy manners, and when introduced to you speak through grunts and long silences. Quite a few of these old men, I'm told by others later, were partisans in the war. When you work with someone here there's no excess chatter. People are quite reticent which, after some of the immediate intimacy on New Age communes, is a relief. Everyone is polite but distance seems measured. But, as often happens in Italy, some shake your hand and hold it in their grip, talking to your whilst squeezing your palm or leaning on your shoulder with their other hand. It's one of those gestures of intimacy which has never really been exported to Britain.

I'm introduced to Beppe. Despite the sun, he's wearing cords held up by Y-shaped braces. He's got a thick woolly hat on, an unshaved chin and deep blue eyes. His whole body is surrounded by the vanilla-like smell of pipe smoke. He's simple but direct, always talking about justice. He has lived here since he was four. He must be about sixty by now. His father came to take him back when he was thirteen, but he refused to go, saying his father was part of a world which created orphans. 'Orphan,' he says, 'is a word which should be extended to include the homeless, the hungry, the unemployed. God says, "I was hungry, and you gave me food." That's what we believe here. It's about justice for all the orphans. Everyone is our brother.' He shows me his creams which he makes out of bees' wax, peanut oil, propolis and, depending on the ailment being treated, lavender, mint, laurel and so on.

Then there's Sergio. I've been asked to help him in the fields for a few days. We've got to dig up and re-lay the irrigation tubes. The soil's exceptionally rocky and Sergio – one of the original 'piccoli apostoli' from sixty years ago – is looking at me with suspicion as I inexpertly yield the pick-axe.

Someone shouts from the road: 'English boy, don't work with Sergio! He'll break your back! He works people too hard!'

Sergio shouts a reply with a smile and then turns back to give me more instructions. Occasionally, he sends me off to fetch something and, as I trample over invisible vegetables, he screams after me: 'Non pestare. Oh! Tedesco! Non pestare!' But I like him. It's much easier to work with someone who shouts rather than charms. I occasionally feel liberated to shout back and, suddenly, my comedy-accent Italian sounds serious, almost credible. Sergio tells me all about what Nomadelfia was like when it all started at the concentration camp; about how he became the trusted lieutenant of Dolci when they both tried to build another village ('the City of God') on a nearby hill, now abandoned. He still has all his original tools from Fossoli: wrenches and crowbars and the rest. 'Every time we move family group, these are the only things I take with me.' They're magnificent, solid, well-oiled tools, probably about the same age as Sergio, or older.

'When we moved here in the fifties there was nothing. We had to do everything from scratch. The roads, the houses, the buildings, the vineyards.' He points at the cloying clay soil and calls it 'the butter of the Maremma'. It's overlaid with decades of manure, but it's not exactly the best soil for self-sufficiency. There are orange rocks everywhere. It's one of the afternoon jobs, called *lavoro di gruppo*, to clear rocks from fields. 'We used to live in shacks, with bunk beds. It was very, very hard and there was never much to eat.' I've got down a metre or so with the pick-axe and can see the pipes. We slowly unscrew the tubes and shift them to other parts of the field. 'Take the female! Oh! German boy! I said the female.' I realise he's talking about the shape of the fitting, the recipient end as it were. Sergio's rolling his eyes in dismay at my ignorance of biology. 'Emilia used to be the centre of the Italian hemp industry,' he says as he puts the coarse hemp twine around the join to avoid leaks.

Sergio can't remember how many children he has. 'Twenty-four or twenty-five, I think,' he says. 'Ask my wife!' He guffaws, resting his elbow on the handle of his spade. Most couples, those in their fifties or sixties, have had dozens of children. Some natural, but mostly children which are fostered or adopted by Nomadelfia. The president decides, in consultation with the resident priest, with Zeno's appointed 'successor' (another priest) and with the families, who should have which new arrival. The first generation of orphans have now, sixty years on, become the elders of the community. I watch Sergio giving lessons in Sol-fa, the notes of the musical scale, after dinner. He's a bear of a man, gentle but strict. Through the glass door you can hear him helping children sing their scales. Another morning we do the chickens. There are hundreds and Sergio and I have to gather the eggs, still warm, brush them cleanish and put them aside for the various groups. He sees, outside the huge chicken pen, one of the orphans from years ago. He lives down in Puglia now and is just visiting. Sergio starts telling him off immediately, half-jokingly but half-seriously. I can't even really understand why . . . I think it's just because this 'child of Nomadelfia' has left and decided to live elsewhere.

I love the manual labour in the fields. I genuinely enjoy it – spending time milking cows or herding animals or picking grapes or sweeping out the various pens. When you're writing about communes you often get cornered by people who introduce themselves as charismatic healers; for me, the best healing is simply manual labour. Nomadelfia would never have worked if it didn't involve such happy tasks. It takes all sorts of tricky types and puts them to work. The monastic tradition of manual labour is distinguished by the ancients' phrase *otium negotiotissimum*: one was at rest while working, it was an example of 'laborious leisure' in which the hands and muscles were at work, but the spirit, by contrast, at rest. That's why Benedict insisted on manual labour for his monks: 'They are really monks if they have to work with their hands,' he wrote.[6] It was peaceful labour, a means by which prayer and contemplation could continue whilst useful works were done. In fact, at Nomadelfia, one was often exhausted by the evening, aching after hours of tilling the soil or clearing rocks or clay, and yet throughout the day one was serene, genuinely rested. As the Cistercian Abbot André Louf once wrote, 'We must work with some material substance that resists us, and against which we have to pit ourselves to reshape it.' We will 'thus be kept in contact with reality.'[7] It's only now that I realise what a virtual world I've always inhabited. I've never measured myself against any material or matter. I used to think that that made me extraordinarily privileged, but now I wonder whether that liberation from labour isn't rather unfortunate.

It's spring now. Fra and Benny are here and we've moved from the guest house to a family house in the Assunta group. The view from our window is perfect: we can look out across the vineyards and trees towards the sea a few miles away. It's hard to imagine a more wonderful place. Living here is a sensory experience. There's a kind of enjoyable primitiveness to it all, as if all the unnecessary scaffolding of civilisation has been stripped away to leave people more fully human. It's a primitiveness which never seems to preclude the most innocent pleasures: at every meal we enjoy the wine; during the winter members of the community combine spiritual exercises with skiing in the mountains at Boccheggiana; on most summer days they go swimming in the sea.

Each morning we're woken up at 6.30 by the classical music which is blared from loud speakers. We go and have coffee in the communal house. It's already warm outside and the sky is on the cusp between night and day. People are heading off to work at 7 or 7.30 . . . to the carpentry department, to the garage and so on. I've been invited to teach at the school for a few weeks and at 8 o'clock I wander down the hill to the classrooms. The entire youth from the community is heading in the same direction, their backpacks bulging with books. The school is a *scuola paterna*, a self-run school but recognised by the state. It takes children from nursery to *maturità*, the equivalent of A levels. Many of the community members teach here, but there are many external teachers too. Maria Giovanna is the headmistress. We talk about life in community and she says, on one occasion, 'we don't use the word community, but *popolo* [people]. Believe me, characters are stronger in a community! Don't let anyone tell you that here we all become some indistinguishable bunch. Quite the opposite!' I like her immediately. She's a very clever headmistress, but without the power-trip that many are on. We talk about books and writers we've come across.

Teaching English at the school is quite an eye-opener. I've taught all over the place – in Hong Kong, Tokyo, to Bosnian refugees, to Ivory Coast immigrants in Parma – but this is very different. Often when I've taught I've had to be a disciplinarian rather than a teacher. I wasted hours telling children to sit down or shut up. Here, though, everyone is vivacious but respectful. There's a great energy but it's the energy of eagerness, not distraction. They want to learn what you can tell them, not what they can tell themselves. Halfway through one lesson a child realises I'm running out of chalk and goes and gets some, breaking it in half as she passes it to me so that it doesn't squeak on the blackboard. Never before, in a decade in classrooms, has that ever happened. Others offer me their *focaccia* at the break because they don't see me eating a snack. Some go off and pick raw peas for themselves in the nearby fields; and when they come back they offer them to everyone, palm open in the middle of the playground.

All the children seem attentive and courageous. Language learning is notoriously difficult if people aren't prepared to guess and experiment, but here it's fantastic: they want to sing, and talk about English football, and they're not nervous about trying out ideas. One English song has 'lollipop' in the title and I ask what it means. Little Gregorio repeats the word – 'lollipop' – and hazards 'octopus'. I can't quite work out why he's said it.

'Nope, I'm afraid not,' I say gently, and everyone laughs at him. And then I realise. 'But a brilliant, brilliant guess, Gregorio.' He beams with pride. The Italian for octopus is *polipo*.

The surprising thing about the school is that, even though Nomadelfia adopts and fosters all sorts of difficult children, there are almost no discipline problems. There are students here from Romania, Slovakia, Colombia and so on. Some have obvious difficulties: a couple seem silent or morose, but there's never any aggression. It's partly because they're surrounded by teachers with whom they eat lunch and dinner and thus there's no division between school and domestic behaviour. There's no anonymity here, everyone is recognised, known and, well, loved. Families are so large and extended that students are surrounded by cousins and siblings. Class sizes, at least in the senior classes, are small: sometimes only four or six in a class. They're unusually mature, too. I ask many whether they will become Nomadelfi, members of the community (a choice which can only be made after twenty-one and which involves a three-year postulancy); many, rather than being rabidly in favour or against, just say they will consider it, that they admire some things and are frustrated by others, but that they will make a decision when the time comes. Some say that becoming a Nomadelfo isn't a choice, but a response to a calling.

School lasts for five hours each morning and after lunch all the children are involved in *lavoro nei campi*, work in the fields. Then, in the late afternoon, a lot of the children head to the sports dome next to the school. As we walk past, we can see gymnastic dancers practising their moves. Every summer the youngsters tour parts of Italy with their mazurkas, tarantellas and sirtakis. It's their way of promoting Nomadelfia, though to me it looks rather old-fashioned: cymbals and accordions and bonnets and so on. During one number, they're using the Pet Shop Boys' 'It's a Sin'. The church is just the other side of the path, another simple, albeit large, Portakabin.

Memo to myself: don't ever, ever tempt fate again. I've been teasing the students for the last couple of weeks because about a quarter of them are either on crutches or in plaster. I suppose it's part of living an outdoor life that bones get broken. So I've been winding them up and each time someone comes into the classroom with a newly plastered wrist or finger or ankle I joke about how accident-prone they are. The following Sunday I'm playing in the weekly students–adults football match. It's a baking-hot March afternoon, and there are quite a few on-lookers. It's a serious game on a full-size pitch, eleven a side, proper kit and so on. I've been defending the reputation of English football for weeks now, and so during the game the students are winding me up about how poor my ball distribution is. They're all quicker than me. One or two shout 'Bye-bye!' as they dribble past me. But, unfortunately, one or two of the tackles are less than fraternal. I'm just gliding past a player in the centre circle towards the end of the second half when one of the kids clatters into me studs up and I hear my ankle crack loudly. For the next two weeks, I'm on crutches and spend many hours rubbing Beppe's cabbage cream onto my swollen ankle.

This comes as close to perfection as I can imagine. I'm sitting on the bench outside Assunta. It's early evening and the sun is going down behind the hills. Alessio is laughing a few metres away, twisting the sun's last beams into a fierce point with a magnifying glass. 'Oh, Tobia, look. I'm cremating a butterfly!' he shouts. Alessio is one of ten siblings in Assunta, and is by far the most rebellious. I've got my aching ankle up on Benny's pushchair and am watching her sleep. She's got wispy, velvet hair in a sort of tonsure. She looks like Yoda or a big potato with four fat sprouts curling out of it. Somewhere in the distance I can hear one of Alessio's brothers practising the piano. Someone else is walking up the path carrying a dozen chickens for the barbecue they're having in another group for Aharon's birthday. An Ape – one of the little vans on three wheels, called a 'bee' – drives past with the Nomadelfia insignia branded on the side. The sun is sinking by the minute and drenching the balcony in sunlight. Everyone is coming back from their afternoon's work. Francesca is in the kitchen making pizzas, and you can smell the baking dough. Wood pigeons are hooting in the distance.

Little Ilaria has been told to find some wild asparagus for the pizzas and she asks me if the correct plural of *asparago* has a hard or soft *g*.

'Soft,' I say: '*asparagi*.'

'But what do you know, Tobia? You're English. If the singular is *asparago*, the plural might be *asparaghi*.'

'Yes, I might be wrong.'

'Hey, Sergio,' she shouts, 'do you say *asparagi* or *asparaghi*?'

'Ask the German,' says Sergio.

'He doesn't know,' she guffaws.

So she goes round all the elderly people sitting out enjoying the sunset, asking the correct pronunciation. Eventually she's convinced it's *asparagi* and she wanders off towards the verges looking for them and singing her new word.

I'm struggling to work out what it is that makes this place so magical. Perhaps it's the fact that people seem more human, I couldn't say why. You meet them without the interface of status. They've shrugged off the camouflage of wealth. It's as if people have stepped into themselves and are encouraging you to do the same. Some of them seem to me like large windows, openings which let in the light. Critics normally assume that religion is flighty and other-worldly, but here it appears rugged and earthy. Everything they speak about seems real rather than at one remove. Nomadelfia is touching because you're constantly surrounded by what Zeno called the '*scartini*', the 'little off-cuts': babies or children who have been abandoned. Here, at Nomadelfia, they're not left on the floor, but have become part of a great tapestry, a testament to suffering and love.

Before dinner there are always prayers. They're led by one of the children and normally recited at breakneck speed. At the end comes the 'prayer of Nomadelfia':

> Oh Jesus, saviour of the world, protect Nomadelfia, so that it may follow you heroically, within your Catholic Church, sanctifying all the forms of human life while preserving your presence in them.

We sit down and eat the *caciotta* and *stracchino* cheeses that Lucio has made during the recent weeks. He's sitting opposite us and describes the process. I explain that I'm a West Country boy and try and extol the virtues of Cheddar and Yarg. But he's done his research on European cheeses and is suspicious about our varieties. That's the problem with Lucio: he's got a reply for everything. 'I thought Yarg was only called that because it was the maker's name backwards. Ha ha. Not very romantic is it? No, in Italy we simply have better cheeses, you can't seriously debate that, can you, Francesca?'

At the end of the meal it's the men's job – their only domestic chore as far as I can work out – to sweep the dining room. Then the adults go and watch the news and the children pull out puzzles and decks of cards and schoolbooks. In every group building there are photos of Zeno. All over the school and the offices his benign face watches proceedings. On many walls there are transcriptions of his dying words.

Lucio begins to explain the relevance of Zeno for the community. Zeno is considered a prophet, a certain candidate for beatification. Many Nomadelfi long for doctrinal recognition of the innovations of Nomadelfia: the use of 'vocational mothers' for abandoned children was inspired by the scene from Calvary when Jesus turned to say to his mother: 'This is your son,' and to his disciple: 'This is your mother.' I enjoy reading Zeno's sermons and books because he's so blunt. 'The desire and need to live as brothers,' he once wrote, 'brings us to the communal form of life. If Christianity doesn't only emerge under communal existence . . . it's here that one gets closest to brotherhood, in the sense that we can live as brothers.'[8] He spoke about the 'revenge of love'. In the offices and Portakabins around the community there is one gospel passage which is ubiquitous: it is the line about 'inasmuch as ye have done it unto one of the least of these my brethren, ye have done it unto me'.[9]

They distribute 60,000 copies of the magazine *Nomadelfia is a Proposal* all over the globe. They have a printing press which publishes occasional memoirs for the archives. There are 7000 of Zeno's sermons and lectures which another former *piccolo apostolo*, Gianni Busto, is painstakingly transcribing. The current archivist is the former president of the 'popolo', Francesco. I've been teaching his son English for the last fortnight and we have a long chat. He explains the political set-up of the place. Like all Italian communes I've seen, it's seriously, professionally done. The president is also called the *capoborgata* because it's he or she that organises the family groups, which are called *borgate*; there's a *consiglio amministrativo*, an administrative council or board. On it sit the president, the bursar and three members elected from amongst the council of elders, the *consiglio degli anziani* (a body made up of twelve people over the age of forty). The Assembly is the Commons, the house where all confirmed Nomadelfi gather to vote. There is a Director of the Assembly. All positions and budgets are put to votes in the Assembly. A motion is carried by a simple majority and then, to maintain unanimity, the issue is immediately put to the vote again and approved without any nays. There is a formal, ring-bound constitution which the printers give me. Under 'guests' it says: 'According to the tradition of Nomadelfia, guests are received in the spirit of the gospels: "I was a stranger and you welcomed me." '[10]

A few days later I'm sitting with Domenico in the electronic nerve-centre of the commune. There are dozens of screens and a sophisticated editing suite. This is where Domenico and his colleagues adapt Italian television for Nomadelfia. He removes all the adverts and any scenes of violence or explicit sexual content. He effectively records programmes from the national television and then re-broadcasts the edited version. From the evenings I've spent watching Nomadelfian television, it's obvious that the taste is for reruns of the Popographies beloved of Italian TV producers. There are also devotional programmes about Padre Pio and about other saints and apostles. Sometimes, naturally, there's just the football,

Lino Banfi or Bud Spencer. The removal of adverts and certain scenes is certainly censorship but, in a country where the Prime Minister owns three channels and organises the advertising for two-thirds of all broadcasting, it seems a benign retreat from the incessant salesman.

Ever since I've been here I've been thinking about how calm the life is and now, watching Domenico remove all the advertising, I'm beginning to understand why; it's a kind of relaxation which derives from wanting nothing; a kind of *apatheia*, the setting aside of all desires. I've been watching the TV at night here, and it's so different: no programme is ever interrupted. If you're used to the BBC that will sound uninteresting, but in a country where ad-breaks almost preclude the possibility of making decent programmes, it's truly revolutionary. It's as if the TV suddenly whispers instead of screams. Domenico talks as he works, explaining the process of recording programmes and then scheduling various programmes for the evenings. He notifies people of the schedule by giving his 'listings' to the printer who hands the day's diary, La Vita del Giorno, to all groups at Nomadelfia.

Domenico's got all the screens in front of him, and shuffles from one to the other, TV listings in hand. He's a great character, Domenico. He's from Bitonto, near Bari, but worked in South Africa for years, so speaks perfect English. He's a writer and shows me some of his books: poetry and essays and novels. I read a couple over the next few days and they're good. He really works at it and it shows.

'The news,' he says, 'is only for those over twelve; the rest have 'current affairs' classes at school. Normally, there will be a film or a documentary after the evening news which is always Rai 1 at 8 o'clock.'

Living amongst people so outside the orbit of the consumer culture reveals how daft our 'symbolic economy' is: Jean-Joseph Goux once wrote that 'to create value, all that is necessary is, by whatever means possible, to create a sufficient intensity of desire', and 'what ultimately creates surplus value is the manipulation of surplus desire.'[11] In short, advertising: the augmenting and directing of our every passing whim. What I never realised, at least until coming to Nomadelfia, is that desire is always famished; it relies upon something empty pretending it can be filled. We become like Pac-men, those computerised pie-charts moving forward, munching everything that is put in our paths. Satisfaction leaves as quickly as it came but we have to keep ingesting, advancing but never being satisfied. Only now do I realise that all advertising is underpinned by melancholy. It nurtures unhappiness and envy, it deliberately creates a sense of personal inadequacy so that it can sell its cure.

The result is that we live in a glacéed world almost pathological in its depthlessness. By now we're so used to disappointment that we insist on transience rather than durability. Because we know purchases will be unsatisfactory, we insist on pre-empting disappointment by buying objects which offer immediate gratification and which dissolve almost instantly. Like the never-ending choice and change at Damanhur, in the consumer world we remedy a problem simply by insisting on more of the same medicine.

The root of the problem is that we still somehow think contentment lies in quantity, not quality. Quantity is the instinctive currency of a mercantile, numerical world. Appallingly abysmal television programmes are defended on the basis that they're watched by millions – as if that concluded the argument. Our democratic aerials are immediately on high-alert whenever someone suggests that there's a difference between what the public likes and what it ought to like. Understandably so, since it all depends who defines the difference. For centuries a tiny minority assumed command of cultural tastes, which is why we now have such controversies about the existence or otherwise of a literary canon. But we've now gone to the other extreme where, for fear of being branded elitist, we banish all words like 'taste', 'style' and 'class'. They're banished because they have no numerical referents and are therefore bewildering; they suggest differentiation and that hints at moral or aesthetic hierarchy. In quantity there is no differentiation, only more of the same things already being counted: viewers, money, whatever. What is being counted isn't intrinsically valued but merely serves to increase a valuable total. And, invariably, that total is a tool by which another total is levered (viewers equal money and so on).

I'm beginning to wonder whether the only possible rejoinder to that numbing, numerical consumerism lies in religion. I used to think that morality or high culture could defend the qualitative against the quantitative; but high culture shorn of its religious gold standard has accommodated itself to the 'revolt of inferiority'. It's no surprise that high culture has lost any distinction from popular culture at precisely the time in which religion has lost its central role in the lives of cultural consumers. Any words which come from the same root as 'spiritual' – aspire, inspire and the rest – appear irrelevant concepts; they're derided because they appear to offend us with their negative judgements of where we are. They hint at hierarchy and heroism; they whisper that we could, actually, be somewhere or someone better.

About a year ago I went to see a very unusual aristocrat in Varese. Count Giuseppe Panza di Biumo has been collecting modern art for over fifty years. He is a very formal man, polite and reserved, and yet his villa is an explosion of abstract canvases: bizarre colours, huge, unusual objects, all juxtaposed with an antique billiard table or eighteenth-century harpsichord. I went to see him because he's known as the shrewdest collector of modern art: he was snapping up Rothko and Dan Flavin and Phil Sims before they ever became famous. He even gave over a wing of his house to Robert Irwin, telling him to do whatever he wanted. The result is an incredible house (now donated to FAI, the Italian Federation for the Environment). Count Panza di Biumo is the kind of person whose aesthetic judgement you instinctively trust. He read me something he had once written, and I suppose that's what I'm thinking about now: 'The western world . . . now faces another risk. Excessive well-being has diminished any interest in a search for new moral and intellectual values; this has a negative effect on the public, which prefers an art without content. There are, however, very many artists who still believe in the values that lie behind the great art of all times, but they are isolated and estranged.'[12] It was an unusual feeling, walking round his villa with him, to hear him talking about the 'idealism' of abstraction. For many, modern art and abstraction are synonymous with absurdity, they give expression to chaos and meaninglessness. But he saw high culture as a pointer to religious values. He would stand in front of a large rectangle of strong colours and talk about 'purity and truth'.

The real defenders of high culture eventually concede that it has to rub shoulders with the religious. It's a notion which is echoed by all of the eloquent writers on the subject, even those who don't necessarily have a religious belief. Culture, Roger Scruton once wrote, 'has a religious root and a religious meaning. This does not mean that you have to be religious in order to be cultivated. But it does mean that the point of being cultivated cannot, in the end, be explained without reference to the nature and values of religion.' That's because religion, he says, offers 'man as an object of judgement'; like high culture it 'teaches us to live as if our lives mattered eternally.'[13]

Herbert Spencer once wrote that religions are 'at one in their tacit conviction that the existence of the world, with all it contains and all which surrounds it, is a mystery calling for an explanation.'[14] Viktor Frankl's 'Logotherapy' considered 'man a being whose main concern consists in fulfilling a meaning, rather than in the mere gratification and satisfaction of drives and instincts. . .'[15] The recognition of a mystery, and the tentative offering of what is almost its contradiction, meaning, is where high culture meets religion. Whatever one thinks of the explanation for the mystery offered at Nomadelfia, the result is remarkable. It's one of the few oases in the Western world where consumerism has been successfully confronted head-on and thoroughly dismantled. And the more I watch Domenico patiently removing the advertisements, the more I feel that their explanation of the mystery warrants attention because it is the means by which they have rid themselves of the tyranny of quantity.

Another truism of our age is that, so incredibly technically competent, we have the means to pursue any end. But as we increase our knowledge of the means, we become ignorant about the end. Just as we seem on the verge of being able to do anything, we suddenly find ourselves unable to say why we should bother in the first place. Fixated on causes, we know nothing of meanings. Only high culture, like religion, offers a passage into a kingdom of ends: a place where we understand how we should act and why. Like religion it gives us a telos, an end: not just the technical means, but the mystical meaning. And it's a kingdom which, according to those at Nomadelfia, has a King.

Unfortunately, it's part of living in community that before you can realistically assess it, you go from extraordinary enchantment to mournful disenchantment. We had been at Nomadelfia for a few weeks when we both began to feel uncomfortable. I had begun to feel restless on reading a particular passage from one of Zeno's

many books: 'homogeneity is the first condition for serenely sharing in harmony and for working together to the exclusion of any
discord which could arise because of the disparity of ideas'[16]. That
reference to homogeneity unsettled me. It stuck in my brain like a
fish-hook because it somehow seemed a long way from my notion
of brotherhood: it wanted uniformity not alterity. It reminded me
of the old Roman idea of the *limes*, the wall which separated the
civilised world from the barbarians. I began to overhear the ways
in which parents admonished their children: 'non fare l'islamico'
they would say.

I was reading a book by Zeno, *L'Uomo è diverso*, when I read
the sentence: 'Do you believe in God? If you don't believe in the
Son of God incarnated and in his Catholic Church, you will not
have "God as Father".'[17] I sometimes wonder whether, having
been laicised for a decade, the price of Zeno's return to Holy
Orders was a renunciation of his earlier radicalism on ecclesiastical
matters. Having been once very suspicious of the priestly caste,
Zeno appears to have become a favourite of the hierarchy himself.
Pope John Paul II visited in 1981 and the photographs of his visit
are now enlarged and proudly hanging all over the community.
There was, everywhere, a kind of certainty which bordered on conceit. Another sentence from Zeno concerned me: Nomadelfians, he
wrote, 'have been liberated from the vacuum of uncertainty about
existence having received Christ according to the gospel; therefore
they travel in the Catholic Church, founded by Jesus Christ. Of this
they have the resolute persuasion of being in truth: they know
where they're going and why.'[18] That was something else I was frequently told: Jesus Christ came to earth to found the Roman
Catholic Church. We were often invited to other groups for lunch
or dinner and, without fail, someone would always start criticising
the Protestant or Orthodox 'sects' and 'heretics'. The intriguing
thing is that Catholics often, rightly, criticise Protestants for being
biblical literalists, taking one verse and quoting it out of context.
And yet here I was being reminded, every day, of the one verse in
the gospel on which the entire edifice of the Roman Church was
based: 'you are the rock on which I will build my church'. I go back
to the prayer of Nomadelfia and it's there '. . . protect Nomadelfia,
so that it may follow you heroically, within your Catholic Church
. . .' Every page of Newman drips with the command *nolite exire*,

'do not go out'. Nomadelfia was beginning to appear insistent whereas a few weeks ago it had seemed, to me, serene. I felt, for the first time, excluded.

I admired Nomadelfia's confidence and conviction; they were, after all, what I had been looking for having left Damanhur. But after a while there were increasingly moments in which that stridency was overbearing. There were increasingly moments in which I had to bite my tongue in order not to loose it in anger, or else occasions in which Francesca, knowing my sensitivity on certain subjects, quickly changes them.

It happened one dinner time when I was sat next to Don Zeno's second successor. He, like me, was on crutches and he joked that we, with about sixty years between us, should have a race. He began telling me about England: 'My brother went to England to sell ice-cream. He told me of one occasion when there were two priests, one Protestant, one Catholic, in the same room. They got on! I couldn't believe it. If one was right the other was wrong.'

'Maybe they had a lot in common,' I venture.

'Rubbish. Either the doctrine is right or wrong. The Catholic religion has been hounded out of England because you don't have families any more. Women go out to work and get seduced by other men. In England,' he changed tack, 'they don't have bread!'

'But there are communities comparable to Nomadelfia in England.'

'*Ma! Non credo.* Don Zeno said that England needs Nomadelfia more than Nomadelfia needs England!'

'I'm sure that's true,' I said, trying to be emollient. 'But there are Christians who aren't Catholics, aren't there?'

He shook his head, I'm not sure whether in disagreement or dismay. There was a long pause. One quiet, kind woman had seen that I was really rather hot under the collar and began saying 'yes of course,' but others were now gathering round and contributing too.

'Non-Catholics can never be *fully* Christian,' one man said, emphasising gently the word *pienamente.* When I asked him about ecumenical Christian communities like Taizé and the monastery of Bose, he said bluntly: 'They're good places but they're making a mistake. Ecumenicalism is misplaced because there can only be one truth.'

I closed the subject, walking away to do the dishes. There we kind of left it, uneasily aware that we had had a little fraternal fall-out.

I had always thought that truth can only be shown, not narrated. I had been enchanted by Nomadelfia because, perhaps more than anywhere else, it really does demonstrate what a life lived according to the gospels would look like. But the aspect of Nomadelfia that I struggled with was this: showing was always accompanied by telling. The proselytism was constant and any dissent was seen as evidence of the onset of relativism or error. It had little of that enchanting humility I had seen in other communities.

And if the rhetoric of Nomadelfia had initially appeared bravely counter-cultural, I began to feel that, as so often with Catholicism in Italy, it wasn't only whispering truth to power, but also allowing its truth to be beckoned by power. At elections, the president debates with the community as to who will receive the entirety of Nomadelfia's votes. A decision is reached and the block vote of all Nomadelfi is given to one party. It naturally gives Nomadelfia political clout, whilst at the same time reducing individual expression at the ballot box. It was, in my opinion, taking homogeneity to extremes and was an example of idealism becoming, to put it politely, strategic (obviously, if you can bring a politician one hundred and something votes, they listen to you quite carefully). I asked Mario who the community had voted for at the last elections and he said that, with '*mal di cuore*' from many people, the entirety of the votes went to the UDC, the Unione dei Democratici Cristiani, the reinvented Christian Democrats. It is a Catholic party in coalition with Silvio Berlusconi's Forza Italia. Two of the main donors to Nomadelfia are former Presidents of the Republic: Oscar Luigi Scalfaro and Giulio Andreotti. Nothing wrong in that, it's just that it suddenly began to appear very much part of the mainstream, rather than a voice whispering uncomfortable truths. The summer tour in which children dance in villages and towns across the peninsula has the spooky label 'Propaganda'.

I began reading the constitution and certain phrases stuck out. '. . . reserved behaviour borne with serene severity . . . the absolute exclusion of any kind of sloth . . .' As Francesca said as we lay on the bed exhausted one evening, life here wasn't really any less frenetic than the world against which it defines itself. It was based

79

on the old, tough life of the countryside and any quiet was hard to find. There was barely any time for idle conversation. The final straw came when, on one blissful Sunday morning after church, we were playing with Benny and other children in a courtyard. An old lady holding a photo came up to Francesca and pointed at her bare, upper arms. 'You can go to Grosseto if you want to dress like that,' she said. 'But dress properly here.' Then she showed us the photo of herself with Pope John Paul II: 'I was the only one he stopped for,' she said proudly.

Whilst we were at Nomadelfia two interesting, international debates flared up. One concerned a UDC politician, Rocco Buttiglione. A minister in Silvio Berlusconi's government, he had been proposed as European Commissioner for Justice. Usually the interrogation and ratification by the European Parliament is a formality but Buttiglione was asked whether he considered homosexuality a sin. He replied that yes, he did. Controversy ensued. He went on to say that such an opinion only had a bearing upon his position if he thought that it was not only a sin, but also a crime. As is well known, Buttiglione was subsequently refused the portfolio and he returned to Italy railing against 'paedophiles'. It was hard to feel much sympathy for Buttiglione; and yet, the liberal reaction to his comments was bizarre and came in one of two forms: either he wasn't in good faith (i.e. he wouldn't actually uphold that sin–crime separation if in power); or else, he was a hypocrite for admitting the legitimacy of that separation. In reality, he was actively paying homage to the separation between moral and civic duty. Far from being theocratic, he was bowing to the secular division between the morals of citizens on the one hand and that of believers on the other. Now, Buttiglione was clearly picking the wrong political fight in the wrong political arena and his political naivety was almost as ridiculous as his opinions on homosexuals. It was easy to understand why he was pilloried, but I, personally, couldn't follow the logic. He was only defending that public–private division which is so dear to rational secularists: sexual behaviour, even sexual ethics, has no bearing on public life. (I've often told Italians about the English notion that a man who lies to his wife – or a woman to her husband – is more likely to lie to his or her constituents, and they invariably find this notion hilarious, albeit highly original). If Buttiglione was sincere about the sin–crime separation, his point of arrival was exactly the same as a secularists' (the 'naked public square', shorn of religious conviction) even if his point of departure was radically different. Buttiglione's real mistake was to go abroad to defend a moral schizophrenia which he, and his political allies, daily attack back in Italy. At home, politicians from the UDC would frequently insist on the correlation between private and public morals. Suddenly, abroad, Buttiglione was pretending to believe that such a correlation had never entered his mind. The real accusation against Buttiglione should have been not homophobia but opportunistic inconsistency.

Then, a little later, an Italian politician from the UDC demands that all public buildings – classrooms, courtrooms and the like – should carry a crucifix. He says that Italy is a Catholic country and shouldn't be ashamed of its symbols. There has, he says, been rude haste in dismantling everything the country stands for; a nation's identity is under threat. Predictable parts of the Italian body politic back the proposal. Indeed, John Paul II had openly made a similar appeal in October 2002 and Joseph Ratzinger, once elected Benedict XVI, returned to the theme. 'Where God disappears,' he said, 'man doesn't become grander but loses dignity. It's important that God be visible in public and private buildings.'[19] The besieged defenders of the (often nominally) lay state were appalled: it goes contrary to the constitution, they pointed out. The Church and State, married under Constantine, have been divorced since the revised Concordat of 1984 and, they insisted, that decree nisi is irrevocable.

The issue of the crucifix in public buildings has been a hot potato in recent years, producing various legal cases. In Abruzzo in 2003 Adel Smith, the president of the Muslim Union of Italy, went to court to remove the crucifix in the school frequented by his children; in the Veneto, in January 2004, a mother of two children in Abano Terme took similar legal action to remove the crucifix which, she maintained, was an affront to secular education. In Tuscany, in Bagno a Ripoli, members of the UDC and Forza Italia urged, by contrast, that the crucifix be restored to schools after thirty years' absence. There's no uniformity in the application of the law: in one part of the country it seems inconceivable that the crucifix will be removed, in others it's unlikely that it will be restored.

Other countries have had similar debates. In America the presence of the Ten Commandments in a courtroom has divided public opinion. In France, the national parliament, in February 2004, passed a new law by 494 votes to 36 which outlawed the use of the hijab, and any other over religious iconography, in French schools. Most people I spoke to either agreed with the secular position or else with the Catholic one. I found myself in the strange, uncomfortable position of disagreeing both with the theocratic intentions of the Italian Catholics and with the French tendency towards liberal totalitarianism. In fact, although the Italian and French positions seemed at opposite ends of the religious–secular spectrum, they were strangely similar in consequence: both involved coercion, declaring that the body-politic was in a position to declare the best beliefs for its citizens. In both, the state's creed was to be imposed on its subjects; nationality was conflated with either Catholicism (in Italy) or with Atheism (in France).

Whether the creed in question was Catholicism or evangelical atheism, no one really questioned the imposition of a creed. Important, only, that it be the right one. There was, even in the secular, a search for absolutism and certainty. No one I spoke to either in France or Italy expressed concern about both pieces of legislation: either they were in favour of restoring Catholicism to its traditional place or they were in favour of banishing all religion from the palaces of the state. There was none of what Keats called 'negative capability': 'when a man is capable of being in uncertainties, mysteries, doubts, without any irritable reaching after fact and reason'.[20] Northern European Protestantism, and British Christianity in particular, is invariably accused of being wishy-washy and watered down. Catholics invariably say that the lack of radical atheism in northern Europe is precisely because Protestantism has so weakened Christianity as to render that atheism redundant. But its great asset is that 'negative capability', that willingness to admit doubt rather than deny it. It allowed for sophistication and subtlety. I was beginning to yearn, not for home, but at least for England.

Francesca and I are sitting in the kitchen after dinner. Lucio and Alessio have us in stitches with a memorable conversation. Alessio plays the role of the adolescent sceptic, his butterfly-cremating magnifying glass now in his back pocket; Lucio is the father-figure who, lovingly, tries to explain the teaching of the Church.

'But how do you know,' starts Alessio, 'that Adam and Eve really existed?'

'Various mystics and saints,' Lucio says, 'have confirmed that there was indeed a couple called Adam and Eve. They were created by God and were extraordinarily beautiful.'

'But are you sure he was called Adam?'

Lucio is smiling wearily, as if this isn't the first conversation of this kind.

'And what about evolution?' Alessio goes on. 'I thought it was proven that we're all descended from monkeys.'

'And where did the monkeys come from?'

'Are you saying Adam was actually a monkey?'

Lucio rolls his eyes and smiles at Francesca and me.

'Because I don't mind,' says Alessio, 'if we're descended from monkeys. The important thing is that monkeys don't descend from us!'

I'm still struggling with my Newman at night. He's not exactly heart-warming, candlelight stuff, but I suppose he's taught me that obedience is a word which disgusts most of us. It's anathema to almost all moderns. But it's the hidden virtue which introduces all the others. Benedict spoke of 'the strong and glorious weapons of obedience'. 'The first step in humility is prompt obedience,'[21] he wrote. It introduces the notion that there really are irreversible choices and consequences, there really is good and evil. There is a right way to live and a wrong way. It means that – unlike in the New Age and its post-modernism milieu – there's no embarrassment about talking about tares and wheat; there's an acknowledgement that moral relativism is somehow ridiculous. As some Nomadelfi said to me, true tolerance isn't about the dissolution of our own beliefs, but an eloquent concentration upon them, a clarification of what we believe in.

It's impossible, in non-religious terms, to understand what they're doing here. Of course, any humanist would recognise how admirable Nomadelfia is, but they would baulk at the implications: that Nomadelfia only exists because they are following the preaching of Jesus of Nazareth. It's extraordinary and unreal, but that message is central to understanding how they have scaled such moral heights. I'm beginning to wonder if it's true that there really is no way in which virtue can be taught if not in a religious context. As Alisdair MacIntyre wrote in *After Virtue*: 'Ethical behaviour should be adopted for no reason, but a choice which lies beyond reason.'[22] I used to think that religion was about offering us an end rather than means, but now I see it rather differently. There might be an end, but it isn't offered for our observation. We're asked to accept the heaviest of burdens without even the compensation of an end in sight. Unlike advertising, which gives us an immediate, tangible object of desire from the outset, transcendental religion insists that its end cannot be glimpsed. Since that implies almost futility, virtue can only be guaranteed by obedience. Only then is it disinterested, unlike Bentham's Utilitarianism. If virtue didn't appear futile, if it wasn't pointless, it would be so obvious as to render obedience redundant. We don't match the means to the end, as in a bureaucratically competent society. It's about an obedience so elevated that we avert our eyes from the end because we trust the means to get us there; and we trust someone – you can choose who – to teach us the means. The gatehouse to the kingdom of ends, suggests Newman, is obedience. There is no other portal. There's an extraordinary rebus wherein the ends are only glimpsed when they're entirely ignored, when purpose is dethroned by obedience, and when utility is, apparently, usurped by futility. It's then that the ends come and find you, rather than vice versa. The promise of faith is that on the far side of meaninglessness there really does emerge meaning; but actively looking for that meaning dissolves it in the acid of enquiry. Faith is blind. We understand the point of obedience only through obeying; and it's incumbent upon that obedience that the 'point' is invisible to our eyes. Only that way are we ushered out of our world to inhabit it more fully.

Maybe he's right. Certainly, using utility as the yardstick for morality is absurd. Virtue can't be dictated by consequences even though in a utilitarian society we have no other yardstick. Virtue is absolutist and sovereign precisely because it suffers no enquiry but is, rather, underpinned by nothing other than itself. That is the reason for its magnificence and vulnerability. Its importance has to be taken on trust, it can never be proven. I had problems with

Nomadelfia, there were sides of it that made me uncomfortable . . . but I could see what they were doing and why. They had stepped outside the utilitarian world and, surprisingly, were suddenly more useful. They disparaged the cold, aimless world of cause-and-effect, but were actually more consequential. It was as if meaning had found them, rather than vice versa. My disenchantment was replaced by realism: this was a place where they take in thousands of orphans and feed and clothe them. They do so because they're commanded to and they obey. They might, occasionally, be a little blunt or blinkered, but there was no doubting their love. By now, I was slightly detached, thinking about moving on. But as we set a date, I began to regret having to leave. It was, despite everything, an inspirational place.

As I write this in the hypnotic silence of our room, I can almost hear Zeno's voice ringing in my ears. He is always direct. His prose is always earthy, the metaphors usually drawn from peasant reference. In one sermon about idealism, he pointed at the green mountainside and said that we're all blades of grass, and we only change the colour of the mountain when we all stand together. It's the Church's job, he lets it be understood, to make sure we all stand in the right place. Nomadelfia's ambition is to live out the life preached at the Sermon on the Mount, to be the lawn at the feet of the preacher, listening to everything he says. The morality is entirely unlike Damanhur because in the New Age the obsession is about humans becoming divine; at Nomadelfia it's about the divine becoming human. It's about this world, rather than any other. It's not about the arrogance of the weak, but about the meekness of the mighty. That's why it is more relevant, rooted and terrestrial. It opens the door to idealism without elitism because there is no snobbery, no hubris.

Despite Domenico's warning a month ago, I had begun by thinking Nomadelfia might be my utopia and had come to earth with a bump. But that's where, again, it's different from Damanhur. It's not optimistic about human nature, it doesn't assert the sovereignty of humanism; what it does is build community based on pessimism about humanity. Their optimism comes from an entirely different, non-human source. One afternoon, sitting outside our house at Assunta with Pietro, the president, I hinted at some of the aspects of Nomadelfia I struggled with: the fact that only Catholics were allowed to become Nomadelfi, that all other Christian churches were roundly ridiculed . . . he said to me: 'We all have defects; if we were perfect we wouldn't need a community.'

I was also, slowly, reconciled with the towering figure of Zeno. He was, as one Communist once observed, a 'revolutionary with the imprimatur'. I admired his social revolution and if it was prompted by his Christianity then I admired that too. I had thought that I was looking for the good life – for enjoyment, relaxation and calm. But Zeno, in one of his speeches, drew a distinction between two very different types of 'good life': there was *star bene* and *far bene* . . . effectively the 'good life' of comfort and the rather different one of 'doing good'. I realised that I had been caught up in the fallacy of eudemonism: the notion that virtue brings happiness. Of course it doesn't and I realised, after a few moments of sadness at Nomadelfia, that our search for the ideal community should be focused not on felicity (as occurs with almost all modern seekers) but on virtue.

Domenico, more than anyone, is sad we're leaving. He had organised everything, he had shared his books with me. He has been a brick and we go and say goodbye. There's another guy in there and we get talking about Christianity in England. He looks at me, confused as I mention all the denominations. He asks me about my own upbringing. As I reply I get the giggles because I can hear how ridiculous it sounds, even though it's all true.

'Well, I was baptised by a woman called Bruce,' I say. 'That was a good start. Then the Methodist chapel in our village closed so I went Church of England. Then I went to Quaker meetings for a few years. And then I got confused and now I'm here.'

'Well, which is it then?'

'How do you mean?'

'Which one is your church?'

Domenico is behind the big guy's back, smiling and drawing his fingers across his throat to persuade me to stop talking.

Some of the students come and say goodbye. They bring clothes and food for Benny. Beautiful Naomi gives me some of the volcanic quartz you find here for my desk. One girl offers us a poster of Benedict XVI.

So we put my crutches in the back of the car, strap Benny in the car-seat and head north. I was feeling sad. Nomadelfia was a place which had enchanted us, it really had touched us deeply. And yet it wasn't what we were looking for. We drove up along the coast, heading to my in-laws in Parma. On the way Francesca joked how you get a better class of graffiti in Italy: we passed one road sign which had been daubed with 'God exists'. On the following road sign someone, in different colours and calligraphy, had written 'Which one?' Then about another ten miles along there was another road-sign with 'God exists' and then, a few hundred metres along, the rival graffiti-philosopher had scrawled 'What's he called then?' We laugh at the thought of these two rival Tuscans painting theological declarations in the dead of night.

It's not really surprising that Damanhur and Nomadelfia are in the same country, because in some ways they define themselves against each other. Italy always takes things to extremes and, as with the politics, the two extremes rely on the demonisation of the other. And yet I still wanted to go beyond those two extremes. I hoped not for a halfway house between them, but something which transcended them. I didn't want either no choice (where choice is seen as heretical and a diversion from homogeneity) or endless choice (which is, again, no choice because choice hasn't any consequence), but something beyond both options. If the only way to create community in the contemporary world is by renouncing everything modern, by closing it out and travelling back in time fifty years, then my entire pilgrimage is pointless. I'm interested in how to build a community in the contemporary world, not the premodern one. Maybe I had found the sacred canopy I was looking for at the beginning, but couldn't cope with the implications. Maybe I had bottled out, I don't know. Or maybe we were just looking for a place in which the exposure of female shoulders wasn't an issue. We were looking for a community which wasn't homogenous or anachronistic, where listening and contemplation were more important than preaching, a place where obedience was still paramount, but where it entailed obeying the conscience as much as a church.

I thought I knew where we had to go, but first I had to make one more stop. I left Fra and Benny at Parma and drove back towards Ivrea. Here, in a tiny village, lives a hermit in her eighties. She is called Adriana Zarri and lives in a *cascina*, an old farmyard, owned by the local parish. It dates from the seventeenth century and is stunning: inside the walled garden is a grassy courtyard. There's a well, an old horse cart. There are flowers and bare wood everywhere. There are cushioned chairs around tables, stone cellars which have become mini conference rooms for retreats and meetings. Zarri is, by all accounts, a very unusual hermit. She used to appear a lot on Italian television fifteen to twenty years ago, reading her short stories as the opening meditation for a factual programme. She was an observer at Vatican Council II, the only woman accorded the honour. She writes regularly for various newspapers and publishing houses. She's old now and rarely appears in public. Her living quarters are a long tunnel-like den on the first floor of one of the wings. Underneath is her tiny chapel. She, like me, has a rather fractious relationship with the Catholic Church. Unlike me, she's a highly admired theologian, someone who has published long monographs on all aspects of the Christian faith.

She's sitting in an armchair in a simple smock, wondering why I've come here to consult her. I suppose I'm here because Zarri has written, more profoundly than anyone else, about what it means to live in a community. She became reluctantly famous in the seventies and eighties by challenging the easygoing, euphoric communitarianism of those years. Writing as a recluse, she criticised the newfound lust for communes saying that they cultivated 'a spirit of the ghetto, a certain intransigence, a subtle discrimination between "us" and "them"; and "our" opinions are the only unit of measurement which disqualifies other opinions.' In a painfully relevant metaphor, she said that for a communitarian to be mature he needs to be given 'a spine, not crutches'; otherwise communitarianism 'is only a spirit of the herd, an inclination to gang together, a defensive reaction to nervous and ideological fragilities . . .'[23]

They were sentences which reminded me of our time at Nomedelfia and I mention to her the excruciating difficulty of being a non-Catholic in Italy. She smiles sympathetically. 'Italy,' she says, 'is an almost uniconfessional country. There's a frightening ignorance because the vast majority grow up sucking on the milk of Catholicism. Our churches are full of non-believers.' She says that she finds the modern papacy 'absolutely idolatrous' and mentions with dismay the 'armoured cars of the Curia'. She lists with forceful indignation and witty neologisms her difficulties with Rome:

'indecent, ridiculous, scandalous canonisations', 'a sexist Church', a tendency to create 'madonnaioli'. ('Modaiolo' is the word for a fashion victim; 'donnaiolo' is the word for a womaniser. So 'madonnaioli' implies people who have a superficial mania for the Madonna, kind of 'Madonnerisers'.) 'I love normality,' she says, 'and I'm very suspicious of the exceptional. Here in Italy we love miracles, we venerate Padre Pio. All of which obscures the fact that one finds the sublime in the banal. In what is normal there's a similarity between first and last.'

If she's so ardently Christian, and so critical of Rome, one begins to wonder why she doesn't leave the Roman Church. 'Because I'm a Christian from the Catholic tradition, I was born into this sphere, and to change would be an anti-ecumenical gesture. For a Protestant to become a Catholic would be equally anti-ecumenical.'

I ask her about the fundamentalist-relativist conundrum: 'Fundamentalism,' she says, 'isn't the truth. It stops at the formal, external elements of the truth. Think about the Trinity, a reality which has been tragically forgotten by the average Christian. The Trinity means that God isn't a static, monolithic being, but that within the unity there is dialectic and confrontation.'

We talk for a long time but towards the hour she's politely becoming restless. As I get up to go, she has a few last reflections: no true community, she says, can exist unless the members are comfortable with silence and solitude. She reads me a passage from one of her books: silence and solitude are the true 'purifying contestations' which could become 'spaces of reflective pause necessary to make of the community a communion'.[24] No one, she said, could truly live in a community unless they were able to enjoy solitude; otherwise the community was merely a refuge which will slowly degenerate. She spoke of silence as 'like white: not an absence of colour, but the sum of all the colours, assembled and unified . . .'[25] Now, years later, she underlines the point, talking of silence not as 'the absence of words, but as the essence of the Word. God is silence, but his silence is called the Word.'

It was that which persuaded me we had to go to York. I wanted to live in a community which sounded almost a contradiction in terms: a gathering of people based, not on homogeneity, but on the riches of silence and solitude.

3

Silence

There are about forty of us in an ordinary room. We're sitting facing each other in a series of concentric circles, saying nothing.

Outside, someone is hammering. Then, a plane bellowing in the distance.

Still silence here. Five minutes go by.

The cheerful, high chiming of a bicycle bell. Children laughing.

Nothing. Most people are sitting with their eyes open, palms on their thighs. I remember something once said to me in Japan: everyone can distinguish between wise and foolish talk; it takes a master to discern wise from foolish silence. To me, at least, this silence seems very wise but I'm not sure why.

Then, the soft drone of a passing car.

'Friends,' someone has stood up, 'obedience and listening have the same root in the Latin, *audire*.' She sits down again.

A whistle and a trumpet: birdsong and moped.

One of the strange things about silence is that, having listened to it every Sunday morning for years, you begin to glimpse variations in its intensity, begin to notice differences within what should, by all rational analyses, be uniform. I first noticed it sitting in the British library one day when an announcement was made calling for a minute's silence after the Madrid train bombs. It was a strange request, because – it being a library – everyone was silent anyway. But the nature of the silence changed and charged, as if you could hear the concentration and intercession.

We're still there. Some are looking around, some straight ahead. The children have just gone out so we've only been sitting for a quarter of an hour. It feels like much longer. I'm thinking about that line from St Isaac: 'Speech is the organ of this present world. Silence is the mystery of the world to come.'

I sometimes feel at meetings that sounds begin to melt together and make their own acoustic connections. I just heard the sound of a free-wheeling bicycle and it sounded precisely like the rhythmic on-off-on-off roar of night-time cicadas. It sounds pretentious, but it was that exact sound. Then, a few minutes later, a passing skateboard imitates fireworks as the wheels crack on the rough road surface. A speedily reversing car whines like a baby. Everything sounds like a baby's squawk when you've got one to listen out for. When you're perfectly still, the noise becomes very interesting. I'm beginning to appreciate John Cage and all he used to say about the proximity of music to noise. His posturing silences were windows onto the world we're forced to listen to and, if we can, to harmonise. Every performance of silence is unlike any other. We participate by sharing it with other people and comparing, afterwards, what it sounded like.

In the concrete underpass there are stalls selling powdery or syrupy drinks for two or three quid. Our train has been cancelled and since there's a massive queue at the ticket office, I have to phone train enquiries on my mobile. It's cold and the platform covering offers little protection from sharp, oblique rain. Benny is crying. When I'm off hold, I speak to someone in Asia. There's a second's delay between each exchange and I have to spell Temple Meads three times. I can feel my blood rising. There is no sense to this situation. Why am I waiting for a train talking to a poor girl somewhere in Asia? It costs us £156 to get to York. That seems to me like a shitload of money. As the train heads to Gloucester, I pick up the glossy magazine, *Hotlines*, which is part of the 'in-voyage entertainment'. My eye is caught by a photo. It's a dark crimson interior, low lighting, roses. The article is called 'decadent desires' and the caption for the photo says 'your very own den of sin'. The superimposed pitch goes: 'Indulge your every whim, feed your every fantasy and spoil yourself rotten. This season, give in to the dark side. You know you want to.' Tragic: nothing quite reveals the sordidness of persuasion as when a journalist turns their hand to advertising.

I do our sums and try and work out how much money we've got for the next month: £982 exactly. Fra opens her wallet and offers her twenty for the pot. It sounds like a lot, but I've just put £156 on my card, so we're now at £846. We've got to find somewhere to live because this community where we're going is full, with a long waiting list for any spare room. So that's, say, another 700 quid for a month's let. That leaves £146 for a family for a month. *Un tubo.*

So we get to York. The city was founded in 71 AD when

Vespasian was emperor. His troops, stopping at the confluence of the rivers Foss and Ouse, named the new military settlement Eboracum, the 'place of the Yew'. It's a small, stunning city, full of timber buildings, ancient churches and – being that sort of tourist place – fudge and teddy-bear shops. It was here that Constantine was pronounced emperor in 306 and, with the spread of Christianity throughout the empire, York became one of the centres of English piety, a city surrounded by forests and Cistercian monasteries. The Romans left in 410 and, centuries later, in 867, my favourite-named Viking, Ivan the Boneless, captured it and renamed it Jorvik, hence, eventually, 'York'. Everywhere the streets have the suffix 'gate', since that was apparently the Norse for street. The actual city gates are called 'bars'.

The three of us are wandering around the city. After Tuscany it feels cold, really cold, and grey. It's supposed to be spring but it's trying to snow. Some sharp estate agent manages to persuade us to rent a one-bedroom place in town. It's OK. We're comfortable. She takes slightly more than £700. We do our sums again and try to be cheery. I unfold my bike and lock it in the cellar.

The next morning I cycle to a model village a few miles outside the city on the Haxby road. You can tell that is was built with deliberation rather than the slow sedimentation of the centuries. It's neatly laid out with crescents and avenues which mostly have horticultural names: Almond Grove, Lime Tree Avenue, Conifer Close, Willow Bank. It feels like many of those American cities which, built from scratch, carefully follow an overall architectural design. Unlike York, it's not built through chaotic accumulation, but by sensible symmetry. And, like many of those New World dwellings, its name is an updating of an existing village: built near the old hamlet of Earswick, it's called simply New Earswick.

By now, over a hundred years since the project started, it's as much a suburb of the city as it is a village: it's a short walk northeast of York, and if you drive you barely realise you've left the city at all. If you cycle, you can smell the aroma of warm chocolate from the Nestlé factory. It used to belong to the Rowntree company until the 1980s. Huge lorries emblazoned with 'KitKat' and 'Yorkie' are constantly emerging from the gates. But further along, as you wander around the model village, everything feels strange. It's different: there's the Folk Hall and a Friends' (Quaker) meeting house. The rows of terraced houses aren't depressing like their urban Victorian counterparts, but rather charming in a Hansel-and-Gretel way. The early Edwardian red-brick is stylish, the houses small but solid. The architects Sir Raymond Unwin and Barry Parker were among the first to use cul-de-sacs (used for reasons of cost, making roads lighter, narrower and cheaper) and the effect is an intimate isolation: some of the garden gates barely come up to knee height; the surrounding hedges are no higher than your thighs.

The village was initiated by Joseph Rowntree, the Quaker businessman from York. Influenced by the likes of Ebenezer Howard and Octavia Hill – who had written extensively on garden cities and social housing – and by the concrete examples of Sir George Lever's Port Sunlight and Richard and George Cadbury's Bournville, Rowntree hoped to provide a comfortable domestic environment for workers from his factory. He had become exceptionally wealthy through his business of selling cocoa, gums and pastilles and, at the beginning of the twentieth century, he set up a series of trusts to ensure the continuation of his philanthropy. One of those was, originally, the Joseph Rowntree Village Trust. Rowntree made his wishes explicit: he wanted not palliative charity, but intellectual investigation of the root causes of social problems: 'The soup kitchen in York,' he once wrote, 'never has any difficulty in obtaining adequate financial support, but an enquiry into the extent and causes of poverty would enlist very little support.'[1] In a similar vein, he wrote elsewhere that 'Charity as ordinarily practised, the charity of endowment, the charity of emotion, the charity which takes the place of justice, creates much of the misery which it relieves but does not relieve all the misery it creates.'[2] In a way, it was a very British kind of charity: his vision of benevolence was always filtered through business viability. The ends he sought were very clear but he allowed his trustees maximum interpretation of the means they could use to attain those desired ends:

> The need of seeking to search out the underlying causes of weakness or evil in the community rather than of remedying their more superficial manifestations is a need which I expect will remain throughout the continuance of the Trusts . . . Realising not only that 'new occasions teach new duties' but that 'time

makes ancient good uncouth', I have given to the Trustees and Directors of these foundations very wide powers and very few directions of a mandatory nature as to their exercise.[3]

Given the avowed intention to offer not charity but solid, financially viable communities, the Trust was under instruction not only to offer houses to the poorest classes, but also to ensure that rents yielded between 3 and 4 per cent. The aim was what Rowntree's fellow Quaker, Cadbury, had called the 'power of almost indefinite expansion' with regard to philanthropy. A successful and thoughtful businessman, Rowntree hoped that successful charity wasn't paternalistic but self-sustaining and, eventually, self-reproducing. He saw his idealistic island, as many utopians do, as an outpost which could enthuse and influence the cynical surrounds:

I should regret if there were anything in the organisation of these village communities that should interfere with the growth of the right spirit of citizenship or be such that independent and right-minded men and women might resent. I do not want to establish communities bearing the stamp of charity, but rather of rightly-ordered and self-governing communities, self-governing, that is, within the broad limits laid down by the Trust.[4]

The Trust, indeed, became like the benevolent government of the village. Verges were clipped, a library opened (with 100 books donated by Rowntree). The Garth, an old people's home, was set up, a dairy farm established and so on. A sense of common destiny still exists: in the Folk Hall they serve coffee in mugs with 'New Earswick 1902–2002' on the outside. There's a large, black-and-white photo of Joseph Rowntree in the corner and, all around the room, a photo-montage of various New Earswickians. One large aerial photo is of hundreds of people standing on the green, writing with their bodies the centenary message: 'New Earswick 2002'.

As you walk through the village on Hawthorn Terrace, you pass on the left the village green and the primary school; on your right there are a couple of shops. The photos from the 1900s had looked romantic and rustic; now, under the grey Yorkshire sky in 2005, it looks barely distinguishable from any other British suburb: cars roar through towards the York ring-road, boys in hooded tracksuits are trying to chat up lippy girls in white mini-skirts. But, this being a puritan village, there is no pub. Further along is the Joseph Rowntree School.

But the reason I'm here is that as you head out of the village you come, within a few hundred metres, to a new community. Built from scratch in the late 1990s are 152 bungalows. They're almost identical and have that clean, cold look of the purpose-built. Unlike York, where ancient timber buildings all keel left and right, here they're immaculate and geometrical: light red brick and orangey tiles. I can't help feeling that it looks all very American (I find out later that it was largely modelled on another Quaker retirement village in Pennsylvania, called Pennswood). Everything is pristine and manicured. The trees are still little more than saplings. The spaces between the bungalows haven't quite been filled by foliage. The lawns are as perfect as AstroTurf and, as you walk in, it's eerily quiet. There's a central rectangle of road with bungalows mostly on the outside, and the central, communal area on the inside. But few cars pass; only, rarely, an elderly person in a buggy. About a third of all the people who live here are Quakers. All are over sixty. This is Britain's first ever 'continuing care retirement community': Hartrigg Oaks.

I've come here for all sorts of strange reasons. At the beginning I was simply interested in seeing a model village one hundred years after its conception. I was curious about how New Earswick and its ideals might have been morphed and moulded by the reality which surrounds it. But almost immediately I was drawn to the newer community of the elderly at the other end of the village. The idea of a new model village entirely made up of the elderly interested me for some reason. It would be elegiac, perhaps, but also, possibly, intriguing. Staying at Hartrigg Oaks would clearly put me at one remove from my own reality. I wanted to know what the autumn of life looks like and, by spending time there, listen to what it says to the other, cheery seasons of spring and summer.

More than that, however, I was intrigued by the fact that much of the community, like Rowntree himself, seemed infused with the values and aspirations of the 'Religious Society of Friends', better known as the Quakers. Quakerism was by no means a criterion for membership of the community, but it was, clearly, an important influence. The Quakers interested me for various reasons. Partly because of the admiration they attract. William James wrote that

Quakerism was 'something which it is impossible to over praise. In a day of shams, it was a religion of veracity, rooted in spiritual inwardness, and a return to something more like the original gospel truth than men had ever known in England.'[5] In some ways, it seemed an interesting progression from the New Age antics of Damanhur: it, too, consulted what Milton called the 'inward oracle', but with a seriousness and serenity I hadn't found in Piedmont. In other ways, too, Quakerism seemed to chime with our own times: it was born in 1650s England in an era characterised, like ours, by frantic individualism and spiritual exploration.

Hartrigg Oaks is the first experiment of its kind in Britain and has frequently been the subject of academic and geriatric studies. And yet, on the first day we were there, my heart sank. I couldn't, for the life of me, remember why we had decided to come here. Of all the places, why a grey ghetto? What on earth could there be of interest in a purpose-built village for the retired? It looked like it was built out of Lego. 'Toytown' some residents mockingly call it. That first morning of our month's stay, I sat down, rather dismayed, with a coffee and just watched the procession of people coming through a large restaurant-cum-lounge. It felt like the foyer of a hotel: thick carpets and stone floors, floral furnishings in yellow, red and green. There were wheelchairs, buggies, walking sticks, some people who couldn't straighten their backs beyond 45 degrees, others were walking so slowly it took them ten minutes to get from one end of the room to the other.

'So whose grandson are you?' Someone had put their lunch tray on my table. It was a question I was asked repeatedly over the next few weeks. I explained what I was doing, expecting scorn at the intrusion. But the woman asked if she could join me. She introduced herself as Sheila. She wanted to know more about the book.

'I'm kind of making it up as I go along,' I said, 'but basically it's a book about communities, about self-contained communities . . .'

'This isn't self-contained!' she interrupted. 'Not at all! You're in the wrong place. The person in the bungalow to my right is in Greece at the moment, visiting grandchildren. The one to the left has gone to Australia to visit his brother. We come and go all the time. No, no, it's not self-contained. Wrong word! I thought you said you were a writer!'

I had forgotten how straight-talking people can be in Yorkshire. A couple of others had joined the table and a debate then ensued between them as to what my book was really about. What made me laugh was that they clearly liked the idea of the book whilst also being aware that I really had no idea what that idea was. Towards the end, Sheila said: 'I know what you're writing about: it's not about self-contained communities or communes or whatever. It's about places with a purpose.' We all considered this. People began nodding.

'Yes, it's about purpose,' said someone else.

'Oh, OK,' I said, pleased they had resolved the subject of my book.

There was a pause and I wondered how, tactfully, to ask the next question.

'Isn't this place, erm, incredibly middle-England?'

'Middle class, certainly,' said one of the elderly ladies. 'Unfortunately it is for the affluent. One couldn't come here without having had a house to sell and with both a state and occupational pension. That's true. But middle-England, no. There are people here from Poland, Russia, Denmark, Germany . . .'

Soon after that first encounter, my gloom lifted. What had looked from the outside an exceptionally dull community became, over the next few weeks, rather surprising and fascinating. I had imagined that no one ever left the place, but it was much less static than that: many were frequently away for reasons of grandchildren-sitting, holidays or charity work (one woman frequently going to Chechnya as a volunteer). Hartrigg Oaks might be very middle-class, but it was full of people with an intellectual edge. There was a large library upstairs full of learned journals. Many of the residents are retired professors and still regularly lecture here and abroad. One person told me that she was 'constantly stunned by the calibre of people here'. Many converted the lofts above the bungalows into studios or offices. When I tried to arrange interviews with various residents, I discovered their diaries were much more packed than mine. It only took one look at the notice-board to understand why: there were dozens of activities and courses and outings. I had assumed the place would be rather like the geriatric wards I used to go around with my GP father years ago: people dribbling in chairs facing a blaring TV. But Hartrigg Oaks was designed precisely to offer an alternative to that. People were busy, active and independent. In my initial condescension, I had imagined the residents were as homogenous as their hair colour; it was gently pointed out to me that the community was surprisingly diverse. It was proud, for example, to have a few same-sex couples (affectionately nicknamed 'the boys' or 'the girls'). At least one love story has had Hartrigg Oaks as its stage.

Every Tuesday morning, in the Music Room, there's the Quaker 'meeting for worship'. About twenty-five of us gather, sitting again in a circle of chairs. On the central table is the Bible, the *Quaker Faith & Practice* book and a bunch of flowers. People are getting comfortable and the silence slowly expands. It has an amazing fragility: it's easier to break than an empty egg shell. A couple of late-comers arrive and you can hear the rattle of the Zimmer frame and the hiss of a wheelchair. And yet, slowly, the solidity and stature of the silence returns. Surprisingly, it never feels solipsistic but rather communal. It's not, or not only, that each individual descends into their own internal sea, but that we're all swimming in a shared ocean. It's an extraordinary mix of communion and contemplation. Pierre Lacout once wrote in his minute book, *God is Silence*: 'Words split apart, silence unites. Words scatter, silence gathers together.'[6] It's that ability to share the silence and be comfortable with it which makes Quaker community extraordinary. It's a recognition, inevitably in a retirement community, that we're mortals. Language, like life, suddenly seems only a brief interval in the silence, an interruption of the resounding quiet. Renouncing language to listen to that epic, awful silence is more than a studying of our own extinction. For the religious, like Lacout, it makes language and life heavy with responsibility: 'Words must be the vehicle of silence if we are to be the messengers of God . . . words must be purified in a redemptive silence if they are to bear the message of peace. The right to speak is a call to the duty of listening.'[7] It makes no sense to many people, but the aspiration of the spiritual is to make speech nothing other than the resonance of silence.

Since the politics of emancipation became ubiquitous, silence has been a dirty word. It has become perceived as a colleague of inequality and is duly something which the brave should break. To be quiet is to acquiesce in, or collaborate with, injustice. Everyone should have a voice and, preferably, exercise it as much as possible. The consequence is merely clamour. We live in an era in which there are volume police in the form of noise pollution officers who prowl our cities; trains have to have special carriages for peaceful types. Silence is seen by most people only as the interruption of noise, as negation, rather than affirmation. But because language is invariably divisive, true community is impossible if members of that community don't flee from noise. As Max Picard wrote in his book *Silence*:

> Within the realm of creative silence the individual does not notice any opposition between himself and the community, for the individual and the community do not stand against each other, but both face the silence together . . . In the modern world the individual no longer faces silence, no longer faces the community, but faces only the universal noise. The individual stands between noise and silence. He is isolated from noise and isolated from silence. He is forlorn.[8]

Since silence is at the heart of Quaker worship, it's very difficult to know quite what they believe in. Rather like when you ask a Buddhist a question, you often get a gnomic reply which only shows how daft your question is. The Religious Society of Friends urges its members to 'know one another in the things that are eternal' and, obviously, that makes words rather inadequate. It's a form of worship without ritual, without priests and symbols. In many ways the Quakers emerged, in the mid-seventeenth century, at the extreme end of Puritan values: rubbing shoulders with the Diggers, the Ranters and the Fifth Monarchists. They refused any terms of deference, refused to doff hats to anyone (a foretaste of Zeno's 'no master, no slave' formula); they refused to take oaths, saying that their word was sufficient; above all, they refused to pay tithes to the established Church, frequently interrupting services to denounce 'hireling ministers' and their 'steeple houses'. Their disdain for sainthood led them to abbreviate place names and refer merely to Ives, Albans or Bury-Edmunds. They rejected, too, the use of pagan markers of time like Thor's Day, Woden's Day or Mars's month.

Where they differed from the Puritans was in their interpretation of the role of the Bible. Disdaining any notion of an established

Church, the Puritans had made the Bible the foundation stone of their faith; the Quakers, however, went further and sometimes even dismissed the Bible as a 'paper Pope'. William Penn (one of the most revered early Quakers) wrote: 'There is something nearer to us than Scriptures, to wit, the Word in the heart from which all Scriptures come.'[9] Here was a recurrence of a 'heresy' with a long history: previous incarnations had been called Joachism or Montanism; comparable movements – very different but stemming from the same motive – was Hendrik Niclaes's Family of Love or the famous Ukranian Doukhobors, championed by Tolstoy. It was a heresy which, according to orthodox critics, was New Age before its time. Since Quakerism is part of the Immanentist tradition of Christianity, it historically believes that God is perceived in inward 'openings'. It urges consultation of one's conscience and the removal of external moral sign-posts and formulaic pedagoguery.

The Quakers originally called themselves 'children of the light', 'the camp of the Lord in England' or 'first publishers of truth'. The epithet of Quaker was originally an insult (as religious labels, even 'Christian', often are), referring to the quaking nature of those possessed by the Holy Spirit. The emphasis was on personal response, upon enunciation as well as quiet: 'What had any to do with the Scriptures, but as they came to the Spirit that gave them forth? You will say, Christ saith this, and the apostles say this; but what canst thou say?'[10] George Fox reportedly said to the other pillar of early Quakerism, Margaret Fell. Fell later said that Fox had 'opened us a book that we had never read in, nor indeed had never heard it was our duty to read in it, to wit the light of Christ in our consciences.'[11] Here were the seeds of theological and political revolution. Gerrard Winstanley, the grandfather of British communalists, wrote: 'You do not look for a God now, as formerly you did, to be a place of glory, beyond the sun, moon and stars, nor imagine a divine being you know not where, but you see him ruling within you . . .'[12] When wondering why he had incited thousands to risk their lives cultivating the common lands, Winstanley merely replied: 'All that I have write concerning the matter of digging I never read it in any book, nor received it from any mouth . . . before I saw the light of it rise up within myself.'[13] It was a truly subjective, individualistic, liberationist creed. The 1660s saw the beginnings of the scientific revolution and religion and politics would now test laws against personal experience. The Quakers had taken Paul's arguments against the legalism and literalism of Judaism ('the letter killeth, but the spirit giveth life') and re-applied it to Christianity itself. They believed that there was a 'light that lighteth every man that cometh into the world'.

Persecution after the Restoration was harsh. The 'chief executive body' of the Quakers is still known as 'Meeting for Sufferings' because its original purpose was to support Quakers in prison and their families. Although persecution soon gave way to tacit tolerance, the Test Act had banned Puritans, Quakers and assorted nonconformists from parliament, the civil service and the universities. With those career options curtailed, many went into business and finance. Two of the largest banks were run by Quakers: Barclays and Lloyds; the so-called 'innocent trades' included foodstuffs, and the Quakers were renowned for their produce: Coleman's mustard, Carr's biscuits, Cadbury and Rowntree confectionery.

The interesting thing is that the antiformalism of the Reformation, which rejected centuries-old liturgies, often resulted in modernised forms of worship which, by contrast with the ancient mass, appeared thin. Many Protestants, having done away with the theatricality of worship and ecclesiastical pomp, yearned for the immediacy of the worshippers' relationship with God. Any hint of structure to worship was suspicious: religious services emerged in which the actual, inspirational element was foremost as laymen and women started preaching extempore. And yet, centuries later, many of those reformed churches now appear proud of their liturgical elements, their history and their structures. Gone is that immediacy but, by comparison with the Catholic Church, their history and liturgy still appear lightweight, rather recent. Those reformed churches are caught between one extreme and the other and end up satisfying neither the yearning for spontaneity nor the desire to be part of an ancient ritual. Of all the movements which emerged in the seventeenth century, only the Quakers still appear to offer both the revolutionary and the timeless. Silence is the one form of liturgy which never ages or dates. And it unites; unlike Damanhur's sacred language and the Gnostic, knowledgeable elite it creates, silence is immediately inclusive. Quakerism sweeps away everything that is a symbol of the sacred: linguistic referents, pictorial representations and all the rest. It believes, with Karl Kraus, that 'language is the universal whore I have to make into a virgin'[14] and that the purgatory for that 'whore' is silence.

Sometimes, the less dogmatic, liturgical and ritualistic your worship, the more exacting one's standards as regards extra-ecclesiastical manners. What you believe can be communicated only through behaviour, through rigorous living. Formulaic worship in the sacred arena often leads, according to the Puritan critique, to deregulated living in the profane arena. The quietism of the Quakers is the reverse: the lack of 'order of service' in one context creates extraordinary commitment in another. Freedom of worship translates into obedience in behaviour rather than obedience in worship leading, occasionally, to freedom outside it. For Quakers, observance in its religious sense is transposed to the profane world: ideally, every act becomes one of worship. Specific sacraments are superseded by their belief that the entirety of life is sacramental. It reminds me of that line from Sebastian Frank, the German religious radical: 'You think you have escaped from the monastery, but everyone must now be a monk throughout life.'[15] Hence what is, to many, the defining characteristic of Quakerism, the witness for peace: the opposition, always, to every war.

Many traditional worshippers feel awkward with Quakerism. Worshipping only in silence, interrupted rarely by a few, improvised sentences, is too unstructured for High Anglicans and Catholics. There's such an emphasis on the immanent experience of God that, in the orthodox terminology, Grace (the interior voice bestowed by and responding to the Almighty) is mistaken, according to those critics, for the godhead itself. What I personally find fulfilling about it, however, is that words like 'God' are very, very rarely heard. Silence can never be the negation of someone else's silence and thus any sign, especially linguistic, is seen as an inadequate, terrestrial representation of the sacred. There's a reluctance to banter around a word to define an inchoate theological position. That reluctance to rationalise and depict God, that refusal – as in other monotheisms – to dare to name or paint him, is accepted wholeheartedly by Quakers. Familiarity with a one-word definition somehow causes more confusion than clarity. It was eloquently put in one of the seminal utopian books, Gabriel de Foigny's *A New Discovery of Terra Incognita Australis*. The native's 'religion is not to speak of religion':

They believe that the Incomprehensible Being is everywhere, and they have all imaginable veneration for him, but they recommend carefully to the young men to adore him always, without speaking of him, and they are persuaded that it was a very great crime, to make his divine perfections the subject of their discourses, for that one may in a manner say, that their great religion is not to speak of religion . . . Men cannot speak of anything that is incomprehensible, without having diverse opinions of it; nay even such as are even contrary one to another . . . we better approve of an absolute silence of the matter . . .[16]

Christianity has often been too loquacious, too syllogistic whereas religion is, in some ways, the constant erasure of everything that previously constituted religion: magic, superstition, images, liturgies. It's a constant paring down, a removal of what we think is sacred but which we realise is not. Religion is the pencil's eraser, not the lead. To the purists, idolatry is as pernicious to religion as atheism, and better to have a blank than a Baal. Hence the mystic's plea that God might remove from his mind all that he thought God was. Bacon expressed it eloquently in his essay, 'Of Superstition': 'It were better to have no opinion of God at all, than such an opinion as is unworthy of him; for the one is unbelief, the other is contumely: and certainly superstition is the reproach of the Deity.'[17]

All of which has led to the suggestion that the cold, secular world is in some way closer to, not further from, God. Dietrich Bonhoeffer, imprisoned and then executed under the Nazis, wrote: '. . . we must not gloss over the ungodliness of the world, but expose it in a new light. Now that it has come of age, the world is more godless, and perhaps it is for that very reason nearer to God than ever before.'[18] The more the image of the benevolent man in the sky was discarded, the more graven images were removed from the theological imagination, the more possible, even probable, was Christian mysticism. The fact that Christianity had always been profoundly profane in the original sense of the word (that it was *pro fano*, outside the temple) was cited as a reason for the faith's survival in the secular world. That, I think, is why Quakerism remains so impressive. It inverts what most people expect from Christianity. It is receptive rather than prescriptive; it speaks to our age because it listens to it. Its attitude towards the sacred is less concrete certainty than humble surprise. And the silence doesn't preclude an eloquent life but becomes, rather, its source: as one of the Quaker tenets has it, 'let your lives speak'.

Even though not everyone at Hartrigg Oaks is a Quaker, the effect of its values on the community is huge and surprising. Above all, it's very rare to visit a community which doesn't have a cult, however innocent and small, of a leader. There is, invariably, a founder who is deferred and referred to. At Hartrigg Oaks there is no such figure. Joseph Rowntree is certainly a presence, but there is only one photo of him, hanging in the offices of the community. He died in 1925 and his isn't an imposing presence. And amongst the residents, there is neither leader nor hierarchy (although some, I'm told, have tried). It's an amazingly egalitarian, democratic place. There's a directory of residents but rank and titles aren't used. 'All the bungalows are practically identical,' one resident told me; 'it's not as if money can buy you something better. There's one car-park space per bungalow and so on. There are no penthouses here, no prestige or pomp.' Unusually for a retirement community, there is no chapel. In fact, one of the most obvious consequences of the Quaker influence is the absolute lack of any religious iconography. Carol, a retired Anglican priest, edits the community's newspaper: 'I can only slide overtly Christian things in sideways,' she says. 'I put up some rather lovely posters in the reception before Christmas and certain people were up in arms.'

There are individuals who sit on the 'residents' committee' or the 'management committee', but no one is ever allowed to pull rank. It's something which caused problems at the outset as there were 'many chiefs and few Indians' as one resident put it. Suddenly men (it was, apparently, usually men) who were used to chairing meetings and commanding factories and laboratories, were unable to impose their opinions. Anyone who tried (and there were attempts) was fairly quickly put in their place. It makes it a kind of bottom-up community. Every initiative comes from below; the Trust, apart from organising the finances and the care, deliberately doesn't get involved. 'There's a lot of initiative here,' said Theodore, a retired accountant, as I drank wine with him on his golden wedding anniversary. We were looking at photographs from the mid–1950s and the certificate signed by all the Friends as witnesses, since there was obviously no officiating priest at the ceremony. 'Quakerism is a DIY church,' says Ted, 'and Quakers have to do things for themselves. Hartrigg Oaks is a DIY community, full of "committee people".'

Since he's an accountant, Theodore explains how, financially, the whole place works. Hartrigg Oaks is effectively a mini-welfare state, a mutual society. Financially it's a fairly complicated but very clever actuarial model. There are four types of bungalow (one-bedroom, 'Rigg'; one-bedroom with loft conversion, 'Rigg Plus'; two-bedroom, 'Hart', and two-bedroom with loft, 'Hart Plus') and eight different costs (2005): £98,277; £116,573; £140,094 and £156,542 respectively for a non-refundable purchase; the same bungalows on a fully refundable basis – either repayable on death or on the decision to leave the community, but paid without interest – cost £141,000; £167,250; £181,000 and £202,250. Currently, 63 per cent of all residents have chosen the refundable option so that either they can change their minds or else their estate will benefit from the value of the property. In addition there's an annual community fee which varies, depending upon age and payment type, from £2,664 to £9,222 per annum. It is, clearly, an epic financial commitment and one quickly realises that Hartrigg Oaks, rather than catering to the poorest, is very much a place for white-collar, professional classes. A research paper published by the Joseph Rowntree Housing Trust estimates that only the top 25 per cent of society could afford the fees.

In return, the residents are guaranteed exemplary care until the day they die. Without ever being hit by extra costs, they will receive up to 21 hours' care per week in the bungalows, and once they need more care they will be invited to The Oaks, the care home at the centre of the estate. The entire community is 'ring-fenced': it isn't run for profit, but for the residents themselves. Any money paid into the pot remains there for future requirements. There is a guarantee that the community fee will not increase over 3 per cent over the retail price index. Whatever illness or ailment arises, the residents will remain where they are, either at their own bungalow or a hundred yards away, at The Oaks. They never need leave their spouses or their friends for a hospital. Whatever medical condition arises, they know that they will be paying what they are paying now. Everyone pays their premiums, as it were, and everyone benefits when they need. For the model to work, new residents must be in a decent mental and physical state: there are health and dementia tests on entry (like spell the word 'world' backwards without looking at it written down). There's a constitution and a contract: it's a very Protestant kind of philanthropy – business-like, practical, blunt.

It has proved such a popular vision that there are now over 250 people on the waiting list, hoping for a bungalow when one arises. Precedence is given to younger (sixty-year-old) applicants. As in any actuarial model, ill-health is penalised, invariably by exclusion from the policy itself (in this case, the community). Currently at Hartrigg Oaks there are 71 men and 140 women, 113 are single and 98 married. The average age is seventy-nine, although there is a forty-year spread from sixty to above a hundred such that, in one case, both mother and daughter live on site. Anyone without grey hair is clearly in a minority, but on site there are almost 100 Rowntree staff, some part-time and many who work on-site but for various Rowntree ventures; there's also a nursery called 'Little Oaks' next to the central reception area so that the squeals of four- and five-year-olds are never far away.

It's a very unusual community since, in some ways, it's not a community at all. It's a very private, Anglo-Saxon interpretation of the word. Many people never come to the central area and others insist that any post is put through their door, not left in their pigeonhole. Some tell me they came here only for the care, nothing at all to do with the communal aspects of the venture. 'I'm here to be looked after, nothing else,' one forthright woman told me. 'I'm here to have my future guaranteed.' Hartrigg is clearly a community from necessity as much as choice. It's a place which, it's obvious, has hermits and loners.

But of the 211 residents, between 120 and 150 have lunch here, in The Oaks, each day. If it's not the care, it's the food which brings people together. Sitting chatting to one of the caterers on one occasion, I was told, 'it's very, very demanding. When residents are well they expect it to be like a hotel, when they're poorly they want it to be like a care home. Young staff are usually shell-shocked. They come in expecting a lovely granny, but at sixty you don't suddenly become a nice person. The rudeness shocks and upsets them.' Some arrive and treat the place like a resort: I overheard one man, newly arrived with his wife, say to the receptionist on introduction: 'So I suppose I pay your wages!'

Some residents regret that the 'glue' of the place is the guarantee of personal care rather than something more altruistic. 'Personal conflicts,' says Rosswitha, a German brought up in the Moravian church, 'do exist. And to give time and energy to community you need to know why you should. Here we haven't got a good "why", only the safety and security. It's sad that we come here because of the comfort and that becomes our faith and our ideal. With a common reason to be together everybody would be embraced and it's here that our community shows up its weaknesses . . .'

The staff at Hartrigg gave me the best tips about how to get into the community. Two girls who alternate at the reception desk would hail me down and point me towards a particular bungalow or bed. They put up a note on the board asking any residents interested in a coffee/chat/walk etc to contact me. 'It's easy to show visitors the physical, visible side of Hartrigg,' one receptionist said. 'It's very difficult to show them the invisible side. Working here has completely changed the way I look at life.'

'In what way?'

'You never look at old people in the same way again – they're more diverse, active and entertaining than you expect.'

So I spent the first week or two just wandering around, having meals or tea and biscuits with anyone who crossed my path. It was great fun – partly because I'm nosy and enjoy seeing where people live. I must have seen about thirty homes in those weeks, and in each it was striking how simple they were: tidy, efficient bungalows, containing the small treasures of a lifetime. They were light; not so much because the windows were huge but because in this former field no one has built higher than their neighbour. Most of the furniture is simple. The bookshelves are simple. Everywhere you look in Hartrigg it's tidy. One woman from Hull, whose husband was at the university, told me about Larkin; one veteran from El Alamein had fostered a famous ITN newsreader; an old lady in her nineties was the grandmother of a famous London novelist.

I went to art classes and sat with a dozen others drawing a portrait of a resident: her skin was too large for her face and she joked, as we concentrated on her lines, about not making her look old.

Lots of residents showed me pictures of grandchildren. Many of their children have married foreigners, and so in these bungalows there are pictures of their descendants in Australia, Finland, Jamaica, Japan and so on. Although Hartrigg, in terms of skin colour, is snow-drift white, the visiting relatives cover the whole range of the spectrum.

But there is another glue here. Many of the residents had spent years looking for their ideal retirement community and many said that the only thing that held most retirement homes together was a bar (or, for the posher places, a golf course). Hartrigg Oaks has a licence to sell alcohol and it even has its own wine label ('Lucombe', which is, I'm told, a type of oak). But there's no bar as such. The glue of the community is the fact that the majority of residents have come not only to be cared for, but also to care. There is an epic, if tacit, promise here to support each other during the final years before the grave. As a glue, it makes for a community built upon sorrow and bereavement, but also on kindness and listening.

Ruth is a strong-minded, retired teacher of literature. She's got swimming-pool eyes. We talk about literature for an hour and (as usually happens) I realise how little I studied at university. We get on well. She begins to tell me what it's really like being eighty. 'The sadness,' she says, 'is that one does learn new things but no longer has the occasion to apply them.' She tells me how she learnt how to be a better mother only when she was no longer bringing up children. I'm sitting with Benny asleep like a koala on my thigh. Ruth quotes Eliot. She asks me which of the *Four Quartets* it comes from. I guess and this time she nods: '"The only wisdom we can hope to acquire is humility,"' she quotes. 'Eliot spoke about the fear we all have of belonging to another, or to others, or to God . . . and that if you don't overcome that fear your life will be nothing more than a "receipt for deceit".'

The atmosphere at Hartrigg is one of gentility. There is, says Dudley, 'a sense of the worth of each person'. 'We cherish each other's spiritual journeys,' says Howard. Ted, a spry, jokey Geordie, puts it like this: 'There's a certain austerity in Quaker values. We ignore what isn't essential. Anything that appears superfluous can be cast off until all that's left is honesty and integrity.' And in fact, as you meet people, you realise the extraordinary social commitment expected of Quakers. Rosswitha goes regularly to Chechnya as a volunteer: 'I'm training people to work with trauma, it's about how people can begin to listen again. I'm guarded twenty-four hours a day, but it's an interesting question of whether a Quaker is prepared to be guarded by an armed guard. I said to him, "Please do not defend me with that. Do not fire it on my behalf." That's one thing about ageing. Your life is complete in some sort of way and you don't mind if you lose it. This is the time in life when you can truly take risks.' Unlike most people of their generation, their memories of the Second World War don't regard battles and bombings, but peaceful missions: many were in the Friends Ambulance Unit, others went to Austria to work in refugee camps after the armistice. Almost everyone I speak to seems to have dedicated their life to voluntary work. One woman, a former teacher, spent years in peace negotiations in Northern Ireland; another couple ran a Toc-H house in Birmingham.

Having a community which is exclusively for those of sixty or older creates a unique atmosphere. In almost all the places we've travelled to there's a come-and-go of residents. Here, there's only the come. A few people have left but financially – once you've thrown in your lot – it's very difficult to leave. This is where people are until the end which, naturally, means that the stakes are higher than they are in every other community. This is a canopy that covers you until you die. Everyone here is a 'lifer'. I know what a revolving-door community looks like; I've seen many of them. But what interested me here was whether a community where the exit door remained shut worked better or worse.

Residents said that such a sense of finality was the reason for both the success and the tensions of the place. It's successful because coming here really puts an end to choice. This is where people have chosen to come and live the remainder of their lives and their emotional investment is inestimable. They want to make it work and dedicate much of their time to helping it work for others. It is commitment of a kind that is incredibly rare. But it also means that disagreements and personal feuds are more personal. Talking to people, you realise that in the first five years the place has really had to shake down, and some people, the so-called 'pioneers', have taken some hard knocks. Dominant personalities have been humbled, anonymous letters put through letter-boxes in the dead of night, some people no longer say hello to each other.

There's quite a powerful undercurrent here, a sort of ongoing debate between two camps: the 'trust the Trust' group and The Open Forum. The Open Forum is a sort of discussion group for all those who want to change Hartrigg Oaks. They have presentations and debates every six weeks or so and in recent elections for the Residents' Association the leaders of the Forum (they wouldn't describe themselves that way) have effected a coup. The dissenters from The Open Forum are now at the helm. George Dow, a Quaker from Barnsley with a grey goatee, has become Chairman; Molly Jones his secretary. I sit in George's bungalow as they both list a rather long line of complaints. George is wearing slippers. The pendulum of a soporific clock is clicking to and fro above the orange coals of the gas fire. There is a cross-stitch sampler on the wall.

'It has become incredibly political,' says George. 'There are people who think that the Rowntree Trust is infallible, that it can do no wrong. I've had some very nasty correspondence from some of the more academic residents here, full of French and Latin quotations, basically telling me to drop it. Others are upset with the way things are run but don't want to rock the boat. We're asking the questions, though, that need to be asked.'

The list of complaints is long. Above all, the fact that property prices have doubled or more since the beginning of the experiment means that, in reality, the more expensive refundable option is redundant. One is refunded only the amount originally paid: no equity increase, no interest. 'We couldn't afford a bed-sit now,' says George. Another dissenter I see a few days later, another former Residents' Chairman and Quaker, Elisabeth, has written an account of the first five years. In it, she writes: 'unless one moves out almost as soon as one has moved in, it can be very expensive to buy back into the housing market. Two couples and two single people have done this within a few months of moving in, but the longer the rest of us stay here, the more we are caught in a trap – guinea pigs in a cage.' What was once a reversible decision is now irrevocable. I ask George if he regrets coming here and the answer is rather saddening: 'Yes, in some ways I do regret it.' For many there is no way out. Ray told me, 'We'd go if we could. It's a trap once you're here.' His wife said, 'It's like a boarding school and many people can't pay for the extras.'

George, though, has worked hard to make the place as fair as possible. He has successfully fought a battle to have the council tax band of the bungalows reduced and is disappointed that he, rather than the Trust, had to fight the residents' corner. The Health Activity Centre isn't, as was promised and expected, free. There are problems of sound-proofing between bungalows. Then, the way the money from the resale of bungalows is (partly) used annoys him. It is complicated but goes something like this: the land on which Hartrigg Oaks is built was sold by the Trust to Hartrigg Oaks and interest is paid on the loan. But in order not to penalise early residents, interest will be paid ad infinitum. At no point will the loan ever be paid off. 'Think of the whole thing as a plc,' he says. 'The Rowntrees say it should be a partnership, but they are the bankers, they put up the finance.'

'We often feel,' adds Molly, 'that we're put on show for the glorification of Rowntrees. Academics and journalists are frequently coming here to gawp at us.'

Another problem is simply one of attitude. Joseph Rowntree himself, years ago, openly spoke of 'benevolent autocracy', but times have changed. As Elisabeth tells me, 'The transition from paternalism to democracy is not an easy one.' Molly, likewise, tells me that the Trust 'is more used to controlling than dealing with independents'. Many residents complain of an attitude of condescension, as if their occasional gripes are being met with a metaphorical patting of the head. There are other tensions. Many non-Quakers felt they had moved into a Friendly ghetto. One person notoriously went around asking 'Are you a friend with a capital F?' There is a community within the community here, a large cluster of Quakers who make up almost a third of the residents. They don't dress in the Hollywood stereotype – all bonnets and cloaks like the Hutterites – but they're an identifiable group.

Easter Sunday. We go to New Earswick, to the meeting house. It had to be extended when Hartrigg Oaks was opened since, obviously, the Quakers in the area suddenly increased exponentially. I realise something rather obvious: that of all the churches to which you can take babies, the meeting house is, in some way, the least appropriate. We've been sitting in silence for about ten minutes when Benny discovers her voice. She's a few months old now and it starts as a gentle gurgle but builds up into her impression of baby bagpipes. We scarper out the door and head into the Sunday school area. There are a few children sitting around a table with colour-in Bibles. One young boy – he can't have been more than eight – says: 'I don't understand why, if Jesus is God and is all-powerful, why he didn't just get down off the cross.'

Afterwards we meet a few friends from Hartrigg. They invite us to dinner at the Oaks next week. We head off to Fountains Abbey. It's still bitterly cold and it's raining heavily, drops thumping on the roof as we sit in the car park eating sandwiches. The football's on the radio. Francesca is shaking her head, saying with a smile that she can't believe she left Parma to be dragged around miserable northern Europe to listen to the commentary from Goodison Park in the car. She has a point. Eventually we get out of the car but we discover that the only way to the Abbey is through a knee-deep puddle because the manhole cover is blocked with leaves (leaves normally fall off the trees in autumn, but not here). Benny, safe in her marsupial, actually smiles as we paddle through the icy water. Fra reads some brochure about the word 'Cistercian' deriving from Citeaux in Burgundy, or maybe from *cistels*, Burgundian patois for reeds, which abounded in marshy land there. Oh well, it's marshy here in Yorkshire too. The whole place is becoming a pond. There are entire, extended families huddling under giant umbrellas. It's freezing.

It's a great Abbey, nestling in a narrow valley. The sawmill has been restored with one of those child-friendly hands-on shows. We press buttons and watch an actor telling us, all cor-blimey, about what life used to be like in the old days. At the Abbey itself, the windows, openings in the stone, are still there. The cloisters have survived, still ordered and regular. The latrines are there, planted just above the river. We wonder where all the monks have gone. I know about the dissolution and all the rest, but where are the monks today? Who are the people who get up in the middle of the night to pray? Are we really so much more knowledgeable about human nature than they were 500 years ago? I don't know. Monasteries were places where one could be alone, *monos*, but together at the same time. They were places where one retreated deep within oneself but, because of that, one had more to share with other people. Within such close quarters there was both solitude and communality, both the 'eremitic' and the 'coenobitic'. And that, I thought, is a surprisingly apt description of Hartrigg Oaks. It was a place where you could be both together and alone.

All over Yorkshire you see the Reformation writ small. Monasteries became quarries for conveniently well-cut stones. Those not plundered now stand alone in our landscape: admired for the age and history they narrate, but derided for their ideals. Each time I walk past Clifford's Tower, next to our flat, I can't help thinking of Robert Aske who, having entered York with 30,000 pilgrims during the Pilgrimage of Grace, was hanged from that Tower and his body left there, on display, for over a year. All the British monastic orders were asked to render to Caesar what was his, and then they vanished. The temporal and spiritual were torn almost completely apart, the only umbilical cord being, as it still is, the 'establishment' – great, subtle word – of the Church of England. I explain to Fra that we still have bishops who retain the right to sit in our upper chamber: we have a combination of 'lords spiritual and temporal'. We agree it's bizarre. So much easier in Italy where you have clericalism and anti-clericalism. For once, my country appears more complicated than hers.

A few days later, we're walking around York Minster and come across the Dean. We share a surname and we talk. He's a middle-aged, grey-haired man. He's got a smile which is incredibly, well, chilled. I'm asking him about purpose. 'It's very difficult for anybody,' he says, 'to believe they live in a world without purpose or meaning. You have to have such terrific stamina to keep reminding yourself that it's all meaningless. You have to live in a state of euphoria just to keep yourself from lying down. The purposes and meanings which people find themselves living for are amazingly thin compared with what the purposes and meanings are for a religious person. Theirs is just a kind of décor rather than really meaning something. The Britain I look out on is one with which I don't quite share . . . well, it's a kind of style statement rather than anything else.'

I'm trying to ask him if religion can really offer a way out of the relativist-fundamentalist aporia, and he pauses and thinks about it for a while. 'The real religious thing is in neither of those places.

The "thugs" are people for whom truth is a whole set of really hard programmes of belief and action; whereas religion is first of all a vision of something that is both beautiful and true, that generates a whole range of imaginative responses which are about the way you live. It's not prescriptive in that hard way. But at the same time it doesn't say, "Ahh, all these things are just open to whim and choice." Religion is different to that.'

I tell him a bit about the book and ask if I can quote him.

He nods courteously.

I ask if I can record him, because his words are chosen with such precision and I don't trust my shorthand. The batteries on the Dictaphone are low, but OK. Just as well, since this was the crunch. Dogma. Everyone is dismayed by the D-word. It comes next to Fundamentalism and Intolerance in Post-Modernists' Code of Crimes. Presumably, I ask him, there's good dogma and bad dogma. How do you know the difference?

'A dogma is only wrong when you are convinced of the evidence which presents itself to reason but you override it on the grounds that your reason must not be trusted. If your reason tells you that the prevalence of homosexuality seems to be naturally caused but that you will not go along with that because your reading of the first chapter of St Paul's letter to the Romans tells you that you should not hold that that evidence is true, then that seems to me dogma in the bad sense of the word. But the dogma that in the life of Jesus Christ God and humanity are equally present . . . I've spent most of my life examining this claim, and I live as if it were true. That is a dogma for which I am hugely grateful because it crystallises a piece of truth which I find life-giving. Dogma is just the conclusion which your community has reached in the past . . . it could be up for grabs. It's the refusal to take new evidence into account which proves whether your dogma is a cramping thing or not.'

A couple of friends phone to see how we're getting on. They still think I'm writing about spirituality, even though I keep saying it's not. 'It's about what religion is like when it's promoted to become a community's choreographer.'

'Yeah, but you're writing a book about spirituality, right? Not religion?' asks Pete.

'Erm, I don't know . . .'

And we get to chatting about the difference between the two. For some reason everyone assumes that spirituality is good, religion bad. I tell Pete about sitting with John one afternoon at Hartrigg. He's a retired C of E clergyman and a sharp theologian. 'Spiritualism to me,' he said, 'only means something if it implies a life lived in a world orientated towards God and energised by his spirit – that's the key to true Christian spirituality. Without that, you're on the open sea without a rudder.' Perhaps by 'spirituality' these friends mean mysticism, but that, at least according to the definitive expert on the subject, 'implies the abolition of individuality . . . purely from an instinct of love.'[19] I can't imagine that people who dabble in such things would countenance the 'abolition of individuality'.

'And where does that get us?' asks Pete, doubtfully, on the other end of the phone.

'Not sure.'

'Do we approve of spirituality,' he says, 'because it's inclusive whereas religion is exclusive, as every community has to be?'

'Hang on. Many religions and communities are founded on the desire to be inclusive and universal.'

'Meaning colonial.'

'Another word from your Code of Crimes. I think the problem is that spirituality has become a kind of shorthand for just being deep. It doesn't really mean anything. It can't be a choreographer. You can't write a flipping travel book about "spirituality". What would that mean?'

Pete is thinking. 'But surely there are plenty of people who are spiritual without being religious?'

'I guess so, but there are also plenty of great novelists who have never committed their novels to paper. Spirituality is to do with the soul, with *anima*, with breath and wind, with *ànemos*. It offers the infinite expanse of the skies. But religion provides the sail which gives the wind its terrestrial sense. It allows a ship to have direction. It allows me to see something.'

'You're talking like one of your vicar friends.'

'I just have a real problem with the fixation on the isolated, aesthetic experience of the spiritualist. There's no canopy there. It's like globalisation, which is a false canopy, not really a canopy at all. You might just as well talk about the sky and the stars – things which cover our heads wherever we are, whatever we do . . .'

'Meaning?'

'I don't know. I'm just thinking.'

'And why do you want this so-called canopy anyway?'

'Because I don't think you can have community without one.'

We're both confused and agree to meet in Bristol at the end of the month.

Listening to the elderly is like listening to someone speaking a foreign language you don't know very well. Because you can't follow their conversation, only dip in and out of the sense of it. It's partly because sometimes it veers from one subject to the next and you're left trying to splice the non-sequiturs. But it's often because they really are talking a different language. I'm sitting in the Oaks talking to Em. She's exactly one hundred years old and still laughing. She tells me about her life in Sierra Leone. Almost all her adulthood was spent there and she still speaks the patois. '"Don't shout at me" was one of my favourite lines,' she says. 'They used to say "make you no holler pan me". And when you went off on a long journey they would say "may God go carry you go".'

But mainly it's difficult to converse because many simply don't have a memory any more. There was one lady who made us laugh: Stella. She had a cheeky smile and used to come to a memory class run by Joanna. Joanna left Germany in the 1930s and is a trained psychiatrist. She had organised this class but it was more a game – Rummikub I think it was – which was supposed to help keep people sharp. When I sat next to Stella she looked at me and said: 'You must be good with numbers, I expect, what with having to count out your pocket money.' She was cheerful and charming even though she barely knew who she was with. She kept forgetting whether the game was going clockwise or anti-clockwise and each time her turn came we had to re-explain the rules. But she just giggled and apologised and promised to concentrate. It was like sitting next to a young child. We played for a couple of hours. I saw her in the canteen a couple of days later and she said: 'I know you, don't I?' And I had to explain where we had met. Then we chatted and she was charming again.

Memory is a big thing at Hartrigg. Joanna tells me how important it is to be open with people about it. She says that many are terrified at the prospect of losing contact with reality and don't want to be informed about what it involves. Stella, though, keeps joking about it, she knows what's going on. Apart from Rummikub, Joanna organises music classes with percussion instruments to help mental agility. Another lady, until recently intellectually very active, now sits in the canteen repeating one single sentence to all passing males: 'Are you Chris Perry?' People go and sit with her, and talk to her, but they know she's somewhere else.

One afternoon Fra, Benny and I were in the literary group. There were about twenty people there, some in wheelchairs, but mostly just in the semi-circle of chairs. The theme for the readings was memory. As each of them read poems it was moving: 'Old Man' by Edward Thomas ('. . .try/ Once more to think what it is I am remembering . . . listening, lying in wait/ For what I should, yet never can, remember. . .'); 'Remember Me' by Christina Rosetti, 'The Things that Matter' by E. Nesbit ('forgetting seems such silly waste . . . let me know something when I'm dead'); 'When You are Old' by Yeats. Marjorie, one year short of a hundred, read 'Dido's Lament' ('remember me'); then someone recited 'All that's Past' by De La Mare – 'silence and sleep like fields of amaranths lie' . . . at which point a debate ensued about the meaning of 'amaranths'. I ask Francesca, who asks me for the Italian translation. Er, pass. One resident reckoned it was a stone. Howard, as one would expect of the convenor of the Trollope Society York seminar group, tells us they were mythological flowers which never faded (or else, more prosaically, an actual genus of plants including love-lies-bleeding and tumbleweed). 'Silence and sleep like a field of amaranths lie.'

The amazing thing about watching everyone during the readings was that many had their eyes closed and were mouthing the familiar words to the poems with their heads thrown back. Maybe it was just cultural coincidence, but cultural coincidence, like memory, is now at a premium. There wasn't really any homogeneity to the residents, but they had cultural peaks in common, they had all compared the view from similar vantage points. The afternoon became a sort of tribute to their youth, when they had memorised so much poetry.

After each poem there's a brief chat about what's been read. The conversation goes off towards the actual years in which the poems were written and I'm feeling very young all of a sudden. Someone mentions 'rods and perches' and I have to ask what they were. The whole room erupts in laughter. 'No, I really don't know what they are,' I say, and that only increases the giggles. Howard later tells me that rods (also known as perches) were both measurements of length and of area: a perch was 5.5 yards or, expressed as an area, 30.25 yards. 40 of these perches or rods made up a rood (1210 square yards), and four roods was an acre. Simple. I try and translate the meanings into unimaginative metric for Fra, but it gets far too complicated.

Howard is smiling. I've never met anyone with as much precision as Howard. He has an anecdote for every occasion: it's always funny and clever. And as you laugh, he adjusts the thick orange frames of his glasses and starts another anecdote. He knows everything there is to know about opera. Fra and he get talking about Verdi and Parma. He knows everything that Trollope ever wrote. He invites us to dinner with Dudley.

The connection between the original model inspired by Rowntree, New Earswick, and the Hartrigg Oaks community is that thirty-eight bungalows were originally set aside, with the help of 'bursaries', for people from New Earswick. That number has now fallen to ten and the connection between the two villages is tenuous. A dozen of the elderly from New Earswick, however, are external members of Hartrigg Oaks: they live in their own homes in the village proper, but pay the community fee and are guaranteed care when the need arises. There are tensions on both sides, however. Originally, many from New Earswick resented the disappearance and development of one of the village's own fields; on the other hand, when Hartrigg Oaks opened The Oaks (the care home) it was, for obvious reasons, empty: some of the elderly were moved from the Garth (New Earswick's care home) to The Oaks, taking up beds which were, by right, those of Hartrigg Oaks. Other, external patients often have use of the beds in The Oaks, not least because at £549 per week for nursing care, it's a huge source of revenue for the community. But, as one person told me, 'there's a fine line between having an asset of ours unused and, on the other hand, having it so taken up that when our turn comes, there will be no room.'

Other tensions between the two villages occurred when one enthusiastic newcomer to Hartrigg Oaks tried to promote more links and events with the village proper; he was heavily criticised. 'I was given a rough ride,' he told me, 'it was made absolutely clear by the residents of Hartrigg Oaks that they were not prepared to enter into it.' In many ways, Hartrigg Oaks is surrounded by a metaphorical moat: it's not exactly a gated community, but many of the residents are clear that they want to retreat from the outside world. Any outsider is very quickly noticed and, normally, confronted. Learner drivers who used the peaceful drives for practice have been asked to find other roads; the 1,300 school-children that pour out of the village's secondary school across the road are viewed, by some, as a danger and a menace. That metaphorical moat even exists between the bungalows. Many told me, with sinewy determination, that Hartrigg Oaks isn't a community at all; and that precisely what attracted them to the place is that they could be private and reclusive. The attraction, for about half the residents, wasn't the community but the care.

One lady confined to the Oaks is a forthright, cut-glass type whose pronunciation of the word 'yes' can last upwards of a few seconds until it veers off to the frequencies only dogs can hear. She has scoliosis. 'Young people,' she admits, looking out of her window at the walls of the nearby comprehensive school, 'make me terribly afraid, they all have such terrible behaviour. They trample on flowers. There are no rules of taste. Their upbringing hasn't brought them into connection with society and its past, so they're rootless.' Another resident, not in the Oaks, openly says: 'I'm a grumpy old man. I anticipate that children will annoy me. We chase them off here quite regularly.' He says it with a smile, being half ironic, but mostly serious. One of Hartrigg's glues, and there are many, is a fear of the dreaded other.

Some people regret that. One woman I spoke to was saddened at the existence of 'a handful of people who want it to be an exclusive environment with no visitors. They want it closed to the outside world and it's so sad. It's a small group of people who are inclined to influence and frighten others. They send around notices saying "There's no reason to be frightened" which is, of course, guaranteed to frighten people.' She calls them 'the awkward brigade' or 'the narrow lot'.

It's clear that many not only have a fear of the young, but are convinced that their fear is justified. When you talk to anyone over fifty in New Earswick itself, they all mention that the place has gone downhill. Some of them talk about being terrorised in their own homes. Another man, with impeccable liberal credentials, urges me to take at face value the fears of the elderly. 'I never thought I would live to hear myself say this, but society has abdicated from the responsibility to exert social censure. Thus we have no means to deal with behaviour which is wrong but not criminal. And that causes the other problem, that these children are criminalised because they're not censured. You think my words harsh, but censure isn't part of a gerontocracy; it's about respect and civility. I would rather exercise the persuasion of social censure than criminalise these people later on. We're all moralists, you see, it's just that some of us are more openly and rationally so.'

Since the Rowntree Housing and Community Services own the entire village (or villages) you wonder how they have tried to remedy a problem which riddles the Western world: how to integrate youth into society, how to offer it rites of passage which are more rewarding than condoms or needles. The Rowntree Trust is in an extraordinary position here. It owns the freehold of all the properties in both New Earswick and Hartrigg Oaks. It owns between two and three thousand property units around Yorkshire. It is one of the country's biggest landowners, and almost the only landowner which studies its tenants and claims credibly to have their interests at heart. Last year alone it donated £100,000 to projects around York. I don't want to over-egg it, but it has pioneered the daring concept of applied philanthropy.

So how does the Trust, with over a century of social pioneering, deal with the yoof thing? I go over to 'The Homestead', the former home of Joseph Rowntree and now the operative base for his Trusts. It's the other side of York, a far cry from social services. The Homestead is a large building with extensive grounds. The lawns are like golf greens, there's a lake of daffodils and a children's play area. Jacquie Dale is the Head of the Housing and Community Services. She lives in Barcelona but flies back here for work. 'New Earswick does have entrenched views about young people. There's a general view that young people are not good and don't have a right to occupy public space. That has an impact on young people's self-esteem. We have to mediate between the two and there's always a danger that we come across as Victorian paternalists.'

I confess to her that I do find New Earswick slightly spooky. 'Everything you see is owned by you lot!'

'Well, that is changing. About five or six years ago we began a thing called SAVE, the sale of alternate vacant properties on estates. Every other property that comes up [and there's a waiting list of 680 and only nine properties freed up in the last quarter] we try to sell 25 or 50 or 75 per cent of the equity at market value. They could increase or decrease the equity as circumstances change. This is called "phase 5" of shared ownership.' The Trust sees its tenants as business partners but have had to issue twelve Acceptable Behaviour Contracts (the Trust's equivalent of Asbos) in the last two years: for bullying, harassment, incivility. A contract is written in agreement with the parents, the young person and the police. Tenants are potentially in breach of their tenancy: expulsion has never happened but it looms. 'That is our rod,' says Jacquie.

'We had a brilliant idea which was a disaster,' she laughs. 'We discovered through research that levels of fear of crime were up partly because the older population harked back to the local bobby, to a visible policing presence. So we, the Trust, bought an additional twenty-seven hours per week of police time solely for New Earswick. It was a complete disaster. Researchers found that fear of crime rose even higher . . . seeing an officer on the street made people assume crime levels had increased. We had funding for the project for three years but pulled out after only eighteen months.'

Susan lives at Hartrigg Oaks but remains Rowntree's Chair of Housing Operations. A former magistrate, she is saddened that the perception of crime eclipses everything else. 'It makes me very cross. The level of crime is very low here. There are smashed windows, there's a certain amount of drugs involved, it's annoying but it's very minor. It's not bedlam out there. It's very peaceful.' The real problem, she says, is the 'modern means of communication. You don't have to get out and about and meet your fellow villagers for your entertainment. If there wasn't the canned stuff, you would meet them naturally.'

She has a point. That evening I go for a walk through New Earswick. It's almost feeling like spring and a couple of hardy types have their windows open. I can hear gunshots and sirens. The village green looks different when you've got a Playstation guerrilla next door.

The position of the elderly is like that of Tithonus: Tithonus was loved by Eos who begged Zeus to grant him immortality. Zeus agreed but since Eos had forgotten to ask for eternal youth, Tithonus ages but never dies. He becomes a desiccated shell, eventually so sinewy that he becomes like a screeching cicada as the wind whistles through his limbs. Not a particularly cheerful image, but one that appears apposite for the situation of some of the elderly today. There has been an epidemiological revolution in which death is often a result of decrepitude rather than one-off illness; it comes not because of infectious diseases but due to chronic degenerative ones. Because of that, the elderly are with us for longer, but their exit is lingering and drawn-out: gerontologists talk of the longevity revolution, and how the 'third age' lasts ever longer or even enters a 'fourth'. The result is that what used to be painful weeks of medical freefall have been replaced by excruciating years, even decades, of decline.

But although they're now so demographically strong, the elderly are culturally off limits. The cult of youth has reached iconographic invincibility. (Ironically, the tyranny of novelty first appeared at about the same time as Quakerism, in the mid-seventeenth century, as the doctrine of the Holy Spirit allowed for unprecedented eccentricity in religious matters.) Technology, sport and personal beauty have become obsessive themes of our times and all add to the iconography of the first age. Innovation and change are central rather than peripheral. But the old are disdained for other reasons. When society's most important value is function, a thing's utility, old people are deemed irrelevant. They are subconsciously considered useless, a drain on resources (an attitude which is frequently and ruthlessly echoed in many fictional utopias). In our scientific age, the essence of a being, its 'whatness' (called, in the Middle Ages, its 'quiddity') is no longer relevant; of importance is only the role it can have in the great chain of cause-and-effect. Now the value of everything is instrumental instead of intrinsic. Tradition is a synonym for detritus. Age has lost the cachet of sagacity. When that attitude informs the dominant mindset, there's a ready acceptance of the brutal notion that the elderly have no further function, either for us or, probably, for themselves. This attitude regarding their perceived irrelevance then finds confirmation in the fact that society and technology are changing at such an exponential speed that the knowledge of the past is considered, more than ever, surplus to requirements. Any practical knowledge they might have is hardly applicable to our problems, goes the thinking.

I finally realised, after a month at Hartrigg, that we have a memory problem as much as the old. Their amnesia is imposed, but ours is chosen. We're amnesiacs who forget that community always has to be temporal as well as spatial. No community, especially one made up of people so near the end, has any purpose unless it hopes to preserve the treasures of the past and pass them to the future. Any community with a sense of collectivity must surely wish this for its descendants: that they glimpse the candles of the past and can do so is because they're kindled by tradition. Only when a community aspires to bequeath something worthwhile to the future can it transcend itself and answer the question of what its purpose and destiny are. Only then can one taste the sweetest flavours of nostalgia and anticipation, regret and optimism.

Many of the people I end up hanging around with have spent their lives struggling to define the nature of community. One had lived with husband and children on a Bruderhof community, another in a kibbutz and so on. Jennifer was one who summarised it by saying: 'Community is just more interesting. And it's much harder work. It's more rewarding, stimulating, you get to know people in a way you never would when you just go and visit them.' Her husband John – having lived in communities of various kinds most of his life – says that the recipe is simple: 'Just muddle through with common sense and goodwill. Communities generate difficulties but also absorb them. They contain more tension and more forgiveness.

'Often,' says John, 'you hear the phrase "it's a Christian community but it accepts all faiths". What's that "but" doing there? It should be "therefore". For us it's been rejuvenating coming here. Suddenly there are people forty years older than you and you, in your early sixties, are referred to as "the youngsters". It's a very liberating and stimulating place. It's a blessing in disguise that there wasn't more acreage, that it's cramped. There's a culture that you can sit next to someone you don't know. People are absorbed and picked up.'

Rosalind moved to Germany as a young child in 1923 and was twelve when Hitler came to power. Her family left in 1936 when fifty-two of the university staff were sacked. Her parents were great friends with Nikolaus Pesvner. 'Hartrigg Oaks,' she says, 'is a successful community because it hasn't sought to be one. It's not too tight, too close. You don't have to see people here if you don't want to. Many people never do.' It's a place which is reticent and yet that's not a contradiction of intimacy, as is the stereotype today. I sometimes think there's actually more privacy in communal life, because you can so easily distinguish privacy from loneliness. One is a voluntary retreat, the other an anxious sense of abandonment. And although Hartrigg is cosmopolitan, it feels very English. Italian friends always assume English reserve is a cloak for animosity, or at least superiority, but here it's reserve in the noblest sense: it's about not imposing oneself on anyone else. That is part of the reason that many are here, so as not to be an imposition on their children. Many say so and it's part of the Quaker philosophy that old age shouldn't become a negation of the lives of younger people. It's an unassertive place. In fact, the few tensions there are arise when someone tries to assert themselves. 'This place set out to answer the questions about old age,' says Rosalind, 'and I think it has answered them very well.'

The Open Forum understands Hartrigg is a temporal as well as spatial community; George's feisty defence of residents' rights is in fact a recognition of it. For all his reservations, he admires the people at Hartrigg. 'There's a lot of informal care here,' says George: 'people notice that someone's curtains haven't opened this morning, so they go round and see them. Very often, in Barnsley, we were the only people on our close all day. Here we're surrounded by friends. My wife and I have seen every care home in the country and this one is excellent. I wouldn't put my dog in the others.' I meet many former dissenters who, having had to go to The Oaks because of a fall or an illness, return converted: 'exemplary' was the most common adjective used. As with all actuarial models, Hartrigg Oaks is, ironically, most appreciated when things go wrong. One can pay tens of thousands of pounds in fees and, if in rude health, it can seem extortionate; but when one needs care and it is provided immediately and professionally at no extra cost, the logic of the scheme becomes apparent.

There have been ninety-three deaths since Hartrigg opened. 'Are you able to contemplate your death and the death of those closest to you?' asks *Advices and Queries*, the tiny booklet which is one of the spiritual guides for Quakers. 'Accepting the fact of death, we are freed to live more fully . . .'[20] Christianity has always looked at life from the perspective of death. It's not an attractive proposition in our age of aggressive self-assertion, but Christianity has always spoken of the need for our own selves to die. The desert fathers pointedly wrote about the need to mortify ourselves: 'The monk must die to his neighbour and never judge him at all in any way whatever.'[21] Only after a life lived that way can death be faced with courage. Most of the real world seems obsessed with blocking out suffering whereas here it's faced head on. It's no longer at arm's length, but is very close. Things happen each day which make you realise the fragility and fortitude of the place. Old ladies would mention an affront and say no more than 'I was surprised . . .' Others, feeling lonely, would say that the rest of the world seems so busy. There was one cheery, maternal woman who described what it was really like beneath the surface: 'You fall over and don't think you'll ever get up. Or else your hands grip the sink in the middle of the night and you're there for an hour because you're glued there, can't move and can't make yourself heard.' 'It's like all the sand is falling from your hand,' said one man, living alone. 'It's slipping out between the fingers, in the gaps between the nails and knuckles. It's falling away and some of us have only a few grains left where we used to have a fistful.'

Hartrigg's a complicated, vibrant, intimate place. Most people retreat in front of bereavement. Partly out of respect for privacy, but mostly because they don't know what to say. Perhaps the objective facts of death are so concrete that consolation appears insultingly callous. But death is always the beginning and end of religion. The end because death rips any possibility of meaning from our lives. I couldn't get that Tennyson couplet out of my head all month: 'Thou madest man, he knows not why; / He thinks he was not made to die . . .'[22] But because death is knowledge that cannot be believed, it often begets religion, which is belief that cannot be known. The meaninglessness of death is, for the religiously-minded, something to be transcended and transposed into an inconceivably greater end. That was the basis of Frankl's logotherapy. Its central aim was the creation of meaning where it was apparently absent: 'Suffering ceases to be suffering,' he wrote, 'at the moment it finds a meaning . . .'[23] It may sound like nothing more than a secular, psychological consolation. Sometimes, however, an unexpected reply creates a conviction that suffering isn't pointless; it's not the way in which God teases mortals but the way in which he reveals himself. Many of the insights of Christianity, including its central crucifix, are offered at the extremities of suffering. Christianity is rarely, if ever, the trite consolation it can appear from the outside; it's not the negation of suffering but the recognition of it. As Weil wrote on another occasion: 'The false God changes suffering into violence; the true God changes violence into suffering.'[24] It's the same distinction Frost made between grievance and grief. And our suffering requires, almost demands that God suffers too. 'Then and then alone will our doubts be stilled, not because we understand, but because we trust.'[25]

William Penn wrote in *The People's Ancient and Just Liberties Asserted* that 'liberty of conscience is the first step towards having a religion'.[26] Conscience was the real revolution of Quakerism. It turned Christianity inside out. The old school saw the sects and heresies of the post-Reformation shakedown as evidence that a little bit of liberty was a dangerous thing. This interests me because, in recent heavyweight debates with friends, I've been fought into a corner. I'm intellectually on the ropes and I'm not sure how I got here. The problem is that I have a hunch that our obsession with liberty or freedom really is a dangerous thing. I don't even know where the hunch comes from, it's just a feeling. 'Liberty of conscience' I admire, because it is, in some ways, an oxymoron, giving with one hand and taking with the next. It takes you with both hands and turns you around. But freedom has become absolute, the all-time greatest conversation-stopper. If you dare qualify it, you can expect the sure jab that freedom is everything, the alpha and the omega. And since I'm ridiculously privileged, never having had my freedom infringed, I'm in no position to pontificate. I'm not even sure why I'm uncomfortable with freedom. Like friends, I think freedom is everything, so why am I saying it's not? I don't quite know why I'm attacking something I love, it's like an argument that's been bottled up too long and you let it all out in the wrong direction. So to get off the ropes I have to confront freedom. That's the next stop, I decide, as we're packing up the flat in York.

Fra looks at me suspiciously. 'Freedom, huh?' she rolls her eyes and asks where we're going.

'I have no idea.' I suggest we go and hang out with her parents for a while and see what turns up in Parma: take Benny back to mountains, play a bit of football, drink some beer in the park, that sort of thing.

'Perfect, but what's that got to do with freedom?' She's looking suspicious.

'Something will happen . . .'

4

Freedom

There's seaweed on the pavement. A dried-out palm leaf is on the road, looking like a large, desiccated fish-bone. As you come to the end of each block you can glimpse the sea or else the majestic mountains. I sometimes hate this city. It really makes me depressed. But I keep coming back because, although the island is dusty and arid, the seeds that are planted do, eventually, flower into thistly, tough plants.

It's six-thirty in Palermo. I'm sitting at il Lava's desk, trying to reconstruct what brought me here. The wind is blowing and his ancient shutters are rattling. It's hot. Il Lava is still at work. He's a mate from Parma, an astrophysicist who fell in love with a Palermitana. He moved here to work in the physics faculty of the university five years ago. He's a large, freckly redhead, a rational scientist who writes equations that are over a page long. His conference essays read like something from a science-fiction novel. I sometimes tease him by suggesting that he just makes it all up, to which he replies with a sentence that is so long, with so many words I don't understand, that I begin to think he really does. So anyway, I'm sitting at his desk trying to work out what brought me here.

We had been in Parma for over a month. To be honest, I had been pretty lazy. It's amazing how in Italy days become weeks, the weeks months, and you don't really 'combine' – as they say – anything. Maybe it's just me, but as soon as I'm here, I kick back and relax. I always know something interesting is bound to happen, so I just hang around reading and chatting to people and don't worry where the next story's coming from. I was still thinking about freedom. Partly because I was struggling to define its relationship to community. Logically, they are opposites. Community is a place, said everyone, where you take chunks out of your individuality in return for a place where you fit it. You sacrifice personality but get belonging. But a true community, they said echoing Weber, would be an iron cage. The cost of company, said everyone from the Stoics onward, is a reduction of freedom.

I wasn't sure. I still thought the two could be complementary. The trouble is that nothing is currently allowed to complement freedom. Freedom has become akin to a flag, raced up the pole to test our loyalty to it. Freedom has become one of those words which is hoisted to end all debate. Politicians call their political coalitions – with a telling plural – the 'house of liberties' (the *Casa delle Libertà*, Berlusconi's centre-right coalition) or name their wars 'Enduring Freedom'. Advertisements and pop songs endlessly invoke freedom. Every politician obsessively repeats the word 'choice' because that has become the leitmotif of our freedom. The only definition we have left for our geo-political position is 'The Free World'. But all sorts of things made me suspicious about this definition of freedom. The fact that its sacraments are car keys and a credit card didn't, certainly, endear me. It was a freedom which appeared to increase with power, rather than exist independently of, even contrary to it. But I was also suspicious because few people appeared to derive any happiness from it. It created loneliness, isolation and continual conflict. What should have made us so happy has rendered us melancholic. It was a kind of freedom which was about conquest. It implied that everyone else is a restriction of my freedom, my autonomy of action. Freedom becomes a theatre for the advance and retreat of our personal battle-lines. This is privatised freedom whereby we only collectivise to form lobbies to promote our own agenda. The trouble with that kind of freedom (always beloved of universalists) is that it can never be universal; one man's freedom is another's loss of it. It is a freedom based upon conflict and an on-going defence of your freedom against another's. It's conflictual rather than pacific.

John Stuart Mill is the patriarch of this definition of freedom. His was a metaphysical creed and his gospel was called *On Liberty*. It stated the new absolutism of his theme: 'The only part of the conduct of anyone, for which he is amenable to society, is that which concerns others. In the part which merely concerns himself, his independence is, of right, absolute. Over himself, over his own body and mind, the individual is sovereign.'[1] By now that expression of autonomy, of privatised amorality completely distinct from society, is so common that it doesn't appear odd. Mill's disciples insist that such behavioural independence is absolute. It's a notion of freedom that has no connection to morality; it is seen as almost its opposite. It implies the removal of all restraint because we have been liberated from objective truth. We are truly ourselves at last, subject to no moral or metaphysical boundaries.

There are many reasons to be sceptical about such a concept of freedom. If the only arbiter for our actions is our own unfettered will, we would have to be convinced that our will was free for it to guarantee our freedom. Our will would have to be emancipated not just from morality, but from all cultural and economic conditioning. That will would have to be undetermined, the agent creating, *ex nihilo*, the action. Decisions would have to be made in a vacuum; they would be, by necessity, uninformed and irrational. None of which sounds like either a realistic or a sturdy basis for freedom, especially since I suspect that whilst we loudly trumpet this radical notion of freedom, we're actually more vulnerable to suggestion and persuasion than ever before.

Whether or not it's possible, however, that interpretation of freedom is rendered attractive because it's seen as a sibling of tolerance. No one in their right mind would challenge freedom if it had such a noble ally. Truth was once the guarantor of freedom; now, with truth announced as extinct, freedom is promoted as the foundation stone of tolerance. But if that's the theory, in practice it's rather different. The frequency with which we give and take offence in the Free World makes me slightly suspicious about the equal frequency with which we talk of tolerance. The flip-side of this tolerance-obsession is that we're all lightning quick to take offence in order to show to others that we're not being tolerated as we would like. What we trumpet as a virtue is often only self-defence. Litigation is the normal tone of communication. We witness the irony of people arguing incessantly because their freedom comes into conflict with someone else's. Fox-hunting, drugs and speech are all examples of freedoms with variant definitions. Many radicals have even taken freedom to the logical extreme where they would be freed from ever being told they're wrong. Slowly what once appeared a universal flag that could be raised above our globe appears a rather damp cocktail umbrella, not large enough to cover even ourselves.

That suspicion was confirmed when I noticed that we don't only take offence, we give it more readily than ever before. It's the way one marks out one's territory. Being offensive, like having a choice, is seen as a paradigm of our freedom. Strange, I thought, that those two, tolerance and offence, should go hand in hand. Just before Christmas a few years ago, Madame Tussaud's created its own nativity scene featuring David and Victoria Beckham in place of Joseph and Mary. It was the kind of schlock tactic which museums and galleries in Britain have been using for years: offence guarantees publicity and, thus, exponential rises in revenue. One media-type I was standing next to told me how he admired the 'conceptual irony' of the piece and thought it an interesting commentary on our worship of stardom and celebrity. I found it boring and cheap. Others, though, found it actually offensive. The level of general despair at the tackiness of Madame Tussaud's stunt was epitomised by James Anstice, a thirty-nine-year-old law lecturer. He decked the waxwork Beckham and beheaded Posh. Offence had been deliberate and offence had been taken. 'I apologise to the court but I find it very difficult to apologise from my heart to Madame Tussaud's,' said Anstice having been given a twelve-month conditional discharge. 'I have done my bit for the war against crap.'[2]

Something very similar happened a few days later. A play called *Behzti* ('dishonour') was suspended at the Birmingham Repertory Theatre because of violent protests by parts of the city's Sikh community. The play featured the rape of a woman in a Sikh temple and had outraged the religious minority. Then, a couple of weeks after the Birmingham fiasco, came the corresponding Christian protest. The BBC had decided to broadcast a musical about Jerry Springer, and the Christian lobby began burning their TV licences in protest. In the musical, God appears as a sort of Las Vegas crooner down on his luck; Jesus, dressed in a nappy, says, 'I am a bit gay,' before being touched up by Eve; Mary is presented with the chorus 'frigged by an angel'.

The reaction to both cases was predictable. Commentators led by Salman Rushdie railed against this infringement (or threat of infringement) of freedom of speech by those concerned to keep certain things sacred; opinion pieces in every newspaper denounced mob rule by a religious minority. No one could, obviously, disagree. Rushdie and assorted commentators were, up to a point, entirely correct: freedom of speech was certainly under threat, it was being relativised by people who recognised a very different absolute value. But I instinctively felt that the logic of such freedom-fighters was extraordinarily wonky. They seemed blind to the fact that there is no such thing as absolute freedom of speech: racial hatred and sexual harassment, for example, are verbal offences which are rightly punishable. No one gets het up about those infringements to freedom of speech when those infringements defend what have become sacred rights. Freedom of speech, secularists were actually saying, can be legitimately attenuated in certain cases, but not in others.

I was beginning to understand why Chesterton, in *What's Wrong With The World*, wrote that our freedom brings anxiety rather than courage. 'Most modern freedom is at root fear,' he wrote. 'It's not so much that we are too bold to endure rules; it is rather that we are too timid to endure responsibilities.'³ We've become so obsessive about the assertion of our rights that modern life sounds like a dog kennel, everyone furiously barking for themselves. The trouble now is that we're ineloquent, even ignorant, as regards the corresponding responsibilities. Even to suggest that they exist at all is to provoke suspicion that you are, at root, attempting to curtail those rights. But talking about duties or obligations needn't be a contradiction of freedom; it's an assertion that we have these rights thanks to the fact that others have recognised their responsibilities. If we really took those responsibilities seriously, rights would be just as guaranteed, but they would become part of the reciprocity which builds a community. Rights wouldn't have been screechingly, selfishly claimed by ourselves because – in an ideal world – they would have already been generously bestowed by other people recognising their obligations.

Responsibility can't exist without freedom; but freedom, of course, can exist without responsibility (and begins to border anarchy). For freedom-fundamentalists, the mere expression of responsibility is an affront to freedom. They don't realise that freedom isn't only the elementary cause of choice, it's also a consequence of choice. Freedom exists through responsibility, it is, paradoxically, protected by it. Freedom isn't morally neutral; the emancipation it offers is a means, never an end in itself. If we believe in progressive collectivity, we have to believe our freedom has a purpose, that it makes sense. One could only have pure, fundamentalist freedom by a blunt admission that freedom has no purpose. If that's true, we can only crown freedom by belittling it, we can only fully grasp freedom by saying it has no end, no *telos*. Freedom would become an ally, as it already has in some quarters, of nihilism and anarchy.

Others, though, suggest that freedom always involves morality, that it is indebted to it, almost synonymous with it. We couldn't have one without the other. Freedom opens the door on a binary world. It grants the possibility of making real choices. But it's more than having a choice, it's about making the right one. It's not about choice but discernment. Every second we're faced with a fork in the road. Freedom was so implicit in morality that almost everyone assumed, right up until Mill's time, that freedom would even uncloister truth. Truth would emerge through freedom because, in that 'free and open encounter'[4] Milton spoke of in 'Areopagitica', error would be defeated: it would be revealed in all its nudity. Those who still identify freedom with morality say that objective truth exists and our true liberation should be deliverance not from restraint, but from evil. 'And ye shall know the truth, and the truth shall make you free.'[5] The definitions of freedom are so far from each other, and the beliefs about truth so discrepant, that there can be no overlap between the two.

My problem with Mill is that he attempts to liberate freedom from justice and confuses (as Milton had anticipated two centuries before) two very different things. In *The Tenure of Kings and Magistrates*, Milton had written in defence of freedom that 'None can love freedom heartily but good men; the rest love not freedom but licence, which never hath more scope or more indulgence than under tyrants.'[6] Mill, and his ubiquitous disciples, have done exactly that. They have confused freedom with licence, and have therefore been blinded to tyrannies which trumpet liberty without knowing its true worth. It's true, or course, that Milton's point is more problematic now than it was in the seventeenth century. We're less certain of what constitutes 'good' and are more aware of the subjective nature of any definition. But the distinction between freedom and licence is still valid: if we don't believe the two are synonymous, we're inevitably drawn into a moral discussion about where the difference lies and about what 'good' might mean.

So we were hanging around Parma, mulling over such things, waiting for something to happen. One day, in the park under our flat, there's the national exhibition of *Commercio Equo e Solidale*, Fair Trade. We go down and walk around the elegant, simple stands. There are a lot of plain, cotton clothes, bare wooden furniture and so on. There's a Senegalese-Italian gospel choir on the stage and about 200 people are sitting on the grass listening and singing. It's all well-organised and tidy: there are hammocks made in Burma, coffee from Nicaragua. A lot of people are wearing sloganeering T-shirts ('Old African proverb: When the elephants are always fighting it's the grass that gets trampled').

We're walking around the various stands and one, instead of smart insignia, has a painted sheet with 'Libera Terra' handwritten in red: 'free earth'. They're selling olive oil, pasta and honey. I know the Libera organisation a bit: it's an anti-Mafia outfit operating out of Rome. They're usually very helpful when one's writing a story in the deep south. But 'Libera Terra' was new to me. The idea, as it's explained to me, seems rather brilliant. Using land confiscated from convicted mafiosi, various co-operatives (made up of students or the unemployed or recovering drug addicts) cultivate that land and survive by selling the resulting produce. We chatted with the guys and bought a packet of *reginelle* (absurdly long pasta) for dinner.

Libera Terra appealed to me on all sorts of levels. Above all because I've been going to Sicily, Calabria, Basilicata and Campania for seven years now and, with one or two happy exceptions, it's always to write some depressingly sad story about exploitation, rackets and murder. This was a positive story, the 'liberation' of the land – as the co-operative's flier had it – from the hands of criminals. Also, it was a secular community, inspired by a sense of civic, rather than religious, duty. And it was, obviously, the mention of 'freedom' which persuaded me. This was the bait I'd been waiting for since leaving York.

So I set off from Parma to Palermo and that's how, I suppose, I came to be sitting here, at il Lava's desk. By now he's back from the campus. We've made a small clearing on his desk of equations and graphs and are eating a large salad dressed with 'free earth' olive oil. On the label it describes exactly what the project involves: 'youngsters who have left the drug trap, in an effort of rediscovered legality, now face the world producing olive oil of a superior quality . . .'

Il Lava starts telling me about various initiatives in Palermo. There's a lobby called 'Addio Pizzo', 'goodbye protection money'. Volunteers have been collecting signatures – so far 30,000 – in and around Palermo. People are signing up to say that they will only buy from shops which put in their window a conspicuous sticker with the Addio Pizzo logo proving that they don't pay protection money. It would create a virtuous circle in which the shopkeepers not only leak less money one way (towards the Mafia), they actually receive it in another (from honest customers). It's a movement which relies on alliance and co-operation, the only way to combat a less conspicuous but more powerful alliance. What's great about Libera, and Italian protest movements in general, is that they mirror the epic fantasy of the criminal. I once made a TV programme for Rai, the Italian state broadcaster, about the famed *fantasia* – the creative fantasy – of Italy, and what I realised during the filming was that fantasy cuts in all sorts of ways: for every bit of creative accounting or inventive scam, there's an equally resolute, left-field reply. Libera Terra, Addio Pizzo and all the other anti-Mafia movements are simple but, in the planning, are extraordinarily effective. I get fairly bilious about the criminality in Italy, and yet it's confronted in very shrewd ways: there was, decades ago, the 'strike in reverse' organised by Danilo Dolci, persuading people to build roads which had been paid for but never completed. There are regular television strikes across the country, organised by an organisation called Esterni. The idea is that you take your remote control into town and you get free access to all sorts of museums and galleries in participating town and city councils. Simple but genius. There's the Time Bank, the *banca del tempo*, invented in Emilia-Romagna. It basically measures your work by time, not money. It's beautifully egalitarian because no one receives a higher 'salary' (time) than anyone else. Each person's input is valued at the same rate and rewarded by equal amounts of the same currency: hours and minutes.

The next day I'm up early to catch the bus to San Giuseppe Jato. It's dawn and people are dragging neat cubes and rectangles of luggage across the pavement. Men are walking to buy their morning newspaper with light coats on their shoulders but their arms not inserted into the sleeves. Why does that make them look so powerful, the simple fact that they haven't fully put on their jacket? Two men are discussing a Communist's by-election victory with a complicated sexual metaphor which I struggle to follow.

I jump on the coach and we leave the city and its suburbs: there is still bunting up from two years ago, shredded pink and black flags everywhere celebrating Palermo's return to Serie A football. There are babies sleeping on the dashboards of double-parked cars. We tear up over the mountains to the south of the city and as we climb the hairpins, you can look over your left shoulder and see the entirety of Palermo and its bay. After half an hour, the coach starts careering along vertiginous dual-carriageways on giant, concrete stilts. We're coming into San Giuseppe Jato.

Gianluca is working out of a ground-floor office in a block owned by the Guardia di Finanza, the financial police. Gianluca is the very clean-cut face of the on-going battle for legality on this macro-criminal island. He's smart-casual in shorts and sandals, wearing designer glasses. He's thirty-one, just married, and is the president of the Placido Rizzotto co-operative. There are others coming in and out of the office; the phone constantly rings. One girl is sitting in a wheelchair, working at a computer. As Gianluca gets on with business, I scour the walls: there are well-wishing letters from the national secretary of one of the largest, left-wing parties and another from a Cardinal. There's a large poster of double-barrelled *maccherone* pasta, the barrels steaming not smoking: 'Anche i Maccheroni Combattono La Mafia' it says: 'Maccheroni also fight the Mafia'.

Giovanni is making calls, talking about prices and harvests and machinery. I pull out my book and read the words of Nando Dalla Chiesa, a famous anti-Mafia campaigner whose father was killed in the 1970s: he lauds (in Italianate prose) 'the confiscation of goods which are forever taken away from the patrimonial circle of the mafiosi and their wooden-heads. And which are, by contrast, given back in another form to the community from whom, in a thousand forms, that fortune had been misappropriated by violent and bloody means . . . The Libera co-operatives should be considered, without mythologising them certainly, but with the due awareness, one of the highest points that the bitter struggles of civilisation have ever achieved in Italian history, struggles in which so many have fought and which are a rock of comparison in the walk of our democracy.'[7]

There were requisitions of Mafia property throughout the 1990s. It's been estimated that as much as 10,000 billion lire was sequestered between 1993 and 1999 (more or less three billion pounds). But it was only in 1996 that confiscation began to make sense. Until then, the land had often been auctioned off and, obviously, in isolated villages and towns no one bid for it. Either that, or the price was kept artificially low and eventually the land returned, by circuitous routes and through hired bidders, to the organisation from which it had been taken. But in 1996, thanks to a petition of a million signatures gathered throughout Italy, law number 109 was passed. It was promoted by the Libera organisation which calls itself the 'association of associations, names and numbers against the mafias'. The plurals are important: it's a portal, a meeting-point for hundreds of organisations which attempt to end corruption, extortion and the rest all over Italy. It doesn't take on one monolithic Mafia, but all of them in all their forms. The law they had promoted foresaw that the land should be used for *fini socialmente utili*, socially-useful ends. The results were spectacular. Between 1982 and 1996, only thirty-four confiscated territories were assigned for use by the community. Between 1996 and 2003, the figure was more than 2,000.

Ten years after law 109, this is the result. Libera Terra now has half a million dollars worth of sales; it produces 13,000 bottles of wine from the Nero d'Avola red grapes. It turns out 250,000 packets of locally produced pasta every year, each kilo being sold for €1.20. All of this on land which has been confiscated from the Mafia and given to people with special needs. Something called the *Consorzio Sviluppo e Legalità* – the Consortium for Development and Legality – has arisen in eight town councils and provides guarantees and an 'anti-Mafia certification' so that, in hiring out work to bottling or pasta factories, the co-operatives know their business partners are clean. The co-operativa Placido Rizzotto is, in legalistic language, a *co-operativa tipo B*, meaning that at least a third of the partners are 'disadvantaged': unemployed, disabled or recovering from serious addiction. The partners are sent on courses which last three months. They spend five weeks in the agricultural heartlands of Emilia-Romagna and roughly two months in classrooms in Sicily. Each has had to pay €2,500 to become a partner in the enterprise. Gianluca has a doctorate in Agricultural Science from the university in Palermo, and was elected president shortly after the formation of the co-operative.

He seems both relaxed and dynamic. 'Think of it from my point of view,' he says, having finished his phone calls. 'I'm in my late twenties, I've studied hard for years, trying to learn about modern, biological farming, and suddenly I'm put in charge of a workforce farming 200 hectares of land. We have national visibility because of the social message; there's been huge media interest. I'm incredibly lucky; no one in Italy ever runs anything until they're in their fifties. Here I am, running an enterprise which I think is both ethically, financially and socially very important.'

You can tell Gianluca is sharp. He's thought strategically about his position. But he's brave as well as lucky. No one gave him a chance when he started the operation just five years ago. San Giuseppe Jato isn't exactly the place one would choose to go to do business if you're flying an anti-Mafia flag. It can sometimes appear a heavy, silent place. *Cantanti*, the 'singers' who collaborate with the justice system, are openly derided, if not worse. Gianluca has, as a Palermo journalist said to me, *tirato fuori le palle*, which basically means he's shown he's got balls. He and his partners are farming land mostly taken from Giovanni Brusca, a man who, for example, strangled and dissolved the son of one of those *cantanti*, Giuseppe di Matteo, in acid.

We go for a drive and Gianluca shows me the co-operative's various fields: there are chickpeas in one, grain in another. Some still haven't been dismantled from their previous use, and there are lines of leaning vines, burnt out by the sun and surrounded by weeds. He points out the places where there have been 'incidents' which remind them all that they are not welcome: someone let out sheep onto the co-operative's field days before they're due to harvest, a tractor is burnt, that sort of thing. It happens with a regularity which excludes coincidence. In July 2004, as many were commemorating the death of Giovanni Falcone, one of the murdered anti-Mafia prosecutors, a fire destroyed one of the fields owned by the co-operative. When you look at the subsequent photographs the field looks like the inverted hide of a leopard: black all over, only intermittent yellow here and there.

It's tough, unglamorous work. There have been endless hurdles. The tractors that were originally set aside by the authorities for the harvesting were found to be without insurance, the ownership hadn't been officially changed and so on. The first sowing of grain had to be done by hand. There was no combine harvester (new Italian word of the day: *mietitrebbiatrice*). Then, there's the feeling of isolation, of being hung out to dry by various manoeuvres such as the one in December 2003 when the Italian government suddenly closed the *Ufficio del Commissario Straordinario del governo per la gestione dei beni confiscati ad organizzazioni criminali*, basically the office which was responsible for overseeing the entire 'confiscated patrimony' operation. It passed into the hands of the *Agenzia del Demanio*.

I could understand the dismay of various people I spoke to. Since 2001, when Berlusconi's government took power, the number of confiscated estates by the Italian state had fallen from almost 1,400 per annum to less than 300. The hand-over of confiscated goods is supposed to take place within 120 days of conviction, but the average amount of time it takes is over five years. When I was there it felt as if the excitement of the early years had worn off, and the actual co-operatives were facing the stark reality of agricultural survival in Sicily. I read one eloquent complaint: 'We feel alone at the moment, abandoned by those who, apart from giving us the land, haven't guaranteed us anything else: an unfinished law, I begin thinking. Why, beyond assigning lands which will remain hers, does the state not foresee an intervention for the launch of the project? Why, to acquire the seeds, do I have to use my own money from my salary and that of my companions? Why should I put in my money to make machines which should be operative work? Why on Saturday and Sunday, in my second job as a waiter, do I have to serve the children of those from whom the land has been confiscated and on which I have been working the rest of the week?'[8]

But despite all that, it's still a very successful operation. Whilst I'm in San Giuseppe Jato a businessman arrives from Barcelona. He's got a beard and that strong dignity of the Catalans. With twenty years' experience in retail, Jorge recognises a good brand when he sees one. He wants the exclusive deal to import Libera produce into Spain. He wants to announce the arrival of the products at a Madrid publishing event later this year: the idea is to serve up the 'free pasta' at the gala-launch of an important Spanish anti-Mafia book. I sit in on the business meeting between him and Gianluca. It's all very informal and friendly. The sticking point is about exclusivity. Jorge doesn't want to do all the hard work of whetting the Spanish appetite, promoting the produce to the public, only for another businessman to enter the market a few months down the line and reap the rewards. Gianluca says he lacks the authority to grant exclusivity; he'll have to talk to 'Ciotti', the brains behind the Libera enterprise. What's obvious from the meeting, however, is the extraordinary power of the Libera logo: it combines freedom with ethics, its simple pasta contains a grain of brave defiance. It has what the marketeers so desperately look for in a competitive market: the 'value-added'. It gives your meal a message.

A few days later we walk up to Portella della Ginestra. It's a pass which connects two valleys. It's high up here, and there's a strong wind to cool you. Everything looks bleached by the sun. On one side of the road there's a gravel clearing which serves as a car park, on the other there's a sort of assembly of huge stones. They have all fallen from the mountain peak, but some as huge as coffins have been stood on end. It was here, on the first of May 1947, that eleven people were killed during the Festa del Lavoro. Someone had opened fire on the crowd, killing indiscriminately. Now there's a memorial here to those who were killed. It's a melancholic place, almost a cradle between these steep, sad mountains. Only a year later, Placido Rizzotto, the man who gave his name to the co-operative, was also killed. He was the local *segretario della camera del lavoro* at Corleone. His body was found, from what they could identify, in a sort of mass grave in a steep crevasse.

We walk on a little further and come to an extraordinary place. It's called Piana degli Albanesi but was originally called Hora, meaning just town. It was founded in 1488 by Albanians fleeing the Turkish army. King Juan II of Aragon and Sicily had given them permission to found a town here, 25 kilometres from Palermo, and continue their Greek Orthodox services. Hence the town was called Piana dei Greci, eventually becoming Piana degli Albanesi. The amazing thing is that after more than five hundred years the first language here is still either Greek or Albanian. We're in Sicily and yet the sign for the town on the road isn't in Italian: Hora Aberesheret it says next to a double-headed eagle. The Cathedral maintains the Orthodox rite, and in the town itself over 100 people have the surname Lo Greco. That's a real kind of canopy. Only in a country with such a strong sense of history could a religious and linguistic enclave like this survive for over five hundred years.

Taking the road back to San Giuseppe Jato, I pass the Libera Terra fields on left and right. One side I can see the *ceci*, the beige chickpeas. The other is the abandoned vineyard. I come to the co-operative's *agriturismo*, basically a rural B&B. This too was confiscated from Brusca. It's been completely renovated with public money and one side is beautifully ancient and modern. The entire courtyard, however, wasn't allocated for renovation and so the outbuildings stand in front of the view: old masonry mixing with weeds. It feels arid and hospitable at the same time.

I sit down and try to see through the ruins to the valley below. This place understands, I think, community in the emancipatory tradition of unionism and association. It is where community meets and enforces freedom. That's what Carlo Barbieri meant when he spoke of this enterprise where 'along with liberty for themselves they [the Libera Terra partners] are giving a little more liberty also to us, and we have the civil and moral obligation to support them . . .' Sicily, for all its obfuscation, sometimes speaks bluntly. This is really freedom from oppression and it's earthy, gritty and sometimes cruel.

A few days later I'm back in Palermo. On the roads there seems to be a competition to see who can get their bumper closest to the jay walker's calf. There's a cacophony of horns. Cars with megaphones mounted on roof-racks are shouting about some clearance sale. I'm standing on il Lava's balcony. Opposite me, separated by less than the width of the street since the buildings have a little lean, is a man on the balcony, in large cotton shorts and a white vest, smoking a cigarette. Down below, there are occasional gaps in the streets where there's been a gas explosion. There are carpenters everywhere and the other smell in the air is linseed oil. Like I said, I used to hate this city, but now I'm rather fond of it. It's a vibrant bridge between the first and third worlds. The street signs in certain parts of the city are even in three different languages and alphabets: Italian, Arabic and Hindi. There's a sense of wistful solidarity to this city. I see some graffiti which confirms my theory that it is a much higher art-form in Italy than it is in Britain. The scrawl of one pavement philosopher reads: 'Is reality independent of our ways of talking about it?'

What I have difficulty with in Italy, and in Sicily in particular, is that there just seems less clarity about the 'categorical imperative'. To recognise it would be an affront to your own interest. It's curious that there's no unambiguous translation of 'mustn't' in Italian . . . *non devi* can mean both 'don't' and 'don't have to': very different concepts, and the difference comes only through the accent, not from the words themselves. There's a kind of moral ambiguity and the true tragedy of the mafias, I've always thought, is that they create an atmosphere in which respect for the law is seen as the behaviour of the immature and idealistic. *Scàntati* is one of the most common phrases you hear: 'wake up', be part of the 'real world'. Perhaps that's why – something I always find extraordinary – there's no future tense in the Palermitan dialect. There often seems to be a limit on optimism, a sense that it's realistic to expect things to stay exactly as they are, and wise to bank on the fact that they will. Libera challenges all that. It brilliantly threatens to overthrow violent oppression by farming the land. It's simple and smart: it serves up the most basic things – lentils, chickpeas, honey and so on – as material assertions of legality and social responsibility. It's a pacific protest which, nevertheless, really does hit the mafiosi where it hurts:

> It's as deadly as a life sentence. What sense would it make to challenge armies, put at risk one's own life and the life of one's children and children-in-law . . . deprive oneself of beauty and the treasures of liberty, stain oneself with infamous crimes capable of marking forever surnames and dynasties . . . what sense would it make if everything that is accumulated could disappear in a breath because of the latest judge? What sense would it make to organise all your life for the entire family, an entire enlarged community . . . if the fruits of the crime can vanish, not even be postponed, and maybe one day cleaned up, generating empires and, who knows, generating honour and respectability as has happened in the past.[9]

Surnames, dynasties, greater communities, children and in-laws: they sound like the raw ingredients for community, but they're used here, obviously, to describe the organisational intimacy of Cosa Nostra. That's why *appartenenza* – 'belonging' – often has negative connotations in Italy. Like the 'amoral familism' described by Banfield, *appartenenza* often implies that you're by-passing the greater good to look after your own smaller profit, often by whatever means possible. St Augustine once wrote that a state which promotes the common interest, rather than true justice, isn't structurally different from a band of robbers. When you spend enough time in Sicily you see his point. It's not enough just to talk about co-operation and community as if they were wonderful things, because Cosa Nostra has them in spades. Such concepts only become ennobled by their proximity to truth or justice. Libera Terra reminded me that Italy is very strong on both kinds of belonging, on the positive as well as the negative. There exist many perverted examples of community – not just Cosa Nostra, but the 'Ndrangheta (the Calabrian Mafia), the Camorra (the Neapolitan one) and so on – but they also give rise to their opposite: the pure examples of community which, having clearly defined notions of justice, become the complete contrary of those 'band of robbers' simply clubbing together to promote self-interest.

A few days later I'm in Castelvetrano. It's a beautiful town, still in the top left corner of the triangular island, but on its southern coast. The entire place seems built from the local, yellow stone. There are solid square buildings throughout the town centre that look like sandcastles. It's small but picturesque. I meet Leo, a man with a Status Quo haircut and small, circular sunglasses. He runs a centre here which works to give drug addicts a second chance. It is part of an overlap of two umbrellas: it too is part of the Libera organisation, although it's called Casa dei Giovani and is part of the Casa dei Giovani 'chain' of communities for addicts. He's profusely apologetic when we meet. I had been phoning him on and off for weeks, but I only ever got through to his wife. I left messages but had never heard from him. Now I realise why. There's no more labour-intensive job than running a community for drug addicts. Leo is brisk, but you can tell the sheer misery he sees each day takes its toll. 'It's very difficult not to let yourself get involved,' he says. 'It's important to have some distance on it because you see pitiful human conditions. It changed my view of the city. I thought I knew the territory well, but when I came here I had the impression that I didn't know it at all. There's an underground we just don't know about.' He describes one person who came in, a multiple addict, who had an horrific family history: 'Why wouldn't you do heroin if that happened to you?' says Leo. 'Can you imagine, an alcoholic father, a mother who goes off with another man, so you go and live with your grandfather who sexually abuses you. Why wouldn't you do smack?' Here, of course, things have come full circle. The wealth of the Mafia is based on narcotics; that wealth is used to buy up large swathes of the island; and now a number of the addicts who, in a tiny way, financed the whole thing have taken possession of that land through the law and, as redemption, are working it in conditions of borderline poverty.

It's only in spending time with Leo that you realise the true business difficulties here. It's one thing to sell olive oil in nicely labelled Libera bottles across Italy; it's another to try and sell simple things like eggs. They're not so exportable and they don't have that same sheen or logo. Leo describes the labyrinthine process he has had to go through just to be allowed to sell eggs. It is a story of days wasted in offices, missing post, deadlines which are never met. '*Tutte minchiate, minchiate,*' he says, shaking his head: 'it's all bollocks, bollocks. I just want to sell blessed eggs! That's all! Can you imagine the difficulties? Here we are, on an absolute shoestring, and it takes years just to get the vendor's permit! *Minchiate.*' He keeps saying how this island typifies *farraginosità*: it means something woolly, tying you up the more you attempt to untangle it. You wonder how much he's hindered by the fact that he's farming land belonging, previously, to Bernardo Provenzano, the head of Cosa Nostra who, until April 2006, had been in hiding for four decades.

It's a scorching day. We arrive at one of their farmhouses. There's a square vineyard in front of us, being watered under the blistering sun. There are pigs all over the place, huddling under olive trees for respite from the heat. There are bee hives up against the bank. There's one guy from the co-operative here, a former addict who has settled into the earthy rhythm here. So little of their conversation is in Italian (it's in one of the Sicilian dialects) that I barely understand them. They're talking about something that's not working, some chainsaw I think. None of them, you realise, are agricultural experts. They're learning by mistakes and, laughs Leo, making many of them. 'We've got one of the most unique olives around this area, it's called the Nocellara del Belice. It produces an exquisite olive oil, but no one has really got around to marketing it properly. No one has the dynamism to make it a success outside this small corner of Sicily.'

Leo knows everyone. As we walk around the town centre of Castelvetrano, he spends his whole time saying hello to people. He's a good operator. I accompany him into the offices of the town's mayor. It's all very informal. Both are smoking, Leo keeps his sunglasses on, they give each other the 'tu'. He's begging the mayor to give free meal passes to the many boy scouts and international volunteers who will be coming here next month for the harvest. They're coming from all over to lend a hand and Leo doesn't want them to have to pay for every meal. They haggle in a friendly way. The mayor offers one free meal per day. Leo begs for two. The mayor says he can't do that, there aren't the funds. Leo asks for some petrol thrown in, at least for those who have to run errands on the co-operative's behalf. The mayor nods. It's all done very quickly. 'He's on our side,' says Leo as we leave the offices.

The Casa dei Giovani movement was started by Padre Salvatore Lo Bue in 1983. It began in Bagheria, a seaside resort a few miles east of Palermo. For centuries travellers and grand tourists – Goethe, Byron and Swinburne among them – came to Bagheria to admire the views: the snowy Madonie mountains above, and the many bays below with their palm trees, gentle waves and fishing boats. The town was, for centuries, a playground for the rich, a chic and elegant place where you could build huge villas away from the bustle of Palermo. It was in many ways the Cannes of Sicily.

Now, however, it's renowned as one of the roughest and, unfortunately, ugliest towns in Italy. When you walk up to any vantage point you can only see mile upon mile of concrete. Almost as far as the eye can see there are the cube-like condominiums squeezed into every spare patch of land. What used to be characterised, in the diaries of those grand tourists, as a paradise of green and sea-blue is now ubiquitously grey.

'We started here,' says Lo Bue, 'because there wasn't only a problem of drug addiction. This was also a huge centre of Mafia influence. Many people were killed here in the mid–1980s, from a senator to grand Mafia patriarchs in their eighties. One Christmas, just after the solemn mass, five people were killed, including the mother and sister of the "Mafia's chemist". I placed the first therapeutic community here because it was very clear to me the problem of drugs was linked to the problem of the Mafia, that these struggles between Mafia clans were part of the battle to take control of the drugs trade. We were convinced that we shouldn't limit ourselves to the saving of a few young lives, not limit ourselves to taking a person away from the dealers.' Lo Bue's aim was more generalised. He wanted to deal not only with addiction but with the context which created it. 'These marginalised people had to acquire an autonomy by escaping not only from chemical substances, but from social pressures. I've always refused a diagnosis of the drug problem that puts at the centre of the problem weak people. We had to historicise the phenomenon of addiction, show people that they couldn't change their lifestyles without a concrete refusal of criminal life. We had to change the attitude of docile consensus that the Mafia bosses enjoyed.'

One afternoon Leo and I go to Selinunte. It's a former coast-line city, founded as Selinus by the Greeks in the seventh century BC. Now, though, the former harbour is nothing more than a dip in the land. One temple is still standing (or rather, was 'stood up' in 1958), but there are columns everywhere: piles of them, and perfectly cut rocks which haven't moved for more than two millennia. Leo knows the guy selling tickets to the temple and, as usual in Sicily, we're waved in for free.

Afterwards we walk a few hundred metres towards the beach. It's fabulous: there are a few people sunbathing or sleeping. A nearby bar is playing loud reggae. We go and get a drink. 'You know what they do here?' says Leo, trying to explain what conditions are like. 'They make you sign a letter of resignation before signing the official contract so that when they sack you they don't have to pay any redundancy money.'

'Who's they?'

'Employers in general. They won't give you a job unless you first sign a resignation letter admitting that everything is your fault. Can you imagine!'

I'm sitting in the main building. This is where addicts first come to detox. This is where they go cold turkey. It's fairly spacious, which makes it feel more eerie. There's a gym, a ping-pong table. There are sculptures, many rather brilliant, in tufa rock: it's the same colour as most of the city, that rich yellow, and they've worked it into sculptures of books or animals.

There's a lively discussion in the offices because one guy, who swears he's clean, has been arrested for possession of a long knife. 'I was only eating an orange,' I hear him shout. His sons are in there with him. I wander out and sit on one of the beds in the dormitory. The next intake is a week away, so they're all empty now. I remember something Leo said a while back: 'I would like to change approach with the user, change the idea that to start over you have to suffer. I would like a softer line at the beginning but harder later.' I look around the dormitory and imagine it full of addicts who have abused themselves for years. It's a harrowing place.

Lo Bue explains why it's only in community that addiction can be confronted. 'I'm convinced,' he says, 'that the symptom is a result of relationships. If a person's relationships are right, there's no longer the necessity or reason to look for a reality different from one's own. Here they can learn again how to live, how to think. Some communities try and propose the head as a charismatic leader, as if he were a father. I maintain that this is mistaken. Either you're a father or a therapist. We insist on families coming into our communities so that we can understand the pathologies within the nuclear families and understand the relationships within them.'

There's an old notion, and I'm beginning to think it's true, that moral beings can exist only in communities. Perhaps it's because of the idea that true virtue has nothing to do with rules and everything to do with roles. It's hard to remember now that morals are isolated into single issues, but in a true community the 'do's' and 'don'ts' were implicit, determined by social bonds. They blended with each other and one grew in moral stature simply by growing up. Behaviour was regulated by what was due and what was duty, concepts which only had significance if social position was understood instinctively. The very word 'moral' comes from *moralis* and *mos*, meaning pertaining to custom. It was about fidelity to precedent, fulfilling expectations. Being honourable was, in some sense, very easy because it was nothing more than obedience to one's role. Virtue removed from context was inconceivable. The notion is fraught with difficulty because, obviously, custom could simply be a means to enshrine the inequalities of the past. And that is why the prestige of the past is currently at a critically low ebb: tradition has been perceived (often correctly) as a collaborator in injustice. The trouble is that we've gone from one extreme to the other. From having been instinctive traditionalists whose morality was guaranteed by context and custom, we've become instinctive innovators. Only now that we've used up or thrown away our social capital have we realised the difficulties of constructing morality in isolation tanks.

And only now do I realise what really perturbed me about Damanhur. It was the fact that everyone had renounced their context, even their names (the most obvious example of social imposition). It was all a merry invention, a community of poseurs. I admired the thespian exuberance, but it was all, I felt towards the end, only about presentation. It was an act and, because it felt counterfeit, seemed inorganic. It was based on rejection rather than on what Cardinal Newman, my old sparring partner, called 'the grammar of assent'. But Damanhur was fascinating because, in some way, it reflected exactly the way we live today, in our era of 'life coaches' and 'lifestyle gurus'. Obsessively contumacious, we suddenly find that having dismantled all the rules, we don't even have any roles left. We're ghostly shadows, uncertain of who we are and what is expected of us. Hence the boom industry for soothing voices, whispering that they can help us become whatever we want.

Back in the corridor there's a large poster designed and painted by local school children. There's a picture of a tree surrounded by needles. The slogan goes: 'Original Sin: Eating the Apple. Unoriginal Sin: Doing the Pear [slang for shooting up]'. It's a thoughtful joke and it's not the first time someone brings in biblical imagery into this very secular place. Carlo Barbieri, who wrote about the Libera Terra experience, spoke of the feeling he got on eating 'Free Pasta': 'I was going to devour the symbol of the fight-back . . .' he mentioned, mid-mouthful, 'the parabola of good and evil . . . the fruit of the ill tree . . . a new life . . .'[10]

It's hard not to talk about temptation and redemption when living amongst addicts. They are the archetypal example of freedom becoming slavery. Transcendence has been on sale. They've tasted forbidden fruit and have enough knowledge of good and evil to last several lifetimes. It's only in the aftermath that one understands the implications of that knowledge. It's not only Genesis which begins with a broken injunction: many fairy tales and legends are set in train by dangling something forbidden which represents, for the characters, a bid for freedom. It's a freedom which teaches us why it was given and why it was forbidden. As Richard Bauckman once wrote, freedom becomes 'the difference between innocence and goodness . . . Without the tree of knowledge, Adam could be innocent. Afterwards, only good.'[11] It's only when you're surrounded by addicts, with that look of desperation never absent from their eyes, that you understand the mystics' refrain about the ancient paradox of poverty: 'We only enjoy true liberty in respect of such things as we neither possess nor desire.'[12]

For the umpteenth time I'm struck by the centrality of physical work in the role of sustaining individuals and building community. Physical labour used to be a sacred activity because it turned the body into an instrument, something which could be subtly worked upon as we were moulding our material. It was mortifying in the sense that it placed the living person within inert matter. That is why various writers have insisted that physical labour should be the spiritual core of a community. Drugs have a similar, more sinister, role: they work on us. We become the material shaped and worked upon. It's no longer a kind of dying which enriches life, but a frenetic attempt to fuel life which ends up by devaluing it. I know drugs from close up and it's only manual labour which offers a way out of addiction. Using our body as a means has become so habitual that physical labour comes naturally. We're addicted to material, to physical stuff, and the rituality of the addict – I've never met people as ritualistic as addicts – can be matched by the rhythms of farming. There's abject withdrawal, of course; there's no longer the acceleration of the narcotic high, but in physical labour we get a minute but comparable buzz: that of giving our bodies over to something. This time, though, it's a rewarding reduction of personality, rather than a chemical boastfulness or bliss.

There's another theory that suggests that our dissatisfying cycles of addiction occur because we have lost any sense of the ecstatic kinship with nature. We no longer feel the natural rhythms of the earth. We no longer have the seasonal highs and lows, the sowing and harvesting. But Lo Bue talks of another reason why farming is connected to drug rehab. 'In Sicily in the last ten years,' he says, 'we've noticed that many of the heroin addicts have almost no education, nothing beyond ten years of age. Many have spent years in prison. They couldn't ever find a job, they can't do anything. The only possibility is working in the fields. But the drug addict has a need to be a sort of superman in order to hide his weakness, he can't undertake such humble work.' That's why farming land confiscated from the Mafia is so important to the rehabilitation project. 'It means that these addicts have to show strength to go to these terrains, to sleep there and work there. It means they have to become exceptional people. The "good" people, the people in the limelight, are scared to go to these places. That means that when you make these addicts the point of the diamond, showing them that they're stronger than other people, they accept this kind of work.'

I'm intrigued by the role assigned to a 'higher power' in defeating addiction. The most successful recovery programme, the '12 steps' started by Alcoholics Anonymous, mentions 'a power greater than ourselves' and talks of turning 'our will and our lives over to the care of God as we understand God'. But despite being a priest, Lo Bue is adamant that religion has no part to play in the recovery from drug addiction. 'It would be a gross blunder to use religion as a therapeutic instrument. That was an experience we had at the beginning, that sometimes it could be a resource. But these addicts are used to exploiting everything and they can do the same with religion. The desire to evangelise shouldn't become mixed up with the therapeutic aspect. That's because the religious reality is a spiritual plane which can be constructed only when another plane is already in existence: the richness of complete humanity.' He makes a distinction between communities which are *laiche* and *laiciste*:

the Casa dei Giovani communities, he says, are lay establishments, not anticlerical.

It was only then that I realised something very strange. I was researching the origins of the Libera movement and realised that the founder of Libera was, along with Rita Borsellino (the sister of a murdered Mafia prosecutor) a man called Don Luigi Ciotti. One of the most radical anti-Mafia campaigners in Palermo that il Lava had mentioned was Don Meli. I had come to Sicily because there were communities whose conception of freedom – from addiction and from criminality – was intriguing. But I had particularly come here looking for secular communities with which to compare the other, more overtly religious ones. Now, after weeks of admiring the operation, it emerged that the brain behind Libera was, like the founder of Casa dei Giovani, a priest. Now, maybe it's just coincidence that that's the case . . . but everywhere I went, every time I went looking for the old or orphans or addicts or whatever, there was always some form of Christianity there even if unobtrusively so. Sure, they're secular places, these co-operatives. But it remained the case that the inspirational spark had emerged from religious men. I wasn't choosing communities because they were religious; I just wanted to find evidence of some serious, gritty philanthropy. And yet each time I found communities which were radically challenging the status quo, the source of that radicalism was always the same.

So I was beginning to take seriously the religious interpretation of freedom. I asked Lo Bue about his interpretation of freedom and found it convincing: 'I know this,' he said, 'liberty can't be liberty from needs, or the liberty to do whatever one wants. It's only when one has a life project, when one has made choices that settle with clarity the end you have in mind, that you're truly free. If we don't make our authentic selves flower, if we hide who we are, we're never free. It requires an acceptance of who we are, a complete transparency in dealing with others. Only then can we be serene and throw away the masks.'

I was beginning to feel that toleration is fine, but it's offensive if it doesn't go far enough. 'I'll tolerate you' doesn't exactly sound like a basis for a community in which people could feel they belonged. Freedom is, as the 'Free World' has recognised, the highest ideal, but understood from a Judeo-Christian perspective it doesn't mean that we all become masters; instead, we all become servants. The most repetitive line in the Old Testament comes in Exodus. When you read it the first or second time, it sticks in your mind: 'Let my people go that they may serve me'.[13] Freedom accompanies service, and we're only liberated from human lordship by recognition of God's lordship. That theme is taken up in the New Testament with the injunction: 'through love become slaves to one another'.[14] Another line hammered home many months ago now was Zeno's 'neither master nor slave'. No human being should be above or below another and that's only possible through absolute obedience to God. As Bauckman anticipated in his book *God and the Crisis of Freedom*, 'If the Old Testament emphasis is on God's people as *freed* slaves, the New Testament emphasis is on God's people as *free* slaves.'[15] The difference between the Judeo-Christian and the modern interpretation is that in the former submission to God's law, theonomy, was a substitute for submission to human law, heteronomy; now, though, we proclaim that we can transcend them both by asserting autonomy. We're not free slaves, just free.

The trouble is that autonomy sounds like nonsense to me. We're finite creatures on a crowded globe. I felt freedom had to be shared, it yearned for relationships. They are the only place our freedom has any meaning. If freedom means only autonomy, it is obviously inimical to community – a tragic, desolate notion of freedom. But freedom has no meaning if it doesn't yearn for company. True freedom would be where we are at liberty with others. It would be engendered by stepping back rather than racing forward, granting people the space to understand the enormity of the freedom they have been given. Etymology shows you the practical ancestry of abstract words, and liberty derives from a whole galaxy of words which mean 'of the people'. Liberty originally implied we were part of a community, not outside it. It was equated with being part of the *oikos*. The Indo-European root of liberty, *leudhos*, became both the Greek 'free' – as in *eleutheros* – but also 'people' – as in the Old English *leod*. Freedom, too, had resonances of collectivity, togetherness and purpose. It comes from the Indo-European *prijos* meaning 'beloved' or 'one's own'. The Sanskrit *priyás* and Persian *fryo* both mean 'dear'. Hence the Germanic Gothic *frijon*, 'to love', the Old English *frith* ('peace'), *freond* and so on. Freedom and liberty properly understood within an historical context would be actually revelling in 'love', in 'people', in community.

True freedom would involve not freeing ourselves from each other, but the discovery of shared freedom. It would require an acceptance that personal freedom is dependent upon its integration with a greater, communal freedom. Our personal freedoms, in order not to become centrifugal liberties, would have to be ordered and balanced, allowing law to be, not the contradiction of freedom, but the necessary background for it. It wouldn't be a negative freedom, obsessed with a 'freedom from . . .', but a positive one, urging a 'freedom for . . .' Only that way could it appear purposeful rather than vapid; the history of liberation would be not only the history of increasing rights, but also of increasing responsibility. It would be a freedom eager to search for, rather than ridicule, direction, even destiny.

At long last, I was beginning to hope that belonging wasn't the negation of freedom, but the only place to look for it. If freedom wasn't something I automatically owned as a right, but something I was given and gifted by my community, it had a completely different, more profound timbre. The nature of freedom was suddenly inseparable from the way it was given and granted, whether it was by bombs, fanaticism, compassion or love. It was a quality not owned by, but leased to, us. It suddenly seemed both more fragile and more majestic. It emerged only through reciprocity, from our own willingness to grant freedom to others and thereby enjoy mutual, rather than competitive, liberty.

All of which sounds insanely theoretical. But I was convinced of it in practice. For months I had been struck – during travels from Grosseto to York and to Sicily – by the fact that those living together, subject to common rules, enjoyed a freedom which lonely isolationists could only dream of. At Nomadelfia there were strict (we sometimes thought old-fashioned) codes of conduct, and yet the Nomadelfi appeared, through those codes, freed up to become truly themselves. One just sensed, instinctively, that they were more human, more honest, than those people obsessed by moral emancipation. At Hartrigg Oaks, residents were confronting, rather than evading, finality, and thus collectivity became something you handed on to other people. It was, in a way, a means to preserve memory even after the onset of amnesia. That acceptance of finality meant that they understood, more than anywhere, the nature of the gift of freedom and – for Quakers – of freedom of conscience. It wasn't something which died with them, but which they gave to the following generations. And here in Sicily, on this island which is both brutally practical and eerily mysterious, community and law and justice and truth had become, not the negation of liberty, but concrete examples of it.

Like Utopia, the ideal community is a receding horizon. Just as you're getting closer it seems to be further from you than ever. But the journey does at least bring into focus, albeit fleetingly, what you are after: in their ideal, mystical forms, religion and community reconcile that contradiction between the wimps and the thugs. In the perfect community, freedom and obedience become, not mutually excluding opposites, but the consequence of one another. It's incomprehensible to materialists, but someone who glimpses the ideal does believe that obligation and freedom are not mutually excluding. It's the blissful, obliterating coincidence of theonomy and autonomy. Georg Simmel wrote that

> this constant intertwining of freedom and obligation, even if it is only symbolic, is one of the social formative processes that is ideally suited to adopting and shaping fundamental religiousness, which otherwise exists merely for itself. For within this spiritual state, I believe it is possible to discern – on close inspection – a harmony of freedom and obligation. These are not meant here as types of relationship to real authorities but as the pure tension and release of the soul, a hovering between boundless extension of the self and the confining constriction of life that cannot find release, a combination of power and powerlessness that cannot be defined in logical terms.[16]

This kind of freedom means that the divine is seen 'not as space invasion, but as the creative giving of space'.[17] It would be exactly the opposite of the stereotypical image: God, rather than being seen as the epitome of non-freedom, would become the guarantor of our emancipation. Long before Mill, true freedom implied signing up to the other side in what was seen as an antinomic world: it's a world of two laws, one of the will and one of the conscience. It was a defiance of tyranny and force and necessity to be conscientious. If, I thought, I could find a place where people were quietly disobedient to the

apparent logic of the world – a place where they formed a community because they ardently believed in the 'survival of the weakest',
where they combined solidarity with silence and freedom – then
perhaps I really would, at last, find the ideal community.

Simplicity

The low winter sun almost blinds us as we head towards the Dorset coast. It's a crisp January morning and all the frosted fields look as if they've been covered with huge, muslin throws. Icy cracks accompany every step. This is remote countryside, the kind of place where grass grows in the middle of the roads. Leafless trees are silhouetted black against the sun.

From the top of the hill we can see the last, deep valley before the sea. The hills on the far side are flat like table tops and between their green cloths you can glimpse the sea. Everything else – breath, wood-smoke, exhaust from passing cars – billows white.

By now we're beginning to recognise the noises Benny makes and this time, maybe it's just me feeling guilty, the whine sounds like: 'Why on earth have you brought me here in the middle of winter?' I'm feeling apprehensive and irresponsible. I say that because by now we've been on the road for over a year. We're really beginning to flag. We go home for a month or so every now and again, but only to catch our breath and plan the next trip. It's the middle of a bitter British winter and I've lost hope of finding that elusive, perfect place. I had heard of Pilsdon on and off for the last twenty years. An aunt of a friend of mine used to live here. A nonagenarian from my parents' village in Somerset once came here with her husband, an old-school vicar of the cricket-loving variety and she had mentioned it a couple of times. They came here back in the 1960s and they spent the whole of their Sunday afternoon washing up. Then at school in Dorset I remember rebellious children would occasionally be sent here to do a weekend's volunteering; not just as a punishment, but as an education about addiction and alcohol. So I had always wanted to come to Pilsdon, but we were tired. I wanted to get a normal job, settle down like most respectable people. But I had written a letter to the warden of the community back in the autumn. A month later a postcard arrived inviting us down. This was the last throw of the dice.

From way up here on the hill we can make out the community: its main house dates from 1642 and it's a large, stone building.

There are fields on all sides, the smaller ones immediately surrounding it belong to Pilsdon itself. From up here it looks like a pebble floating in a green pond. This side of the house we can make out a courtyard and, on the south side, the famous, fourteenth-century chapel. From this height, it looks perfectly integrated into the countryside rather than insulated against it. It looks timeless and still, a combination of fragility and endurance. I pull my bag off my shoulders and find some notes I had scribbled before coming here. I find what I'm looking for and read it out to Fra. It is this, the moving description of Pilsdon by the Chairman of its trustees:

Life at Pilsdon is simple, so that everyone can share it equally without the divisions and anxieties that acquisitive materialism may bring. But it is a precious thing to meet real needs – for food, shelter, comfort, health and peace – and to meet them well; the daily routine of necessary work to that end offers dignity for everyone. Pilsdon is necessarily secluded – set in a garden overlooking the Marshwood Vale, the hills and the distant sea – but it is not isolated; it is there for the world, not set apart from or against it. Nothing is imposed on guests by way of religious activity; but Pilsdon's soul is Christian: with its small mediaeval church in the garden and its household chapel, it is for many people a holy place; a place where prayer has been valid, with a continuity stretching back not just over 40 years but to the Little Gidding community of 350 years ago and the monastic communities of the early centuries. Pilsdon cannot be pinned down, institutionalised, summed up, professionalised, rationalised, reduced, or ossified. It is full of tensions and paradoxes. It is alive, vulnerable and miraculous.[1]

I put the notes back and we walk down the hill. There was a phrase in that paragraph that sounded familiar. It reminded me of something that I had read years ago but I couldn't remember what.

Before long the path levels out and there's a modest white sign-post to the community. We follow the directions, flanked by two irrigation ditches. The path takes us in front of the house. It is clearly seventeenth century, a substantial farmhouse with stone window frames and a steep-pitched roof. In front there's a large lawn with wild borders and benches and a thatched hut. The main entrance is at the back. We walk round and, although it's bitterly cold, there are people out in heavy coats carrying buckets or moving wheelbarrows. There's a large courtyard, a combination of creosoted wood and Somerset Ham stone. This large square, with its buildings on all four sides, looks almost like an Oxbridge quadrangle or an ecclesiastical cloister. But it's very different: wild, almost unkempt. At the far end we can see the cowsheds. The concrete path is occasionally covered with mud or straw matted by manure, and there's a discernible squelch underfoot. In the middle is a lawn, more a field. There's a tall weeping willow, its bare branches looking like thin dreadlocks. There are geese and ducks and chickens just wandering around, some clucking around our ankles.

'Che bello!' says Fra taking in the scene.

'We're looking for Teresa,' I say to one of the guys with a wheelbarrow.

'You the Joneses?' he says straight off.

'Yeah,' says Fra.

He takes us inside. I dump the rucksack on the flagstone floor and we wander into the sitting room. As soon as you go in, you feel the warmth of the fire. It's the centrepiece of the room, framed by a massive stone fireplace, about ten feet wide and five high. The whole room smells of logs. Either side there are long sofas and armchairs. It's a large room. There are cushioned seats on the window sills beneath an entire wall of mullioned windows. There are various tables and other sofas. There's a piano, a chess set. A couple of people are sitting together behind the door, deep in conversation. They nod and say hello. On impact, it's literally and metaphorically warm. We stand by the fire and Benny goes berserk watching the huge flames. It feels like the living room of an almost aristocratic family, but with the aristocratic owners absent. One of the guys, with a straggly beard and more tattoos than skin on show, gets up to make us tea. Someone goes off to find Teresa who's the person I had spoken to on the phone. By now I know that how a community welcomes outsiders is the true touchstone of what those outsiders are being welcomed into and at Pilsdon, it felt as if our feet were being metaphorically washed. We were both feeling, almost instantly, more optimistic.

The numbers in this community are permanently fluctuating, but it's normally between fifteen and thirty-five. In many ways, the purpose of Pilsdon is to act as a refuge for people with broken lives:

people struggling with addiction, bereavement, separation, penury or else seeking asylum. It's a community made up of both regulars (the community members and the long-term guests) and of 'wayfarers' – tramps, men of the road, drifters. They're used to people arriving in all seasons, at all hours. The entire community can fit into the large dining room and be told of who's coming and going in the next twenty-four hours. In that dining room, the recess of the fireplace – still full of massive metal instruments for hanging meat – is big enough to house another table, a fifth, for when the place is crowded. Our first meal there was memorable: not just because the entirety of the food – pork, potatoes, bread, butter – was their own produce; nor because we were assiduously waited on. It was more the fact that the place felt intimate and calm. Unusually, there was a complete lack of conceit, a tangible humility to the place.

The next day we looked around properly. The whole place felt solid and spacious: there were dark-stained doors with brass handles, huge windows, the Aga, the creaking staircases with old carpets. On the north side of the house is the large kitchen, equipped with pans almost the size of steel drums: knives, notices, a blackboard for culinary preferences. The other side is the house's chapel, a small room with a little window onto the courtyard. To the south side are the sitting and dining rooms and the library, with its book-lined walls, armchairs and five daily or Sunday newspapers (the *Mirror, Guardian/Observer, Telegraph, Independent* and *Express*). Above, on the first and second floors, are the community offices, as well as various flats and rooms.

Now, in the daylight, we can see the courtyard properly. On one side is the dairy and, beyond that, the brown wooden loose boxes. They are basically the former animal pens which have been converted into small rooms with single beds. It's a harsh kind of home, but cosy at the same time. Some live alone, but most people share. Beyond them are the cow and chicken-sheds. On the far side are the barn and the pig pens. Then, the final side of the courtyard is made up of Ham stone with distinctive green window frames and red-brick architraves. This is where the wayfarers' dormitory is. There's a pottery shed, two TV rooms (because – a far cry from Nomadelfia – the founder wanted to avoid arguments between ITV and BBC viewers there are two sets). In between them, there's a full-size snooker table. It's a great space, whitewashed walls with random bits of magazines pasted up. People have scribbled funny memories and there are a few hundred paperbacks on the shelves.

Behind those loose boxes are other Portakabin flats and a large vegetable patch. Beyond are the sheep, the donkeys and the few fields owned by the community. The other side of the stream is Bill's cottage, a white thatched house with its own garden. Finally, coming back towards the main house, there's the church. It's tiny, little larger than a long double room and the nave is only four or five metres wide. There are no pews, only hay-bails along the walls with the occasional Psalter or Bible on top. There's a stone font, a tiny bell-tower and a wooden hexagon holding candles which can be lowered so they can be lit. It is exceptionally simple and peaceful.

The house normally has its fair share of gentlemen smoking rollies, laughing at some story or incident that's happened to them on the road.

'Where's ye fram?' asks Matt as I sit down on the sofa. He's got a navvy hat on and gappy teeth eroded at the edges like stacks in the sea. His accent is ice-pick Glasgow.

'Horsington,' I say.

'Dunno it.'

'Wincanton.'

'Oh aye,' he says, glinting. 'You know what the truckers call Wincanton on the CBs? Chinatown. Ha ha. Geddit? Win-Canton!'

He challenges me to a game of chess. Arrogantly, I assume I'll hammer him. I normally think that when I set up a chess board, but especially against a 'wayfarer'. He plays speed chess and absolutely destroys me inside ten minutes. The whole experience is humbling and exhilarating at the same time. As he rolls another cigarette, he explains where I went wrong.

'I only play chess when I come here to Pilsdon,' he says. 'I normally come for a week or so each winter, when sleeping rough gets too much.'

We play another game. I manage to capture his rook and a couple of pawns, but it still lasts only a few minutes longer than the last one.

By the time I wake up the next morning, he has already left.

A few days later. It's not yet 6 a.m. Even Benny is still asleep. It's bitterly cold and pitch-black. Adam and I get the buckets from the dairy and paste the grease on the teats. We sit on our wooden stools and squirt the first spurt of milk onto the floor to check there's no blood. Once he starts, Adam does it like he's doing a drum roll, his hands racing up and down to create a perfect rhythmic sound of liquid hitting metal. The teats are like plastic fingers, long and rubbery. It's still dark. I'm not dexterous at the best of times and now I can't even feel my thumbs it's so cold. They're aching horribly and I huddle closer under the cow. Honeysuckle – what else could she be called? – turns her head and kindly breathes on me. For a nanosecond I feel thawed. We dip the teats in the iodine disinfectant and put the cows out in the field. We carry the buckets back to the dairy where Steve will pasteurise the milk later on. The pond has an inch of ice on it and hardy geese are already trying to break the ice at its muddy borders. They have exactly the same colour eyes as Benny. I'll never forget that cold. I have a bath and crawl back into bed.

An hour later I go downstairs. Porridge is steaming in a vat. People are coming in and out. Benny and Fra are sitting on the windowsill. Adrian's in the kitchen, using wooden bats to make today's butter. Geordie Dave's doing the eggs, freshly delivered by his chickens ten minutes ago. Teresa's laughing at something. Big Rich is, as always, in the draughty phone booth, his feet up on the saloon-style swinging doors. The whole place has woken up. I look out at the pond and it's still frozen, but the sun is catching the crests of the hills now, and the tops of the pines and oaks are suddenly lit up, their black silhouettes becoming golden.

I spend a lot of time playing snooker. It was suggested as something I might usefully do in order just to chat to people. There's no therapeutic cure offered at Pilsdon; it doesn't have any method or course. Much of the way it works is by working: there are jobs that need doing, and people work side by side, talking. One of the members of the community, I can't remember who, said: 'There's a guy called Brian who's coming tomorrow for a few days. He plays a bit. Maybe you could offer him a frame or two.'

When Brian turns up, brought by his mother, he looks like a twenty-five-year-old in a twelve-year-old's outfit. His hair looks combed by his mother. He's nervous, and when I offer my hand he leaps back two paces. We go and play snooker. Everything I say to him makes him more nervous. Over the next couple of days we play a dozen frames. In all that time, we barely communicated but he became visibly more relaxed. I even caught him moving a ball with his hand and he smiled at me as if we now shared a secret joke.

There were others: a guy who had had a stroke and whose snooker style consisted in never getting his chin closer than two feet from the cue. He almost played upright. He was monosyllabic, almost absent, but a great, aggressive player.

But my main adversary was Paul, whom I came to call The Loud-Speaker. He wasn't a visitor but one of the long-termers. He's from Edinburgh, a die-hard Hearts fan. I had seen him play pool against quite a few wayfarers and he was spectacular. He would take on eight-foot pots with such confidence that he would keep talking all through the shot . . . describing his cueing action, how you should watch this because this was brave, attacking play. And invariably the ball went in and the white bounced off the cushion to leave a nice angle on the black. 'You watching pure class,' he would say, chalking the tip in preparation for the next seven points.

Playing The Loud-Speaker was a nightmare. I get competitive quite quickly and he would wind you up, just niggle you all game. If he caught you looking around the room for the chalk he would go: 'What have you lost? Is it your bottle? Ha ha.' As you were lining up an easy black, he would whisper to himself in the corner about how these are the shots that count and it would be shocking not to sink it. He would drive me round the bend. If you ever said 'good shot' to him he would say, 'Aye, it was'. You miss the black and he goes: 'Aye, Tobes, you're a nipple. You're not big enough to be a tit.' He would chip away at you all game. If you somehow managed to stay neck-and-neck, your confidence would still be draining away because of this flipping Scottish voice in your ear, so you would start playing defensively, leaving the white somewhere near, never actually on, the baulk cushion. He would go for ridiculous pots, with commentary, and invariably pull them off. After the best of five we would shake hands and he would apologise for talking through the match. 'I always forget that banter's irritating for the loser.' And he would start laughing again.

That was how I got to know him. He was a livewire. He had read voraciously and was very eloquent. We compared experiences of depression. He never really told me why he was here, only why he stayed. He said he had been to all sorts of communities – especially Buddhist and New Age ones. 'The real hippie places are much more saccharine, much more happy-clappy than here. They'll be talking all day about their spiritual experiences. But Pilsdon just gets on with it. No one ever talks to you about God or your soul. It just works. I don't really ever go to the Church except to pray. I like the praying, you know.'

I ask him how important the Christian side of things is.

'The bottom line here is about not trying to live some magazine lifestyle. That's something Christians know how to resist. But you need to dehippify the concept of community. This place isn't a commune, it's just a village, part of a village. We keep animals, cook our food and eat it. Some people are Christians, most aren't.'

The fact that not all the community are Christians is important. This is a place which is overtly religious – life is lived according to the rhythm of bells for four daily offices – but it is also practical. The bell for Morning Prayer and Eucharist and compline are complemented by bells for breakfast, lunch, supper and a couple of tea-stops in between. Depending on where you are, the bell is either the large, hand-held thing in the kitchen or else the bell in the church's tiny tower at the end of the garden. Everyone comes together at the same time each day to eat, but attendance at the church or chapel is never mentioned; there is simply that bell if anyone is interested. Everyone hears it and knows what it is for. But attendance is expected at the meals. People are missed if they aren't there. Being present for the sharing of food is almost the only condition of living at Pilsdon. That and, obviously, renunciation of alcohol. At each meal, someone gives thanks for the food and company before everyone sits down. It is the only public prayer ever said with the whole community present.

It feels like a much more rugged place than those we had been to before. You occasionally catch phrases from another room about 'parole', 'bail' or 'sectioned'. There are regular trips to Bridport to take people to AA meetings. I once asked Little Dave, a short man renowned for his fish and chips, what he used to do in Plymouth and he just replied: 'Drink mostly.' And yet it is also a soft, gentle place. It feels as if there is an unobtrusive magnet at its centre, moving those who felt its pull.

People sit under the stairs smoking, comparing experiences of prison or life on the road or whatever. Sometimes you just sit there and talk about football. The whole atmosphere is unreal. You are living amongst people who would be terrifying to middle England – many men are covered in tattoos and a few have harder-than-thou scars. But often I have to nip off to finish mucking out the cow shed or whatever, and Fra is in the pottery shed or kitchen, so I leave tiny Benny with one of these guys. And they all gather round and laugh at her smile and mini-teeth, and she starts showing off, and by the time I come back an hour later she's asleep in one of their arms. Another time, during dinner, she was sitting on Jonathan's knee. She dipped her hand in some custard and, rather than pick her up and faff around cleaning her, he just put her whole hand in his mouth and got back his custard. It was that kind of place. There was an absolute absence of pretence because it would have been found out so quickly. For the first time in months we could relieve ourselves of what was most precious: we could just pass Benny around and relax a bit.

In the library there are two oil paintings of two members of the Ferrar family. They hang over the fireplace. It was Nicholas Ferrar who inspired Pilsdon. Ferrar was born in 1592, he had gone up to Clare College Cambridge and quickly rose to become deputy treasurer of the Virginia company. In 1625, only thirty-two, he founded the Little Gidding community, inspiring – centuries later – the Eliot poem (that, I realise now, is the phrase I caught earlier – 'where prayer has been valid'). Ferrar became a deacon and tried to live a simple Christian life in communion with other people. He died thirteen years later.

During the 1950s, a Church of England clergyman, reading about the historic community, decided to try and reinvent Little Gidding. After the Second World War, Percy Smith and his Welsh wife, Gaynor, were in Hong Kong. On returning to England, he had been assigned a parish in Dorset, but he was eager to start his community project. The seventeenth-century farmhouse called Pilsdon Manor came up for auction on 16 October 1958. Sir Anthony Eden was thought to have been bidding. There were nine and a half acres of grounds, the outbuildings and so on. Most importantly, there was the tiny church a stone's throw from the house. The Smiths' bid of £5,000 was accepted.

For a few years Pilsdon enjoyed its fair share of publicity. The BBC sent down the vicar of St Martin-in-the-Fields to interview the maverick clergyman and see his impoverished project. Smith had contacts throughout the ecclesiastical and academic worlds, and people began to arrive and swell the numbers of the community: the disabled, the demobbed, the alcoholic. By 1960, Percy was writing his *Letters From a Community*, a sort of summary to the outside world of what was going on. He described the planting of japonica, forsythia, aubrietia; he described the animals and the harvests and the potato-peeling. 'If Pilsdon teaches anything,' he wrote in December 1960, 'it teaches through failure and disappointment how far we fall short in our love.' It was, he said, 'a school for sinners and not a museum of saints'.[2]

Fra's gone off to the pottery shed. She comes back an hour later with tales of a wonky jug that she has managed to throw. Nick, who comes back to guide potters, was at Pilsdon for years in the 1970s. He met his wife here. He's become one of the country's leading experts on Hardy. He has vivid memories of Percy: 'He thought depression could be sweated out with hard work. There was lights-out at 11 p.m. because the generator went off, but people would sit around the embers, maybe slip another log on the fire . . . it was a place for all those who didn't fit into therapeutic niches. There were more army types, more women in the old days. Percy had contacts everywhere and people were just referred by word of mouth.'

Apparently Percy's great phrase was 'of your kindness'. That was his line when he was standing up at breakfast, distributing duties. 'Of your kindness, would you. . .?' You could object that you had never done brick-laying, but he would just say, 'Maybe not,' raise his eyebrows and send you off to start learning. The day started at 9 and finished at 4.30. 'His instinct about people,' says Nick, 'was infallible. He had an incredible discipline, he would go running every night. He gave amazing energy to the place. His father was a headmaster and he used to say fanatically, "Schools are evil." He was surrounded by a coterie of women who would do anything for him.'

There's now only one picture of Percy at Pilsdon. It's a small photograph on a wooden dresser, almost hidden by jugs and plates. He looks like a rugged, strong man. He left in 1979, after twenty years leading the community. Having memories of Percy is a way of saying you've been here, or been coming here, for decades. Pilsdon, from what they say, has become a different place, perhaps tamer, since the Smiths left. The couple separated, Percy moving to Scotland with one of the founder members and his wife moving to Sussex where she wrote her memories of a quarter of a century of communal living, *Pilsdon Morning*. She spoke of disagreements with her husband; she admired that 'intellectual edge' he gave the community, but also said 'he was impatient of the frivolous . . . his tremendous energy was nervous rather than physical: his batteries were highly charged.'[3]

Over forty years later, the leadership still struggles and aspires to keep authority and love complementary. There was, as far as I could see, a style of leadership which was completely removed from vanity or power. It didn't shrink from taking responsibility in what were, without being melodramatic, potentially life-and-death situations. 'The leader of Pilsdon,' I was told by one former warden, 'will always have to have the authority to ask people to leave against their will. Within an hour if they are drunk, on drugs or violent. The sense of security and safety for many guests at Pilsdon relies on this authority.' It's a kind of leadership underpinned by service to the whole.

The noticeable thing about staying here is that, almost immediately, you no longer feel like an outsider. So many people come and go that you're suddenly the one welcoming people. It's late one night, gone eleven. It's February and cold. A car rolls up just as I'm coming out of the snooker room. A guy gets out and asks if this is Pilsdon. I take him inside and get Adam. He's shown to the wayfarers' dorm and is given some food. He's driven down from Preston to see his girlfriend somewhere down on the south coast. He tells me about his previous two wives and many children. He's younger than me. He stays the night and leaves the next morning after breakfast.

It's always like that. Not usually in a car; most people call from Bridport bus stop or from Crewkerne station, and someone drives out to pick them up. The only rule is that they must arrive sober. Since many of the long-term residents had, previous to coming here, lived rough, there's an affinity between insiders and outsiders.

Wayfarers are shown to their rooms by people not very different from themselves, by people who have no superiority or judgement. Those tough men who are the residents of Pilsdon form both a welcome and a cordon sanitaire: they recognise, from having been there themselves, drug and drink habits, they often know who is high, who's here to steal or just sleep. It's easy to understand why Jonathan says that 'the social ecology of this place needs wayfarers – the new faces and stories.' Pilsdon often seems a place where the world has been turned inside-out, with outsiders suddenly at the very centre. It's men and women who have been outcasts that now build the fire every night. They welcome the wayfarers, offer them tea, find them a pillowcase. All of which makes Pilsdon a home for the homeless. People go away but many return. Of all the way-farers who roll up, about 80 per cent have been here before. In that sense, Pilsdon is almost a contradiction: it's a community of itiner-ants, a mix of stability and fluidity. Someone will be welcomed back at lunch having arrived unannounced after a year or two away. A couple of old friends slap the guy on the back and joke: 'You've been a long time at the shops!' or 'Got my change, George?'

From this vantage point the lauded tolerance of the secular world appears very different. All its gates are financial: the protec-tion of possessions rather than ideals. At Pilsdon, like Nomadelfia, it's the other way around. They protect ideals by disregarding pos-sessions. They believe in the root of community – *koinonia* – which means having things in common. They take their lead from Acts: 'no one said that any of his possessions was his own, but every-thing was held in common . . . distribution was made to every man according as he had need.'[4] The doors of physical access are perma-nently wide open to everyone. That, you could almost say, is the defining ethic of both Pilsdon and Nomadelfia: you accept and feed and give lodging to anyone who rolls up. You never know what's going to happen next.

Gaynor Smith describes well what many of the old-style drifters were like:

> They were half naïve and half cunning, half sad and half funny, like tragi-comic clowns and who can resist a clown? They were

touchy too and moody and often irritable but they knew they were safe with us, safe from scorn and censure. There was an affinity between us: we too had chosen an unconventional path and, like them, were living a life that had shed many of the sophistications of society and was simpler and more primitive than most of modern life. Almost unconsciously we understood each other and were relaxed and at home in that understanding.[5]

Those old-style men of the road still come to Pilsdon. Many are Irishmen in their fifties, men with a trade and families but who are restless, always on the move. Some are tough as nails: arriving in winter with huge overcoats having walked twenty miles on the Monarch's Way to get here. They are mostly boozers, but renounce the habit, even if only for a few days, for the respite of Pilsdon. Many go to work in the vegetable patch, or help out digging a ditch for electric cables. One old boy shows me around all the bits he had painted more than a decade ago. Much of it is pastel green or pink, even on the old oak panelling, which sounds garish and it is . . . but like the man who painted it, it's got a strange charm.

'What unites this place,' says Nick the potter to me on one occasion, 'is sorrow. And yet that's not to say it's a miserable place. There's a lot of laughter, but everyone is gentle because they understand the sorrow.' That, in fact, is a perfect description of what it's like to live here. In the outside world, what unites us is stress. We're obsessed by speed and travel and spend our spare time in much the same manic way as we work. I understand people, on the whole, only because I'm as stressed and rushed as they are. At Pilsdon, there was no stress; only the bond that comes from drinking from the chalice of suffering. Stress makes one strident, whereas sorrow is very different. It makes Pilsdon not frenetic, but quiet and solicitous.

One of the strange things about living here is that it's not just that the weak need the strong – but the strong need the weak. It's not to do with feeling smug because one is being charitable, but something very different. Almost exactly the reverse: one feels exponentially less conceited. Those who have been emotionally skinned, who are in exposed agony, have a gift. They break down the prison of prestige. Jean Vanier, who founded the L'Arche communities for people with learning disabilities, once wrote: 'The poor man has a mysterious power: in his weakness he is able to open hardened hearts and reveal the sources of living water within them. It is the tiny hand of the fearless child which can slip through the bars of the prison of egoism. He is the one who can open the lock and set free. And God hides himself in the child.'[6]

The Christianity of the place is never hidden, but nor is it ever worn as a badge, something which could create barriers. There is never any preaching from either side. 'No one who comes to Pilsdon,' says Peter, a former warden, 'is actively hostile to faith, even if they are convinced atheists.' Yet again, my entire expectations were inverted: one thinks religion implies telling people what they ought to think. But here it's the opposite. It's about allowing people the space and peace to be able to think for themselves. Because of the fragility here there's a sensitivity and subtlety to relationships and any heavy-handed proselytising would ruin the intricate balance they've created. It's typical of Pilsdon that you could be here for weeks and not know, unless you asked, who's running the show. A few men and women would occasionally take people aside for 'chats', but you wouldn't necessarily know who was ordained, who was a believer or an atheist or a leader.

In fact, there was one guy who looked like a typical Church of England bishop. He had a posh voice, white hair, a seraphic smile and a gentlemanly manner. I had seen him in church and for days I assumed he was part of the invisible pastoral team, but he told me, when I sat next to him one lunch time, that he had been in the merchant navy all his life. He made us laugh by using arcane language, and you were never quite sure if he did it because that's how he spoke or just to get a laugh. 'Is he away with the fairies or just pretending to be?' one wayfarer whispered to me. He would always forget what you said to him, so he kept asking Francesca what Spain was like. He was incredibly serious and playful at the same time and we nicknamed him the Bishop after one memorable observation about Benny: 'Your daughter has fine loins,' he said.

One of the men who, it emerged, actually was an Anglican priest told me a story about such mistaken identities. One day, a while ago, he was sitting in the close of Salisbury Cathedral. He was dressed in the typical Pilsdon attire of beard, woolly hat and manured boots, and was eating a sandwich on a bench. A train of bishops and priests gathered nearby in full, glorious regalia to take a photograph of themselves. The guy from Pilsdon offered to move, to get out of the background, but was told: 'No, it's OK, you'll make the photo more relevant.' The Church of England minister had been mistaken for a tramp by his own colleagues. And he took it, of course, as a compliment. The other 'members' of the community are comparably 'embedded'. If you didn't know who the warden was, you would think that he was another ex-serviceman or a tradesman. Jonathan looked both tough and gentle: ear-ring, dark hair, a gingering beard, eyes which closed as he smiled. He dressed like a farmer and had the same practical, occasionally taciturn, manner of the hardy agriculturalist. There was no uniform, no dress code.

I enjoyed the fact that I could, whilst mixing the cement, spend ages talking to an ex-prisoner whilst thinking, for the first hour or so, that he was a priest. Or vice-versa. There was no ceremonial grand-standing. You listened to everyone and they listened to you. It wasn't calculated, it just happened. It was as if everyone was on the margins together. 'I have always believed,' said Peter, 'that the Church works best when it is a minority. Its history tells me that when it is a majority and has real power, it is as liable to corruption and injustice as any other institution. This is true of communities. When Glastonbury Abbey was landlord to most of the south-west it didn't find it easy to be the servant church in solidarity with the poor peasants. Why was it relatively easy for Henry VIII to dissolve the monasteries so quickly and confiscate their enormous wealth?'

Thursday afternoon. There's a delivery of straw and three of us go out to unload it. Graham, a talker from Cheltenham, stands at the back of the barn. Henry is in the middle. I stand on the lorry and chuck down the bales. It takes a couple of hours. Grab the two bits of binding twine, lift the bale over your head, and aim for Henry's feet. He, as ever, just grunts if you miss and he has to go and pick it up from under the lorry's exhaust pipe. The gold dust is everywhere as the thin, brittle tubes snap in your hands and under your feet. I join Graham at the back of the barn and we stack the bales in alternate directions: longitudinally then laterally. We rise two feet with each layer and towards four o' clock we're up under the beams in the barn, and can see the bird shit under the eaves.

Through the dust you can just make out the lorry. Henry goes to get tea. We sit at the entrance to the barn in straw armchairs. The sun is out for the first time in a fortnight.

I'm beginning to realise that this place is impossible to describe. And the longer you stay the harder it becomes. Days become weeks and the pace becomes habitual: porridge for breakfast, work in the garden or with the animals until eleven, a tea break, then another two hours until lunch, a siesta or read the papers in the library . . . maybe you're next to someone on the sofa and you suddenly find yourself in at the deep-end of conversation as they tell you their life story. Or else you go through to the kitchen and begin cooking dinner for thirty people, all of whom have been hoovering, milking, mowing, chopping wood, whatever. Doing jobs for you as you are for them. Tea and toast by the fire at 4.30, evening prayer at 6.30, supper at 7. Then snooker, chess, chats. Compline at 9.15 and bed. Stone sober and asleep by ten. Each day is the same but slightly different. The Loud-Speaker's still beating you every four out of five frames.

You see so many people come and go, so many faces and names that you're struggling to remember them all: Colin and Graham and Himalee and Barry and Mary and Tom. It's still cold. Most mornings the water troughs are frozen. You help big Rich clean out the pigs. They're Royal Berkshires with thin, bristly hides. The new piglets are about the same size as Benny, all nine huddling under the hot bulb in the corner of their sty, climbing on top of each other to get closer to the warmth, then racing to the sow, nuzzling and poking her underbelly in search of milk. She lies, placid but snorting. Just behind this building is the 'boutique' in the caravan – an assortment of spare clothes all in keeping with the style here: rustic.

You slowly get to know the ones who stay here long-term. Trevor's a red-haired painter. He used to do stage designs at the Mermaid Theatre in the 1960s before moving to Rome to dub spaghetti westerns at Cinecittà. He came back and taught art and pottery at a private school before, as he says, the booze took hold. He's been here for years and always sits in the sitting room with a huge bottle of Coke and a crossword. He smokes rollies which he squeezes, rather than stubs, out. He takes me to his studio and shows me intricate abstracts which weave dozens of colours. The strokes look as thin as micro fibre. It's powerful stuff. He did one of the icons in the church and, although he never goes, there's some fairly strong Christian iconography in his work. I ask him the faith question and he laughs: 'Every painting is an expression of faith . . . that you'll be alive long enough to finish it!'

Then there's Geordie Dave. Head shaved, tough face, thick accent. He looks after the chickens. One day we get chatting about things and I realise I haven't lived. 'By your age, Bud,' he says, so that Bud rhymes with 'hood', 'I was almost a grandfather. Thirty-six when I became a grandparent!' We're sitting under the stairs by the wood basket. Faith's there and a couple of others. Dave is telling his stories: about falling in quarries, smashing up the school, being told off by the headmaster so he trashed his office as well. He was sent to St Williams, a sort of correctional school run by monks, between York and Hull. We laugh at all his stories now, because he seems so calm. He's talking about running away from the monastery and breaking into a Little Chef at night. He talks openly about alcohol and needles and prison and overdoses. A while back in Exeter he deliberately put a brick through a Lamborghini window just to make sure he got put back inside, where he couldn't drink. Now he's here, making sure we all have eggs in the morning.

So the weeks go by. Gandalf, the guy who looks after the sheep, has a birthday and someone ices a cake so that it has sheep in a green field and they've used sheep's wool for Gandalf's shoulder-length white hair. Richard shows you his favourite Fritz Eichenberg woodcuts. The Loud-Speaker and Liam take bets. You see tablets being passed around in brown envelopes. People go to Bridport. A new calf arrives late at night, and it takes three of them to pull it out. You spend the evenings blowing on the fire to give a last glow to the embers. Little Dave's normally there, reading in the corner and simultaneously punching numbers into a calculator, nobody knows why. Any eccentricity seems normal. Someone gets a gorse bush to clean the chimney and it's yanked up and down with a string. You wait for the ewe to lamb. She's got the oily crayon smudge on her back from the ram's painted harness so everyone knows when she's been 'serviced'. George, the cockerel, wakes you up each morning and struts around his harem imperiously. Someone tells you about the famous Pilsdon cricket team which plays inter-village matches in the summer: they have fifteen 8-ball overs and haven't won since the early 1990s. 'Don't ask Tobes to play,' shouts The Loud-Speaker from the other side of the room. 'I've seen him play snooker!'

I'm out chopping wood in the sheep field. There's a few tonnes of tree trunk in front of me and the snow is horizontal. I chop away for half an hour until the blade comes away from the shaft. Someone walks by. He rests his elbows on the upturned arms of his empty wheelbarrow and we chat in the blizzard. I can't even see who it is, just make out a beard around his lips which – at Pilsdon – barely narrows things down. The rest is overcoat and hat and scarf. But it doesn't matter who it is. He tells me to come in soon because we've got enough wood for at least a fortnight. You feel the seasons here. I just wish it was a kinder one. Huge flakes are swirling in the wind and the whole courtyard has turned white. I go inside. The fire is cracking and hissing. Benny is propped up in her tiny chair, nostrils whistling as her tiny rib-cage rises and falls.

We're in the house chapel with its wooden panelling and tiny icons. Ellen is sitting next to me. She arrived a week ago and will be here for a month or so. She's a large American lady. When you first meet her, she seems the stereotype of the big country: she dresses in jeans, smothers her toast with peanut butter; she's not exactly backward in coming forward. But then it turns out she's a nun. Like Pilsdon, she seems to have perfected the art of undercover Christianity.

The place goes quiet. It's compline and the candles are lit. There are only four of us here. Our whispers are superimposed as we read together: 'Is not this the fast that I choose: to loose the bonds of injustice, to undo the thongs of the yoke, to let the oppressed go free and to break every yoke? Is it not to share your bread with the hungry and to bring the homeless poor into your house; when you see the naked to cover them and not to hide yourself from your own kin?'

It's a very short service, ten minutes or so, and I find myself trying to work out why what I'm seeing is so different from what I'd expected. Part of the problem is the 'flanderisation' of Christianity. Ned Flanders is that character from *The Simpsons* – a dull, holier-than-thou character satirising the American evangelical movement – and is now seen, by the religiously-illiterate media, as the leitmotif of all modern Christians. Some people then add to that paper-thin portrait by voicing single-issue opinions and convincing the media, and onlookers, that all Christians really are cartoon characters. (It reminds me of William Vanstone's famous line that the Church is like a swimming pool: all the noise is at the shallow end.) But the Christianity of Pilsdon seems to stem from that sentence of Schleiermacher: 'Religious feelings should accompany every human deed like a holy music; we should do everything with religion, nothing because of religion.'[7] One is mysterious, the other mechanical. One attitude is a complicated infusion in all directions, the other only a lineal, often brutal, jerk of the knee. Usually, in these times of fundamental scripturalism, sacred books are often seen as akin to moral encyclopaedias: reference works from which you can learn precise behavioural codes. But that is still the mechanical interpretation of religion where believers behave in certain ways 'because of' religion. Behaving 'with religion' is something very different.

Richard and I have been in the kitchen cooking Sunday lunch for twenty-three people. We make Eton Mess as a dessert and rename it Pilsdon Pile-Up. After lunch, it's like any other normal house on a Sunday afternoon. Some drift off to the TV rooms to watch the afternoon's film or sport. Some flop in the library with the Sunday papers. Others go for a walk and we decide to join them. Adam's organising and the minibus is waiting in the courtyard. The road to the coast is barely wider than the vehicle. We pass Shave Cross pub where the monks used to get their tonsures freshly shaven before visiting St Witha's shrine (one of only two shrines to survive the Reformation). This is deepest Dorset. Another of the pubs near here, laughs Adam, has an annual nettle-eating competition.

We start off in the woods. Henry has come along. He's a strong, silent type, a man who is up at all hours doing the animals. He studied art at Goldsmiths College but, for whatever reason, ended up coming here in his twenties. He's been here longer than anyone else in the community. Normally his reticence can seem almost rude, but now – walking through the sun-speckled undergrowth – he starts talking. He mentions all the people he's met at Pilsdon – a member of a notorious band, a well-known screenwriter, a musician and so on.

We're walking the short valley between Langdon Hill and Golden Cap. It's the end of February now and the sky is deep blue. A few hardy people aren't wearing jackets. We come to the ruin of an old Saxon church, St Gabriel's, and head up the hill. As it gets steeper I off-load Benny to Adam, who grunts as her ten kilos thump into the rucksack. The view is stunning: the Dorset cliffs receding into ever-fainter blues. There are long, sandy beaches way below and you can hear the wind whistling between the ferns and thistles. There are buzzards soaring on the cold wind. Way up above us we can see couples and a costal path signpost silhouetted against the glare. Look back with binos and you can just make out Pilsdon.

Down below us are Chesil beach and Portland Bill. Adam tells me that you can always tell what end of the beach you're at because the pebbles are larger at one end. Debate ensues as to the verity of this, and as to how they discovered that . . . and anyway, who was this pillock who didn't know one end of the beach from the other?

Jonathan and I spend the day laying the willow hedge around Bill's cottage. To get there, you have to go over a little bridge across the stream. We clamber up the bank and cut the outside bark of each branch and bend them horizontal. I take off all the foliage and Jonathan weaves the trunks and branches until, after a few hours, we've done twenty or thirty feet. It looks neat, all plaited into itself, with the blackthorn on the outside to keep away the animals. As you work, you occasionally pause, because there's now a view. A hedge that was thin but fifteen feet high is now thick and pared down to two. You can see the other fields and copses. There's a pheasant scampering across the field, three deer bouncing along beside one another. You peer over the road and see someone coming along.

'You all right? Looking for Pilsdon?'

'Yeah, just here on the left, isn't it?'

'Yeah.'

He wanders up the path by the church and you see him cross the front lawn. He's got the windswept face of someone who's been sleeping rough for a long time.

The next day you're back to do another twenty feet on the hedge. And the next day. Then there are nettles. You find a hypnotic rhythm in which your brain seems to be in your hands. Sole on the shoulder of the fork, down and twist it, turn the earth, sole on the shoulder, twist the fork, turn the earth . . . the nettles smell juicy. You stop. It's dusk and the last hills before the sea are ablaze. The stillness is silently thunderous. You've got your feet on the ground, on the cold mud. You feel the same, blissful sense of enchantment you got during the first few weeks at Nomadelfia. It's to do with the sheer simplicity of the place. Simplicity is the defining characteristic of Pilsdon. There's no luxury to speak of, and yet you're always comfortable. There are minimal funds, and yet everyone eats well. You live in such close proximity to animals that no one can ever give themselves airs. I remember something Adriana Zarri, the hermit near Ivrea, said to me. Talking about the trinity, she said that life is a journey from the simplistic, through complication, to simplicity. Pilsdon wasn't simplistic, but it was always simple. It was an extraordinary place to live because I had never, I realised, lived such a pared-down life. Here there was no style, no gloss or sheen or ambition. It was about literal shelter, about finding provisions and keeping ourselves warm.

One of the objections to the idea of going off and living in communities – raised by almost every friend I spoke to at the outset – was that these places would be ghettos, isolated retreats for people who couldn't face reality. The longer we stayed at Pilsdon, the more I thought that the objection was misplaced. It is, of course, idealistic here, and yet at the same time it's more realistic than almost anywhere I've ever lived before. It's comfortable but tough. You have to do everything yourselves, apprentice often leading apprentice. Since it deals with the back-end of addiction and stress, bereavement and depression, it confronts the truths about the way we're living and picks up the pieces. It's not the negation of the 'real world' but its reflection. Almost fifty years ago, in May 1961, Percy Smith said exactly that.

The temptation for all of us, everywhere, is to contract out of this real world, to try and create an easier world of one's own, and to keep out of trouble at all costs. The alternative is to accept the challenge of life, to avoid all escaping, however subtle, and to go further and further into reality through decision and crisis and conflict. By doing so we inevitably question the cynicism and superficiality and escapism of our contemporary attitudes.[8]

I was convinced, by now, that the escapists weren't the residents of Pilsdon – they hadn't retreated into comfort – but actually all those people who ghettoised themselves in the so-called 'real world'.

I'm learning new words that I never wanted to know: daglock. We're dagging. John and I are holding the ewe, and Adam has huge sheers for the job. Then we do the hooves. An old lady passed by here four days ago. No one knew who she was but she looked like something from a Hardy novel. Headscarf, thick accent and so on. She was divining and said the sheep would have three lambs, one a runt. She went off and two days later we had three new Jacobs lambs, two strong, one weak. We made a hay-bail pen for them for a couple of nights.

Once we've done the dagging, we need to put them out into the fields. Lambs are jerky things. They're almost tame already, though, coming up to lick your hand. We take two out, leaving just the runt in the warmth. John is shooing the mother from behind and she's following her two lambs which Adam and I are holding. We keep lowering them to the ground every 10 or 20 feet, so that the mother sees and smells them and follows us into the field. Their little rib-cages are like miniature, carpeted rugby balls in your hand. We muck out the pen whilst they gambol around uncertainly and try to out-bleat each other.

Today it feels almost spring-like. There are daffodils and snow-drops everywhere. You can finally take off your thick jacket and feel the sun through your other four layers. Francesca is in the veg-etable garden and comes over to say hello. She sits down on a large rock outside the greenhouse. Benny's watching the lambs try to walk and, unintentionally, does a funny impression of them on all fours. Gruff Trevor's at the fence, drinking his tea. 'Don't use this as a scene for your book!' he laughs.

'How come? Too bucolic?'

'Yeah, no one would believe it. They'd think you had made it up.'

There were so many moments like that when you just stopped what you were doing and stopped thinking at all about the past or the future. It was as if you suddenly realised where you were in both time and place and, for once, you weren't looking to escape. You didn't want to be with anyone else in any other place.

None of which is to say it's not occasionally awkward here. There are things it's hard to put up with. There is so much smoking that even Benny's nappies, which normally have a distinct aroma all their own, smell of Golden Virginia. There will be some young lad's techno music hammering out from his loose box at all hours. Some people work very hard but a few – since they devolve all their benefits to the community – treat it like a rural resort that they're paying for. In a sense the place, though getting close to self-sufficiency, is still in part bank-rolled by giros. It's hard to tell whether some people don't help out of laziness or lack of self-esteem, or a combination of the two. The longer you stay here, the more you see the mechanics of the place and understand the epic amount of work needed to sustain the simplicity. 'Peace has to be worked at, it doesn't just come out of the beautiful Dorset country-side!' says Peter. Part of the enchantment when you first arrive is that an invisible hand does all the work. The smallest things get done. Flowers suddenly appear on the oak tables; fantastically fresh bread is put on your plate. But then you begin to see the care-ful, intricate organisation, and realise that it doesn't all happen by chance. Members spoke to me of the difficulty of both supporting and challenging people, of getting the balance right between listen-ing and guiding. Even though a few women live here permanently, and others come and go, it still feels a very masculine place. A few people clearly don't get on and, obviously, there are tensions. Inevitably a lot of people fall off the wagon.

And yet, despite all that, it felt like a true, prophetic community. If I had written down a year ago exactly what my ideal place would be like, I would have unwittingly described Pilsdon. It was what I had been looking for ever since we had set out. I can't rationalise it, I can't explain why. You would have to come here to see for your-self to understand what I'm talking about. There's something in that ether of human interaction which feels true and peaceful. It isn't just me who feels it. Francesca normally has to put the brakes on when I get too enthusiastic about something, but she knows this is it. We have found something we had almost given up hope of finding. Hundreds of others, too, feel the same. Every week would bring back people who had lived at, or visited, Pilsdon months or years ago. It has a diaspora of admirers and supporters throughout Europe who keep returning. Dozens would come each Sunday, either for the service or just to help out. Some come, they say to you as you sit around the fire, just to make sure their time at Pilsdon hadn't been a dream. 'It seems unreal once you've left. You can't believe it still really exists.' Most come to take its abundant salt back into the world.

Filippo is visiting us from Parma. Since we're not at home, he comes to see us at Pilsdon and is introduced to everyone. He's hoping to improve his English and, taken by the bare beauty of the place, asks if he might come here for a month or two. Jonathan stands up and announces to the dining room that Filippo might come back in the summer to improve his English. The whole place bursts into laughter at the thought of this Italian lawyer learning Irish and Scottish slang, and having to understand the thickest Cornish and Geordie accents. One of the guys who's laughing is from Belfast. He lived here years ago and is a good oral historian of the place. He's just come back for a couple of days. 'There's always been an Italian connection at Pilsdon,' he says to Fra and Filippo. 'Decades ago Father Borelli, the Neapolitan priest, came here. There used to be a path named after him somewhere. And now you're here. It's really wonderful to think Italians keep coming here and bringing us such riches.'

Coincidences. I was sitting in the library reading Jonathan's dissertation. One of the wayfarers came in and we got talking. He was delighted because he had been given a new pair of shoelaces. He showed them to me and tugged them to show how strong and reliable they were. We say goodbye and I go back to the text: 'possessions for him [Francis of Assisi] were obstacles to communication between people and diminished our sense of reliance upon God. The more radical the poverty the closer the individual comes to reality, and all things become more transparent . . . through a process of interior purification and denial of the world, the world is more fully appreciated.' Shoelaces.

This is a place where parables – about agriculture or candles or leaven bread – seem relevant. It's less removed from that world. One of the members does Sunday morning services in various nearby churches. She's young, attractive with short, white hair. 'This place,' she says, 'means you have to be clear and serious about what you believe. I wouldn't ever bring it up at table, but if someone at dinner says "What's all this Pentecost stuff?" you have to find words to explain what that means in concrete terms to concrete people.' I occasionally pondered the subtlety of Pilsdon. Life went by and no message – no social lecturing – ever took place. And yet there were people here who were burning with news. They had given up everything not for an easy ride, but for an exceptionally tough one. They really did believe in something, and yet they never mentioned it. I asked one person why not. He said: 'Because if you look around you the truth is self-evident. There's no need for us to say it.'

I'm sitting in the tiny church at the end of the garden. Richard is reading psalm 127: '. . . as arrows are in the hand of a warrior; so are children of the youth . . .' What an image. That sense that, now yours, the children will one day be out of your hands and moving away from you even though it is you that has given them, hopefully, the right strength and direction. Afterwards, on the way back into the house, I finally understand the meaning of the Italian phrase which describes certain people as *un gallo nel pollaio* ('a cockerel in the poultry pen'). I see George the cockerel strutting his courtyard. He looks so commanding.

I love just hanging around, playing games. One of my favourite Italian verbs is *cazzeggiare* (actually a bit ruder than 'hanging around'). I seem to spend hours each day playing games and I'm beginning to think that companionship is heavily dependent on recognition that we're *homo ludens* – a game-playing species. If it's not mind-games with The Loud-Speaker around the snooker table, it's silent, serious chess with Geordie Dave. He learnt in prison and we're very similar players. One game – this happens about once in a lifetime and shows our parity – ends in stalemate. We would spend hours playing and it was plodding, determined stuff. No clocks, so people would come in and out assuming we were on our third or fourth game, when actually we had only just got past the opening gambits of the first.

Communal living brings into sharp focus all our faults, which is why, presumably, we're naturally inclined to flee from it and hide those failings from ourselves and others. In community you very quickly discover your less attractive traits. I've rediscovered mine: I don't have a bark, only a bite. And I'm impatient. I bear grudges. I have a terrible temper which only emerges once or twice a year, but when it does people run for cover. At the beginning of this trip I thought living in community would be tough because you're living cheek by jowl with people you might have little in common with, people who you wouldn't necessarily choose as friends. I thought I would roll up, find fault and go home. But the true difficulty of living here is that there's nowhere to hide. The place holds a mirror up to yourself and shows you what you're really like. It reminded me of Ward's description of religion: it 'does not provide answers to life's questions; it puts our lives in question . . .'9 Strangely, the thing that made me most uncomfortable about living in community was myself.

Towards the end of our time at Pilsdon, I began to feel that society and the individual really aren't at odds, because society is where we realise our deepest identities; it is the site of individuation. 'Interdependence is more important than independence,' says Peter. We're all encrypted and it's other people who introduce us to ourselves by providing the code. You find that it's the background which brings you out. Jonathan said something very similar one afternoon: 'I feel no longer defined by what I do, but by those with whom I live.' That's why I'm still enchanted at Pilsdon. It's difficult because you see your own faults close up, you see how you appear to other people. But a true community grants you freedom to understand those faults, to admire other people's virtues and learn from the way they live. Failings and virtues are somehow shared and pooled.

Here the real strengths of personalities emerge, they're never disguised and for that they appear attractive. The community becomes like a jigsaw puzzle, each piece different but useful, one eccentricity filling the space of someone else's timidity and so on. Our strange shapes seem, finally, to make sense; each piece in the puzzle seems important. It's a jigsaw, of course, which is never finished: new pieces arrive, others leave, others change their daily labour and therefore their position in the puzzle. And the picture the puzzle makes changes subtly from day to day as pieces morph. But what is extraordinary is the importance accorded to every piece. Gaynor Smith used a better metaphor. She said Pilsdon was like a library in which different books of odd shapes and strange stories come together and rub shoulders. Some stay, some leave. The library is protean but permanent. It's not that problems are ever resolved, simply that they're put into perspective. They don't get smaller, but over the months and years they appear so because, in community, you can see them from a distance, from someone else's vantage point. There's an instinctive understanding here of Kant's 'categorical imperative' because people are appreciated for who they are, not for what use they might be:

> For all rational beings stand under the law that each of them should treat himself and all others never merely as means but in every case also as an end in himself. Thus there arises a systematic union of rational beings through common objective laws. This is a realm which may be called a kingdom of ends (certainly only an ideal), because what these laws have in view is just the relation of these beings to each other as ends and means.[10]

Here everybody has a role, a use, a purpose and in fulfilling that role plays their part in something far greater than themselves. Everyone is integrated and – like millions of cogs – each is engaged and affects every other. They all turn at the same speed, regardless of their size. No one is surfeit to requirements, no one outside the intricate machinery.

There's the surprising satisfaction of being given duties, of being told bluntly what needs doing: that, so much more than prating about rights, truly recognises someone's worth because it's precisely when people are esteemed that they're asked to perform certain tasks on behalf of other people. People at Pilsdon were proud of their jobs – just washing up or vacuuming or laying the tables – because that was their role and twenty or thirty people relied on them. That was how they were recognised and valued. There's a famous story about Abbé Pierre, the French priest who, shortly after the Second World War, founded the Emmaus communities. An ex-convict was so depressed he told Pierre that he wanted to commit suicide. 'But hang on,' replied Pierre, 'I need you to help me a minute.' That minute of feeling useful, needed rather than needy, saved his life: showing him that he was worth something to someone. Only in context are we indispensable, even integral.

It's counter-intuitive because we're ceaselessly told that self-assertion is the highway to happiness. And yet ecstasy means 'being out of oneself'. I had been addicted, for years, to what Burke called 'the dust and powder of individuality', I had lived the 'unsocial, uncivil, unconnected chaos of elementary principles'.[11] I couldn't understand why it hadn't made me happy, why it had sunk me into a black hole. Nor could I understand now why the reduction of my own importance paradoxically made me so relaxed, almost serene. I felt happy and I wasn't on anything: no pills, drink, nothing. I had spent most of my life looking for niches where I couldn't be judged; where I was the only judiciary. But suddenly I was surrounded by people who had the measure of me, who knew my foibles and vanities and began – never through verbal injunctions, but just by their own humble example – to liberate me from some of them.

That emptying out of your own personality in order to discover it, almost inadvertently, in company was something Jonathan had mentioned to me. In the theological language, kenosis meant that emptying humility whereby the divine becomes human. Christians try to imitate that kenosis. As St John of the Cross wrote in his 'Ascent of Mount Carmel':

> To come to the pleasure you have not
> You must go by a way in which you enjoy not.
> To come to the knowledge which you have not
> You must go by a way in which you know not.
> To come to the possession you have not
> You must go by a way in which you possess not.
> To come to what you are not
> You must go by a way in which you are not.[12]

We have a day off and head north to Chard in Somerset. We see a sign to Forde Abbey and drive in. It's an extraordinary building, almost a compendium of architectural styles from the twelfth century to the present day. It's English Gothic blended with Baroque: built in the twelfth century and updated between the Reformation and the invasion of Classicism. The present-day touches are less ambitious: the current owner has decided to use the great lake as the theatre for a jet of water fired into the air, 'higher than anywhere else in England,' says the gardener we talk to. That, he says, is the way to attract tourists nowadays.

We wander around the state rooms, the refectory, the monks' dormitory, the cloisters and the chapel. It all feels like a sacred place which has become a palace. It used to be a Cistercian monastery, and there's still the cartulary (the old record book) here recording every transaction in the abbey's 400-year history. Chard, the last Abbot, handed the place over to the crown and a century later it had passed to the avowed Parliamentarian, Edmund Prideaux. During the nineteenth century the place was rented to Jeremy Bentham, who entertained John Stuart Mill here. Not for the first time, it feels like this journey is taking me in circles; I keep going to new places and yet coming up against the same names, the same themes. As we walk round, I can't help thinking what an amazing location this would be for a Pilsdon-style community. I can't even admire architecture any more without thinking about where you would put the animals, where you would put the snooker tables and chess sets, how you could give a room to the warden without making him seem superior to the wayfarers.

I'm sitting alone on one of the bales in the church. Everything is very still. There's absolutely no noise. Only the sound of straw snapping and of breathing. There's something about the hard, cream stone that is conducive to something. It's so solid but almost soft. It takes a while for my mind to stop racing, but it goes down through the gears. This is one of the only places in which all barriers drop. The brakes come off and you float. I had been waiting for something to happen for years, I thought that I might be the centre of some 'experience'. But when it comes you almost wouldn't know it. You absent yourself and suddenly see with your own eyes, and hear with your own ears. You don't hear a voice, but hear listening.

Little Dave only comes up to chest high. He's got his 'get off my land' outfit on: flat cap, Barbour, smart Wellingtons. He hardly ever shaves, so he looks – dressed like this – like a posh lout. He makes everyone laugh by continually shouting 'Get off my land!' in a thick Devon accent. After a short climb we get to the summit: we're standing on top of Pilsdon Pen, at 277 metres the highest point in rolling Dorset. The view is spectacular. It's a March afternoon: blue sky, a sou'wester which is almost warm. You can see the sun glinting off the English Channel. Everywhere you look there are tiny specks of bright light where ponds and lakes catch the sun. Herds and flocks are so far below you that they look static, painted into the still landscape. It's a gentle county: the hills seem like risen dough, curved rather than angular. They're still brushed with snow. The many copses look, from up here, like large tussocks, more bluey-grey than green. This used to be an Iron Age hill fort defended by the Dumnonii, a tribe which gave its name to the shire of Devon. Someone asks Dave to say Dumnonii repeatedly to see if it sounds anything like Devon when said in a Devon accent, but we can't hear it. Maybe they made that bit up, we decide. Some Dorset Heritage board mentions the Durotriges in the east towards Maiden castle. Then in 43 AD along came Vespasian – the same Roman who founded York – and captured all these hill forts.

'York. Can you believe it's almost a year since we were at Hartrigg?' asks Fra. 'I wonder how they're getting on.'

We look at each other and nod slowly. We're both working backwards in our heads: Pilsdon, Palermo, Parma, York, Ivrea, Grosseto, Val Chiusella. We're still nodding and looking at each other. It's one of those moments that you know exactly what the other one's thinking. It's time to go home.

A few days later we're saying our goodbyes. Trevor and Richard, who have both lived in and looked at communities for years, start suggesting places to head to next. It's mind-blowing the number of communities there are just within a few dozen miles of here: Monkton Wilds, Othona, Tinkers Bottom, Gaunts House, Magdalen House, Hillfield. There are even satellite communities of Pilsdon, at Glen Crutton in Oban and West Malling in Kent, which have been set up by former members of Pilsdon. 'Do you know Elsie Briggs in Bristol?' asks Richard. Simon mentions the Northumbria community. In every direction there seemed to be houses worth visiting, gatherings of people trying to live in ways which challenge the modern world. There were just so many of them. The list went on and on, making you wonder whether perhaps the 'real world' was a lot more nuanced than you had thought, peppered with exceptions challenging the rules.

As we say goodbye, there's a tangible warmth from people you have hardly spoken to all month. They say they'll miss you and that the place will be different when you're not here. It's said not as a compliment, but just because the community really will be altered since it's an intimate place where everyone counts.

We've felt amazingly happy here because it's never pious or impious, it's just a bunch of people surviving together. Phil, who lived here years ago and still comes back most Sunday nights for the evening service, once said to me that he had never felt so at home anywhere else. And that, after only a month, is what it feels like to us. It's a place with a radical simplicity which comes at a stark price. It costs, as Eliot wrote in 'Little Gidding', 'not less than everything'.

Going Home

I had originally left home because I couldn't abide the way I was living. I wasn't really, as Karen Armstrong once said, expecting to transcend towards anything, only to transcend away from something: away from that 'revolt of inferiority' I saw wherever I looked. I wasn't sure that I would end up anywhere, but I knew I had to move on. I wasn't optimistic or idealistic, but curious about people who were. I thought we would just go 'beautifully astray', hang out, and come home. I had been a bit breezy about the whole thing. But then things suddenly got serious. After this journey, I couldn't remain a cynic. I believed in something: that there really are ways of living that are more noble and more valid. There are ways of living that make life seem both urgent and relaxed, both awesome and beautiful. Both Fra and I had seen it. It felt as if we had been out of this world for a long time and on returning to it found ourselves strangers in a familiar landscape. It suddenly became impossible just to go back to where we had started.

When we were back in our own place, and had overcome the elation of having our own space and time, it felt very strange. Things kept happening which reminded us of what we had been through. Walking under a four-lane roundabout we saw a homeless boy begging. He looked like someone from Pilsdon. A year ago we wouldn't have looked twice. I couldn't get used to the pavements full of people balancing shopping bags in each hand, their faces stern with the determination to get their burden home. We drove to Somerset and, all the way there, the hedges were brutally chopped rather than laid. It looked ugly, the branches snapped and left hanging in the air.

I was kind of stuck. The deceleration and landing had slightly thrown me. We were at home and not sure what was next. A couple of months went by and we studied the situation. It was a good time, we were laughing a lot. We were still digesting everything we had been through. Each intriguing, international news story about communities caught our eye. There was the story about the founder of Domino's Pizza, Thomas S. Monaghan, who was bank-rolling the building of a completely new town outside Naples, Florida on 5,000 acres of land. Called Ave Maria, it was intended to be an enclave of 20,000 Americans living without pornography and contraception. There was the tragic story of the murder of Brother Roger, the founder and prior of the Taizé community in Burgundy. A year ago we would have been on the next plane to either France or Florida. But we had decided to call time, to stop travelling, and it felt eerily calm.

I felt shattered. It wasn't just this journey, it was all the others: decades of manic movement. I sat in a chair and stayed there for weeks on end. It was always the same chair, the linear monster from the junk shop in Via Maestri. Pascal once wrote that 'the sole cause of man's unhappiness is that he does not know how to stay quietly in his room.'[1] I had given up looking for happiness when, halfway through the journey, I read Zeno's distinction between doing good and just being comfortable; and I had realised that there's no correlation between community and contentment except at the absolute end: where there is no community, there can be no contentment. But for the first time in years I was sitting quietly not doing anything and happiness had taken me by surprise. Before, I had sought it through grudge; the good life was something owing to me and the less it delivered, the more grudging I became. Now, back at home, the overwhelming feeling was gratitude. There can be complacency or superiority in gratitude; but it wasn't to do with realising how lucky I was. It was a gratitude which enriched everything, which made the colours stand out. It was about feeling obliged, as if I knew what people had done for me and was finally working out what I was supposed to do for others. I had seen that gratitude and memory are almost synonymous, giving rise to action which was properly organic: they emerged from roots deep in the vanishing point of the past, and broke the surface of the earth in the present.

It was only once we were static, determined to be still, that I realised how much our manic, modern mobility is a mask for irresponsibility. I decided – rather a daft decision for a travel writer – to give up travelling. We drew a circle with a mile radius from our house and decided that that was our community. We were, in some way, responsible for everything inside that tiny circumference. We no longer wanted to travel in search of something, we didn't want to race after idealism. We wanted to renounce selectivity and discover that arbitrary community which surrounded us. It's the very lack of choice inherent in neighbourhood, the fate of whom modern life has thrown our way, that makes the neighbour a person of such symbolic importance. As Chesterton wrote in *Heresy*: 'We have to love our neighbour because he is there – a much more alarming reason for a much more serious operation. He is the sample of humanity which is actually given us. Precisely because he may be anybody he is everybody. He is a symbol because he is an accident.'[2] I'm so obsessively neurotic about accidents, about the lack of my control over my own environment, that such a proposition really was disconcerting. But I had to see if there was a practical application to the journey, whether the values we had learnt would really survive exposure to the macroscopic, multicultural world.

I couldn't help, within that circle we had drawn on the map, seeking out unusual communities. It had become a habit after a year or two. It was staggering how many there were just in this restricted space. Every time somebody asked what I do for a living and I mentioned the book – to the guy coming to fix our leaking roof or the lady at the post office – they said, 'Have you heard about those people in . . . ?' There was an environmental group, building self-sufficient homes in the patch of green between the railway and the allotments. There were two communities just the other side of the park: one a contemplative, Christian place, the other a charitable community for the disabled. The level of eccentricity and adventure in this restricted, inner-city space was incredible. There were New Agey places, unusual religious communities, zero-impact environmental gatherings, all within walking distance. It emerged that one of the guys I play football with every Tuesday night was a member of a renowned diaspora-community which began in post-war Italy: called the Focolare, its founder Chiara Lubich once described it as

a modern community of a few people living in the world, camouflaged to resemble the world, dressing like everyone else in the world, working like other people. However, unlike others, they are people who have left the world; they have left their country, their own families and work, in order to give themselves to the cause of unity in the world.[3]

It was when I discovered a community at the end of our street that I realised I was onto something. I had been haring around Europe looking for communal values and all along there had been this quiet place, with residents from four different countries, on my doorstep. OK, so it was tiny: just a four-storey town house with a library, communal kitchen and a chapel, but it was a hundred yards from our own home.

There was one community, at the southern end of the circumference of our circle, that I was particularly drawn to. It was an Emmaus one in the rough part of town. I had always liked their slogan: 'Giving people a bed and a reason to get out of it'. It seemed to epitomise that paradoxical combination of relaxation and urgency. It offered people not only the means, but also the reasons, to live. The Emmaus movement was begun by a Frenchman, Abbé Pierre, at the end of the war. A gritty, determined character, he opened an 'Emmaus Youth Hostel' in Neuilly-Plaisance in 1947 when he was a member of parliament. The idea was to turn the homeless into real recyclers: they, the so-called 'companions', were given a room in the community home. They collected all the furniture and belongings people no longer needed and sold them to people who could afford and appreciate them. The homeless – various boozers and addicts and gamblers and tinkers – became, in a tiny way, businessmen. It was literal, as well as metaphorical, recycling. The movement grew over the next decade, gaining much publicity in the bitter winter of 1954 when an 'insurrection of goodness' saved the lives of those living under bridges and on park benches. Abbé Pierre wrote that 'faced with this world of sorrow and injustice we felt like the madman who tried to empty the sea with a teaspoon.'[4]

The attraction of Emmaus is that, a bit like Rowntree's philosophy, it insists on work rather than charity. Rule One states bluntly: 'Never, as long as we have strength, will we accept that our subsistence depends on anything other than our work ...' Anyone becoming a part of an Emmaus community signs off all benefits. For all their work – collecting other people's discarded possessions, doing them up, selling them on – they receive board and lodging, plus £37 a week, five of which is paid by the staff into a savings account on their behalf.

The companions were, on first appearances, a pretty rum crowd. They all knew abuse of some sort or another. Almost all the younger boys had been in prison; the older men had often been on the road for years. There were always very few women. The first night I spent there, one man got up to announce he was off for a 'sherman' (rhyming slang that you can work out for yourself). Many of them were still boozing, getting into fights and scrapes in all the nearby pubs. It was in a part of the city that seemed forgotten: the house was between a building site and the city's rubbish depot. Kids from the nearby houses would occasionally kick footballs, or throw stones, at the windows where the 'weirdos' lived.

But there were characters we grew fond of. There was Tony, a man in his fifties with a spitty lisp. He was missing his front teeth, had Dennis Taylor style glasses and a grey, straggly crew-cut. He would keep us all amused by saying things which were clearly nonsense and, when challenged, speaking more nonsense to defend the first batch. There was Welsh Jim with his Swansea accent, his 'come yer' beckoning. He was a cook, a keen fisherman who looked like the stereotype of the homeless: white hair and white stubble, missing a couple of teeth. And then there was Elvis, a solid Midlands man who did all the electrical work on the computers, radios and televisions they sold. He had slicked-back black hair and when he came in bladdered from the pub would sing old Elvis numbers at the top of his voice. Quite a few of them were Bristol types. There's a linguistic tic in this city that's strange: they put an L at the end of every word. Hence even the city's name has morphed. Once called Brig-Stowe ('the place of the bridge' in Anglo-Saxon), it's now Bristol.

'What's the name of your daughter then?' said one of the Bristol boys in a thick accent.

'Benedetta,' I replied.

'Benedettol? Sounds like a floor cleaner to me!'

A few weeks later I took Elvis to my snooker club. He started off as if he were playing pool, firing the cue ball far too hard so that it would bounce around the table randomly. But he gradually got a feel for it and started caressing the ball gently. He began telling me about his mother, about how she had died a few years ago and he hadn't had enough money to get back to Birmingham for the funeral. He trashed the place where he was staying in frustration. Since then he's never even seen her grave.

Another weekend Simon, who had been at Emmaus for a couple of months, wanted to cycle to Bath. He's a troubled-looking lad and can be unpredictably gentle or aggressive. We set out on a typical winter afternoon: cloudy and cold, not raining but damp everywhere. Along the tow-path and old railway routes out of Bristol there's that eerie mixture of urban ugliness with oases of beauty: hints of older worlds amidst the brutal, modern spaces. There's the abandoned station at Mangotsfield. There are parks in the middle of tower blocks, swans on the canal. People have painted bridges. At one point, written in big letters on the asphalt, someone has painted 'Another world is possible'.

Simon insists on saying hello to everyone. If they've got a dog he stops and strokes it. He falls off his bike and pulls the loose skin off his wrists with his teeth and spits it out into the brambles. He tells me he's still paying a £200 fine for shoplifting. It will take him almost six months saving at Emmaus to pay it off. I get that melancholia that often comes with a wet, Sunday afternoon. When we get to Bath most of the shops are open. They're doing a roaring trade selling mobile phone upgrades. The pedestrianised centre is a river of people, desperation etched on most faces. Needy couples are arguing with each other. Even genteel Bath has become infected by the 'Swindonisation' of Britain: all the same high-street chains, the same retail outlets and products.

We decide to put our bikes on the train to get back to Bristol. We have tea in the station. The train chundles along the cycle path and canal we've just been on. There are beautiful pubs here, those places with beer gardens which extend all the way to the canal. It's full of people now, all watching the afternoon football or staring out of the windows at the barges. We go into the tunnel and I tell Simon about a rumour I once heard . . . that Isambard Kingdom Brunel built one of his tunnels, the Box Hill one between Bath and Chippenham, so that the sun rose straight through it on his birthday on 9 April.

'Might be rubbish that,' says Simon, nonplussed. 'It would have to be true to be interesting.'

'I'll check it.' I later discover it's the object of some serious, solar discussion.

'Want to watch Everton-Man U next Sunday?' He asks.

'Four, isn't it? You've got Sky there, right?'

So we go our separate ways back in Bristol and I look forward to seeing him the following Sunday. But by then he's gone. He's slipped back into the real world. We check with the police but they hadn't, so far, picked him up. I see him again eight months later. He had been in prison. I didn't ask him what for.

I was kind of between jobs. I was between books and articles and TV programmes. Not for the first time, self-employment was teetering on unemployment. I spent a lot of time driving the Emmaus van. On the rare occasions we get tipped, Tony spreads the paper across the dashboard and picks the horse which is guaranteed, he says, to turn our three quid into twenty. It's always strange driving the van. You see all the nooks and crannies of the city. It sometimes makes me melancholic because we go to the saddest places – six children, no income, no father – and see what would, in the old days, have been called slums. But at the same time it's uplifting. Like Nomadelfia and Pilsdon, Emmaus opens up the world. It introduces you to people you would never otherwise meet. Some of the 'companions' become good friends. Chris comes and plays football with us once a week and stays for dinner; now he's back from his stint in prison, Simon takes Benny for walks up on the Downs with the community's dog, Dylan.

And something unusual starts to happen. As I begin spending more and more time either in the Emmaus warehouse or their home, I actually need less money. Not because I nobly downgrade desire. It's true that I'm hardly buying clothes, books or CDs any more. But really we need less money, and I have to work much less, because we are constantly being given things. I go out driving their van for a day or two, and at the end of it, instead of money, they give us precisely the chair or a desk we needed, invariably worth a lot more than I could have earned in that time. There are things we need like a bike, a baby-seat for it, pictures . . . but the guys at Emmaus keep digging out stuff and giving it to us. For months we don't buy anything more expensive than a pair of socks for Benny. After a while it feels as if we are going to Emmaus neither for selfless reasons (being pious volunteers) nor for selfish ones (to get free stuff) . . . it's just that we are meeting one another's needs and never mention money.

I remember on one occasion Smiler, a young lad who had wandered around seaside towns most of his drinking life, looked out a pair of baby monitors so that we could hear Benny crying from another room. They cost twenty or thirty quid new. He wanted to check that they worked and so he hid the speaker behind Elvis's wall of electrical wires and we went into the office with the transmitter about fifty metres away.

'Did you know Elvis dresses up in women's clothing at night?' Smiler said to me, leaning close to the transmitter.

'I didn't, no. So he sings Elvis songs dressed as a woman?'

We went on like that for a few minutes and then went to see Elvis. He was tearing around his area trying to work out where the voices had come from. 'I don't dress up in women's clothing. I don't. Who's saying that?'

They always put aside stuff they thought we might need: printers, scanners, armchairs and so on. From having been a volunteer, I've become, in a tiny way, a charity case. And that, I realised as I read his letters from fifty years ago, was what Abbé Pierre called 'the deepest soul of Emmaus': 'to highlight the fact that the only real gift is the one that gives the "other" the means and the will to become a giver in turn. We only give by making a person capable and willing to give. That is how you can give as much to the rich as to the poor . . .'5

Emmaus had all types. There were also businessmen and bank managers laid low by bereavement or booze or both. I remember once talking to one of the 'companions' I had known for a while. He was called Nick. He had been an accountant for years but had hit rock bottom. He reminded me of the Tim Robbins character in *The Shawshank Redemption*. He did the accounts for the community and under his guidance it was thriving: it had a turnover of about two or three grand a week. We were chatting one day in the office of the warehouse and he mentioned other volunteers, all the guys who spent nights sleeping in the home, days driving the vans. There had been dozens already this year. The interesting thing was that almost all of them were Christians. Nick wasn't overjoyed by the fact, and he and other companions often teased the earnest do-goodery of theological students: there was 'Bible Dave' and

'Jabba the Hun' and so on. But Nick had seen all the volunteers and was baffled: 'I don't get it. Where are the humanists and the Fabians and the Socialists?'

We had enjoyed our utopian journey. These were, fortunately, beautiful places and there was, within the Christian communities, both a rigidity and fluidity, a kind of perfect symmetry, an immaculate mixture of the traditional and the revolutionary. But what was strange about living in these communities was that they were exactly the reverse of what I had expected: they weren't places, with the exception of Damanhur, that boasted of being a 'utopia'. Their idealism existed not because they thought they had reached perfection, but because they realised how far short they were. Not even Nomadelfia, as my old mate Domenico reminded me, was a paradise; paradise would imply perfection, it meant, in the original Persian, a walled garden. The best of these communities were built on imperfection, on a recognition of what was wrong. They weren't ghettos or gated or walled, but actually much more open than the self-proclaimed tolerant society from which they had retreated. Their merit lay in the fact that they were so confident of their role that they would reject no human material, nothing was beyond hope. There wasn't a static complacency but a creative response to new arrivals and old problems. There was much more critical self-examination, much more enquiry into the way they lived their daily lives, than usually occurs in the normal, outside world. They were places where the radically uprooted recognised a way of life complimentary to their own: equally radical, but radically rooted. Places like Nomadelfia and Pilsdon had no barriers, they welcomed anyone who wandered in because they knew a way to recycle and renew. They turned everything, somehow, inside out. They didn't boast how strong they were, but recognised how weak, how contingent. They weren't isolationist, but stretched your horizon as far as possible. Not, you felt, so that you could understand, but so that you could be understood. They taught you truly to see through other people's eyes, to experience 'perichoresis': a perfectly reciprocal existence.

The thing that most attracted me to the people and faith in these communities was rather unusual: it wasn't just the philanthropy, or the revaluation of human life, but something to do with style. It sounds daft if conceived in the sense of fashion. It was style in the original meaning. A *stilo* was the actual instrument you used in order to write. It was the tool with which you wrote the word. These communitarians were stylish in that sense: trying to define something, struggling to find the tone, the way to skewer one word onto one page. The people in these communities were writing with their lives and as a result seemed more rugged and brave. The men (regardless of sexual orientation or marital status) seemed to be more like real men. I can't explain it. The women (again, regardless of whatever) seemed to be real women, fully themselves. They were writing their lives, as it were, because they believed that authority wasn't authoritarian, but authorising; it was the very thing that allowed them to make sense of their lives.

In our 'real world', ascension is merely an attempt to rise above other people, an attempt to grip the greasy pole more ably than the less fortunate; in these communities, aspiration wasn't divisive but shared. I had always, until now, assumed that one could only ever challenge 'the revolt of inferiority' by being superior. It didn't get me anywhere; I knew instinctively that it was the wrong answer to the right question. These communities did something very different. They challenged that revolt of inferiority not through hierarchy but through humility. They showed the absurdity of the revolt of inferiority by distinguishing, perhaps unconsciously, between two words which are usually thought synonymous: the vulgar and the common. The meaning of the former is obvious, but the other is – as the root of the word suggests – a gathering together of responsibilities (*munia* implying 'public office'). The noblest of the communities we had seen never looked down on anyone; they stood alongside you and taught you to look up. They embraced, rather than rejected, what was common. They taught you to hear the symphonic splendour of the mundane, the normal and the banal. Rather than racing off to rarefied locations in search of spine-tingling spiritual highs, they taught you to find the splendour anywhere . . . even at the end of your street. I had seen, in the 'real world', what a society looked like when it was based on a gathering together of rights; these communities were about almost the opposite: congregating responsibilities.

I don't know if any of this makes sense any more, but I felt it again and again: we can only be responsible if we have something

– place, context, companions – to which we can respond. In community, everyone is part of the whole, drawn into discovering who they are at the same time as they discover who others are. Responsibility depends upon others, upon a conversation. If we live in a vacuum, deliberately isolated from society, we only have our own, predictable monologue. I used to think that isolation and autonomy increased charisma; 'personal space' seemed a logical guarantee that nothing would get in your way. But all that autonomy caused the complete erasure of personality: it was like trying to grow a plant without light or nutrients. Whereas the acceptance of our extraordinary, unique surroundings causes something unforeseen to happen: real characters emerge, choices become vocations, we become less self-centred but, strangely, suddenly feel more at the centre of the world.

I no longer had an issue with hypocrisy. It's the standard adolescent criticism of any idealism that it's practised by hypocrites. I had rejected idealism as a teenager because idealists were, without fail, disappointing. Let down by the gap between theory and practice, I had rejected the theory as well as its practitioners. Now, though, I realised that there was an ideal which understood that gap, which anticipated it. The inevitable existence of hypocrisy was no longer a reason to throw out idealism, but a reason to investigate it. As Gaynor Smith wrote in *Pilsdon Morning*: 'Do not be hard on the ideal. It points in the right direction even if it never quite gets there.'[6] That was what persuaded me about these communities. They were rooted both in reality and idealism, they were extraordinary but very common.

That said, I have no illusions about the profound difficulties of living alongside other people. There were many I really didn't get on with. Some rubbed me up the wrong way, and vice versa. We met all the usual suspects from the street: the habitual liar, the trickster, the freeloader, the piss-artist, the charmer . . . many took advantage and I repeatedly realised how gullible charity is. There were personality clashes and one particular guy had a temper so fierce it regularly pulled me into the turbulence. It's not as if these places were wonderfully pious. Invariably they were simply practical – feeding and housing people who had nowhere else to go. The communities themselves needed not only vast supplies of vision, space and energy, but also limitless forgiveness.

Most people assume forgiveness is the archetypal Christian virtue, but it also appears in a very different context. Some of the most interesting approaches to community and cooperation come from game theory. Robert Axelrod's *The Evolution of Cooperation* studied the ways in which a player's self-interest can encourage loyalty rather than betrayal. It took brute Darwinism into the more ethereal world of human virtues; it was a mechanical game based around self-interested choices which, rather beautifully, discovered things like forgiveness and memory. What we had found at Hartrigg Oaks, Axelrod unearthed in an imaginary prison: 'The foundation of cooperation is not really trust, but the durability of the relationship.'

The journey had been surprising and counter-intuitive, almost the opposite of everything I had expected. I had found myself in places where I didn't measure truth, it measured me. I had decided to give up on the hunt for happiness, but it had surreptitiously arrived. I had turned to one religion which promised to be irrational and it had been reasonable. If I had been struck, at the outset, by the incredible conformity of disobedience, by the end I was amazed by the brilliant creativity of obedience.

Anyone writing about religion and community eventually has to tackle Durkheim. He was wrong about all sorts of things, mainly because he dared to predict the social structure of the future and was pretty far off the mark. But where he appears acute is in his insistence that, without bonds which are sacred, human community is impossible. Whether it's a totem pole or a temple, the sacred is the place where humans interact at the deepest levels and without such places humanity no longer has any invisible tools to create and shape a community. Others have repeatedly said that community is predicated upon aspiring to something more than a vague being together. Bruno Bettelheim, in *Home for the Heart*, wrote: 'I am convinced communal life can flourish only if it exists for an aim outside itself. Community is viable if it is the outgrowth of a deep involvement in a purpose which is other than, or above, that of being a community.'7 The more exacting the ideal, the more profound and intimate the community. A gathering of people could be either merely social – the opposite of being alone, but not necessarily signifying anything more precise than being present in a crowd – or an example of fellowship. Where the entry requirements were toughest – requiring the renunciation of money or drugs or alcohol or careers – there were the truest communities, bonded by the same strict and logical laws. You can only have regulars with rules.

No community exists unless it is able to live out an interpretation of the sacred: it could be the reclamation of land from violent criminals or the desire to live without causing pollution . . . but whatever it was, no community made sense without it. There had to be an aim, a direction, an orientation. If the sacred was centred not on material concerns but on interaction and relations (between God and man, or between man and man), it could only be revealed in that relational realm. It was dependent upon community, on other people, for its expression. It wasn't the usual parody of the sacred – the external, authoritarian tyrant – but something that emerged through us and the way in which we dealt with each other. For a community to work it wouldn't have to consider the same thing sacred. That would be the kind of homogeneity which denies an interactional element. But it would have to consider the search for the sacred an integral part of what it means to be human.

Secularism began as a noble ally of that search. It was a promise made by the state not to kow-tow to one religious group; that promise was the only way to represent fairly multiconfessional constituents. None of us really doubts the importance of secularism. No one in their right mind wants theocracy, with the multiplicity of mankind forced to obey one earthly authority which claims the exclusive ability to speak on behalf of God. Even in the microcosm of my own family, we have a diversity which makes me grateful for secularism: my parents, from a purely Celtic gene pool (with a drop, allegedly, of Huguenot) now have grandchildren with Hindu and Jewish roots, who will speak Punjabi and Italian as much as English. I don't think we're weaker as a family, an extended community, because we confess different religions or none at all. I do think it would be bizarre, though, if we met at Christmas or Diwali and hadn't been educated as to why this was a holy day and didn't know how to communicate its holiness to each other.

I say that because I have often glimpsed a different kind of secularism. Secularism understood in its contemporary, fundamentalist sense is something very different. The secularist has passed, in the three centuries since the Toleration Act of 1689, from passive umpire to high priest; where once he guaranteed tolerance for all, he now claims to be the only person capable of tolerance. His vaunted defence of pluralism has become a rhetorical device that ushers in his own authoritarianism.

Secular fundamentalism insists on the renunciation of any social dimension to religion in return for toleration of its private practice. Religion is reduced to what one does with one's solitude. It is treated like soft drugs: a blind eye will be turned towards private use, but woe betide anyone who gets caught dealing. The secular vision of tolerance isn't based on integration, the carrying of one's true identity into the whole, but obliteration. It leads, on a macroscopic scale, to communal nihilism, where we can't agree on anything. We become terrified of solitude, because that is where we see the communal nihilism translated into individual meaninglessness. The result is frenetic sociability, a faux communitarianism. Intimacy becomes unconsciously signed up to the search for individual meaning and often creates only more loneliness.

I felt as if the secular universalists were approaching the problem of tolerance from completely the wrong end; they yearned for the unified trunk of the human tree and yet rejected every root on the basis that they were evidence of particularity. They wanted, it seemed, to decapitate the present from the past. I felt that uprootedness was one of the most serious and contagious maladies of modern life. I had gone deep into one particular tradition not to negate that universalism, but to start from the bottom up. The deeper I went into that one tradition, the more I glimpsed the yearning for universalism; but this time, rather than being a universalism based on uniformity, on the wiping away of our true identities, it was founded on the strength of each root. That, I realised, was the central difference between the two approaches: secular fundamentalism asks you to leave at the door of entry everything which is most valuable to you; religion asks you to leave all that is most ephemeral.

The Bright movement of rational atheists was established to cement this supremacy, shining its investigative torch into any dark corners where 'supernaturalism' might still be lurking. According to the website, Brights are 'an international internet community of individuals' whose worldview 'is free of supernatural and mystical elements'.[8] They say that what once constituted religion – power to control events – is now the arena of science, which has shown us its truth: that we are bipedal apes with an astonishing neuro-linguistic ability honed by aeons of evolution. We have glimpsed the smallest particles and taught them to annihilate millions of other bipedal apes in one go. There's nothing we don't understand any more. Our sole purpose is the propagation of DNA. One of the leading Brights, Richard Dawkins, uses the drugs metaphor. Inventing a substance that was an anagram of religion ('gerin oil'), he wrote recently that the serenity of the religiously minded is just 'the smile of a junkie'; religious 'addiction', he wrote in a reprise of what is constantly said to me about religious communities, 'can drive previously sane individuals to run away from a normally fulfilled human life and retreat to closed communities from which all but confirmed addicts are excluded.'9

That wasn't our experience. The places we had been to appeared much less certain, much less absolutist, than that world. Each value around which these communities were built seemed to cut both ways. What was important wasn't the sweeping statement that something – authority or dogma or freedom or religion – was either always good or always bad. The role of the communities was actually to distinguish where and why those good values became bad or vice versa. They were doing grass-root research into political theory, trying to understand at what point authority or dogma or freedom become soiled by human weakness. I relished that sense of discovery which happens when lots of people live messily together and share each day: communities aren't static but journeying towards a delicate, fragile understanding. It was a question of balance. It was precarious and I was convinced by that precariousness; by the fact that every virtue was finely tuned to and dependent upon all the others: leaders need authority, authority depends upon assent. That assent requires freedom. Freedom needs truth if it is to have any meaning.

Without truth, any zealotry is brute imperialism. In the absence of truth, utility is the best judge of what we may adhere to. Long before September 2001, but especially since, the central argument against religion revolved around the uses to which it was put: crusades, colonialism, terrorism and all the rest. It wasn't, to put it lightly, socially useful. But I had seen other consequences of belief and realised that, just as religion has an extra gear when it comes to cruelty, it also has an extra gear when it comes to compassion and philanthropy. Faith, for better or worse, is an agent in history. But I had become interested more in truth than utility. I was interested in the cause, not the consequence. For as long as I stayed with utility, one set of advantages would simply be traded off against another.

I was finally beginning to doubt that the sacred is, as Marcus Terentius Varro or Durkheim would have it, a transfiguration of social bonds, a way to guarantee the moral authority of the state or tribe. I had begun to ponder the opposite, that social bonds might be the consequence, not the cause, of the sacred.

As far as I can see, faith doesn't respond to human hands but vice versa. Anyone who talks seriously about faith says that it's a gift, something almost entirely outside their control. It comes from outside themselves and isn't something which could be tinkered with to notch up a military victory or build better social bonds. They aren't using it, but consenting to being used by it. The problem of writing about such things is that everyone has said it all before. I had gone from thinking, as Os Guinness once wrote, that 'Christianity is true because it works' to something rather different: 'It works because it is true.'[10] There was reason to Christianity, it had been a banister on the first few steps, but no reason *for* it. And that, in a strange way, is what convinced me: not that it seemed unfounded, but that it taught you to understand why it was unfounded. It was suddenly obvious why even talking about proof was daft. That lack of incentive, of imperative, convinced me. The prophets who spoke to me were those whose journey to understanding was about accepting that there are things we cannot know and reasons why not: 'I want to understand in such a way that everything inexplicable presents itself to me as being necessarily inexplicable and not as being something that I am under an obligation to believe.'[11]

Belief has always sounded assertive, almost arrogant, to me. I certainly felt – again, not a particularly promising proposal for a writer – that the only way to show what you believe in is by living with other people, rather than by lecturing them. But I was beginning to find a creed in the oldest sense of the word. A creed was originally something simpler and stronger than an intellectual position: 'creed' comes from a galaxy of words which are all related to the cardiac: the Welsh *craidd*, the Latin *cor*, the Indo-European *kred*. Having a creed meant finding something for which one was prepared to give one's heart.

By now I have such a confidence in paradox that credence doesn't appear so dangerous. It is only a prompt willingness to forgo life that makes life worth living. Believing something could suddenly be inclusive rather than exclusive. So I can finally describe my idea of a perfect community and its unifying canopy. It would have, from experience, between fifteen and twenty-five people. It would, like Nomadelfia, be overrun by children. It would have a full-size snooker table, a chess set, a library, a football pitch and a piano. It would, obviously, aspire to self-sufficiency, even a shared abundance. Silence would be relished as the source which enriches our words and music. The entire community would accept that a definition of good is the only way to distinguish freedom from licence, even though we would recognise that our definitions are temporary and inadequate. Peace would be the only canopy: it would be fragile because any one person could break it. But the strength of the community would be found in that fragility: it would live its peace to its radical conclusion where the community chooses to sacrifice rather than betray itself.

I'm walking back from the circumference late one night, trying to work out how to finish this book. I've been playing pool with Elvis. It's been a fun night. He was on form, stroking the balls into the pockets of the pool table, gripping the cue with knuckles made blue by homemade tattoos: 'bosh' say the four fingers of his right hand. I walk across the no-man's land towards Castle Park. The roofless church has barely been touched since it was bombed in 1943. It now stands in its own grounds as a reminder of the retreat of the old religion. It becomes an ice-rink in winter. I walk through Broadmead, that too bombed but rebuilt disastrously in the sixties and seventies. They're now tearing it all down and spending half a billion pounds (£550 million is the budget) to turn it into more retail space. This is where Wesley founded the world's first Methodist chapel.

I cut up to the main road and can see St Michael's Without boarded up, nettles peering out from behind the wooden windows. I head down Jamaica Street. It appropriately points like an arrow to the Caribbean quarter of Bristol, St Pauls. There's a beautiful church there in Portland Square which they now use to train circus performers. Another one, further along the Gloucester Road, has become a centre for martial arts. In St Werburghs, the church is a rock-climbing centre where dozens of people scramble up the inside of the tower. All the churches are full in a funny way.

The pavements are full of addicts. Most of the city's social housing is here and they gather outside the shops blagging loose change to go and score. There are abandoned blocks every way you look. I stand in front of Banksy's spray-paint depiction of the 'mild, mild west': a teddy-bear with a petrol bomb in its hand. That's the atmosphere here: edgy but funny at the same time. I wander up to Freemantle Square, site of the 1645 battle between royalist and parliamentary troops. It's high up above the basin of the city. It must be one of the most beautiful, contrasting squares in Britain. It's got a raised, walled garden in the middle, a grassy lawn with an ancient hollyoak tree in the middle. All the tall houses are painted different colours. There's a red phone booth, a charity, a pub, council estates just below the brow of the hill. You can see through the empty windows of an abandoned, burnt-out block to the hills of north Somerset. It's a city which seems both rustic and urban. There are buddleia shoots sprouting out of the cracks.

I'm feeling less apocalyptic than I was a year or two ago. As I head down the hill I count the communities around here. Walsingham House, 1B, the group in Cotham. With each passing month I hear about a new gathering of humans, trying to work out the best way to live together. They don't live in secrecy, but nor do they have bell-towers, spires or grandiose sandstone architecture. If you didn't look for them, you wouldn't ever know they were there. It's as if they've gone right back to the beginning.

I turn the last corner. The guy whose blue Citroën is painted with huge yellow letters is writing on the cardboard people have put out for recycling. You couldn't make it up. After ages considering the question, I'm finally on the home straight and this guy is still at it, where he was two years ago: writing his two-word answer on every passing piece of paper. I no longer know whether he's a madman or a prophet. I'm feeling in my pocket for the keys. There's our red door, the centre of our circle.

Notes

Introduction: Going Astray

1 Samuel Johnson, *The History of Rasselas, Prince of Abyssinia* (Wordsworth, London, 2000)

2 Matthew Arnold, *Culture and Anarchy* (Yale, New Haven, 1994)

3 Samuel Johnson, *The History of Rasselas, Prince of Abyssinia* (Wordsworth, London, 2000)

4 Nathaniel Hawthorne, *The Blithedale Romance* (Oxford University Press, Oxford, 1991)

5 Émile Durkheim, *The Elementary Forms of the Religious* Life (Allen & Unwin, London, 1976)

6 Dietrich Bonhoeffer, *Letters and Papers from Prison* (SCM, London, 2001)

7 'The Religious Nature' in Friedrich Nietzsche, *Beyond Good and Evil* (Penguin, London, 1979)

8 Friedrich Schleiermacher, *On Religion* (Cambridge University Press, Cambridge, 1996)

Chapter 1

1 Ivan Illich, *Energy and Equity* (Boyars, London, 1974)

2 Office for National Statistics

3 Italo Calvino, *Invisible Cities*, trans. William Weaver (Vintage, London, 1997)

4 E. McKenzie, *Privatopia: Homeowner Associations and the Rise of Residential Private Government* (Yale University Press, New Haven, 1994)

5 Office for National Statistics

6 Oberto Airaudi, *La Via Horusiana* (edizioni della Scuola di Meditazione di Damanhur, Baldissero Canavese, XXVII anno horusiano/2001)

7 Massimo Introvigne, 'Damanhur: A Magical Community in Italy' in *Journal of the Communal Studies Association*, Vol 16, 1996

8 Émile Durkheim, *The Division of Labour in Society* (Macmillan, London, 1984)

9 Thomas Hardy, 'God's Funeral' in *The Complete Poems*, edited by James Gibson (Palgrave, Basingstoke, 2001)

10 *Private Eye*, 16 April 2004

11 Frank Musgrove, *Ecstasy and Holiness* (Methuen, London, 1974)

12 Quoted in Paul Heelas, *The New Age Movement* (Blackwell, Oxford, 1996)

13 Ralph Waldo Emerson, *Selected Essays*, edited by Larzer Ziff (Penguin, London, 1982)

14 Robert N. Bellah, *Beyond Belief* (Harper Row, New York, 1976)

15 See Wolfhart Pannenberg in *First Things 64* (June/July 1996)

16 Dietrich Bonhoeffer, *Letters and Papers from Prison* (SCM, London, 2001)

17 Wouter Hanegraaff, *New Age Religion and Western Culture: Esotericism in the Mirror of Nature* (Leiden, New York, 1996)

18 Viktor E. Frankl, *Man's Search For Meaning* (Pocket Books, New York, 1985)

19 Oberto Airaudi, *La Via Horusiana* (edizioni della Scuola di Meditazione di Damanhur, Baldissero Canavese, XXVII anno horusiano/2001)

20 Edmund Burke, *Reflections on the Revolution in France* (Penguin, London, 1986)

21 Oberto Airaudi, *La Via Horusiana* (edizioni della Scuola di Meditazione di Damanhur, Baldissero Canavese, XXVII anno horusiano/2001)

22 Simone Weil, *The Need for Roots* (Routledge and Kegan Paul, London, 1952)

23 Peter Berger, *A Far Glory* (Free Press, New York, 1992)

24 Gian Luca Favetto, 'La Città delle visioni' in *Diario* (no. 31/32, 9 August 2002)

25 Friedrich Schleiermacher, *On Religion* (Cambridge University Press, Cambridge, 1988)

26 Dietrich Bonhoeffer, *Letters and Papers from Prison* (SCM, London, 2001)

27 Samuel Taylor Coleridge, *Seven Lectures on Shakespeare and Milton* (Chapman & Hall, London, 1856)

28 Søren Kierkegaard, *Philosophical Fragments*, edited and translated by Howard V. Hong and Edna H. Hong (Princeton University Press, Princeton, 1985)

29 Thomas Traherne, *Centuries* (Faith Press, London, 1963)

30 Evelyn Underhill, *Mysticism: The Nature and Development of Spiritual Consciousness* (Oneworld, Oxford, 1993)

31 Danièle Hervieu-Léger, *Religion as a Chain of Memory* (Polity, Cambridge, 2000)

32 T. S. Eliot, *Selected Prose of T. S. Eliot*, edited by Frank Kermode (Faber, London, 1975)

Chapter 2

1 *Il Cardinale Newman nei suoi scritti*, a cura di Giuseppe Regina (Edizioni Paoline, Rome, 1956)

2 Irene Bignardi, *Le piccole utopie* (Feltrinelli, Milan, 2003)

3 *Ibid.*

4 *Corriere della Sera*, 10 February 1952

5 Anon., *Nomadelfia: Un Popolo nuovo* (Nomadelfia Edizioni, Grosseto, 1999)

6 Parry, David, *Households of God: The Rule of St Benedict, with explanations for monks and lay-people today* (Darton, Longman and Todd, London, 1980)

7 Dom André Louf, *The Cistercian Alternative* (Gill and MacMillan, Dublin, 1983)

8 Don Zeno speech, 30 September 1959

9 St Matthew 25:40

10 *Constituzione della Popolazione di Nomadelfia* (Nomadelfia Edizioni, Grosseto, 2000)

11 Jean-Joseph Goux, *Symbolic Economies after Marx and Freud*, trans. J. C. Cage (Cornell University Press, Ithaca, 1990)

12 Giuseppe Panza di Biumo, *The Panza Collection* (Skira, Turin, 2002)

13 Roger Scruton, *An Intelligent Person's Guide to Modern Culture* (Duckworth, London, 1998)

14 Herbert Spencer, *First Principles* (Williams & Norgate, London, 1867)

15 Viktor E. Frankl, *Man's Search For Meaning* (Hodder & Stoughton, London, 1964)

16 Anon., *Nomadelfia: Un Popolo nuovo* (Nomadelfia Edizioni, Grosseto, 1999)

17 Zeno Saltini, *L'uomo è diverso* (Nomadelfia Edizioni, Grosseto, 2000)

18 *Ibid.*

19 *Corriere della Sera*, 17 August 2005

20 John Keats, *Selected Letters of John Keats*, ed. Grant F. Scott (Harvard University Press, Cambridge, 2002)

21 David Parry, *Households of God: The Rule of St Benedict, with explanations for monks and lay-people today* (Darton, Longman and Todd, London, 1980)

22 Alasdair McIntyre, *After Virtue* (Duckworth, London, 1981)

23 Adriana Zarra, *Erba della mia erba* (Cittadella, Assisi, 1981)

24 *Ibid.*

25 *Ibid.*

Chapter 3

1 L.E. Waddilove, *One Man's Vision* (Allen and Unwin, London, 1954)

2 Anne Vernon, *A Quaker Businessman; The Life of Joseph Rowntree 1836–1925* (Allen & Unwin, London, 1958)

3 L.E. Waddilove, *One Man's Vision* (Allen and Unwin, London, 1954)

4 *Ibid.*

5 Adrian Davies, *The Quakers in English Society 1655–1725* (Clarendon, Oxford, 2000)

6 Pierre Lacout, *God is Silence* (Quaker Home Service, London, 1970)

7 *Ibid.*

8 Max Picard, *The World of Silence*, trans. Stanley Godman (Harvill, London, 1948)

9 Aldous Huxley, *The Perennial Philosophy* (Flamingo, London, 1994)

10 Hugh Barbour and J. William Frost, *The Quakers* (Friends United Press, Richmond Indiana, 1988)

11 Isabel Ross, *Margaret Fell* (Longmans, London, 1949)

12 Gerrard Winstanley, *The Works of Gerrard Winstanley*, ed. George H. Sabine (Cornell, Ithaca, 1941)

13 *Ibid.*

14 Karl Kraus, *Half-truths and One-and-a-half Truths: Selected Aphorisms*, ed. Harry Zohn (Engendra, Montreal, 1976)

15 Alan Gilbert, *The Making of Post-Christian Britain* (Longman, London, 1980)

16 Marie-Louise Berneri, *Journey Through Utopia* (Freedom Press, London, 1982)

17 Francis Bacon, *Essays* (Dent, London, 1972)

18 Dietrich Bonhoeffer, *Letters and Papers from Prison* (SCM, London, 2001)

19 Evelyn Underhill, *Mysticism* (Oneworld, Oxford, 1993)

20 *Advices and Queries* (Society of Friends, London, 1964)

21 Benedicta Ward, *The Sayings of the Desert Fathers: The Alphabetical Collection* (A.R. Mowbray, Oxford, 1975)

22 Alfred Tennyson, *The Poems of Tennyson* (Oxford University Press, Oxford, 1929)

23 Viktor E. Frankl, *Man's Search For Meaning* (Pocket Books, New York, 1984)

24 Simone Weil, *Gravity and Grace*, trans. Emma Crawford and Mario von der Ruhr (Routledge, London, 2002)

25 John Austin Baker, *The Foolishness of God* (Darton, Longman & Todd, London, 1970)

26 William Penn, *The People's Ancient and Just Liberties Asserted* (Flower, London, 1670)

Chapter 4

1 John Stuart Mill, *On Liberty*, edited by Gertrude Himmelfarb (Penguin, London, 1974)

2 Quoted in the *Independent*, 25 January 2005

3 G. K. Chesterton, *What's Wrong With The World?* (Cassell, London, 1910)

4 John Milton, *A Critical Edition of the Major Works,* edited by Stephen Orgel and Jonathan Goldberg (OUP, Oxford, 1991)

5 John 8:32

6 John Milton, *A Critical Edition of the Major Works*, edited by Stephen Orgel and Jonathan Goldberg (OUP, Oxford, 1991)

7 Carlo Barbieri, *Le Mani in pasta* (Libri Coop, Bologna, 2005)

8 *Ibid.*

9 *Ibid.*

10 *Ibid.*

11 Richard Bauckman, *God and the Crisis of Freedom* (Westminster John Knox Press, Louisville, 2002)

12 Evelyn Underhill, *Mysticism* (Oneworld, Oxford, 1993)

13 Exodus 8:1

14 Galatians 5:13

15 Richard Bauckman, *God and the Crisis of Freedom* (Westminster John Knox Press, Louisville, 2002)

16 Georg Simmel; *Essays on Religion* (Yale, London, 1997)

17 Colin E. Gunton, ed. *God and Freedom* (T&T Clark, Edinburgh, 1995)

Chapter 5

1 John MacAuslan in *The Pilsdon Community, The First 40 Years 1958–1998* (private circulation)

2 Percy Smith, *Letters from a Community* (private circulation)

3 Gaynor Smith, *Pilsdon Morning* (Merlin, Braunton, 1982)

4 Acts 4 : 32, 35

5 Gaynor Smith, *Pilsdon Morning* (Merlin, Braunton, 1982)

6 Jean Vanier, *Community and Growth*, trans. Ann Shearer (Darton, Longman and Todd, London, 1979)

7 Friedrich Schleiermacher, *On Religion: Speeches to its Cultured Despisers* (CUP, Cambridge, 1988)

8 Percy Smith, *Letters from a Community* (private circulation)

9 Keith Ward; *A Guide for the Perplexed* (Oneworld, Oxford, 2002)

10 Immanuel Kant, *Foundations of the Metaphysics of Morals* (Prentice Hall, New York, 1989).

11 Edmund Burke, *Reflections on the Revolution in France* (Penguin, London, 1986)

12 St John of the Cross, Selected Writings, edited by Kieran Kavanaugh (SPCK, London, 1987)

Chapter 6

1 Pascal; *Pensées* (Penguin, London, 1966)

2 G. K. Chesterton, *Heresy* (House of Stratus, Thirsk, 2001)

3 'Cos'è il focolare?' in *Città Nuova* no. 14 (1977)

4 Abbé Pierre, *Emmaus* (Le Centurion, Paris, 1987)

5 *Ibid.*

6 Gaynor Smith, *Pilsdon Morning* (Merlin, Braunton, 1982)

7 Bruno Bettelheim, *A Home for the Heart* (Thames & Hudson, London, 1974)

8 http:the-brights.net/

9 Richard Dawkins in *Prospect*, August 2005

10 Os Guinness, *Doubt* (Lion, Tring, 1976)

11 Leo Tolstoy, *A Confession and Other Religious Writings* (Penguin, London,
    1987)

Index